OPPOSITIONS BOOKS

Introduction by Peter Eisenman
Translation by Diane Ghirardo and
Joan Ockman

Revised for the American Edition
by Aldo Rossi and Peter Eisenman

Aldo Rossi

The Architecture of the City

Published for The Graham Foundation for Advanced Studies
in the Fine Arts, Chicago, Illinois, and
The Institute for Architecture and Urban Studies,
New York, New York, by

The MIT Press
Cambridge, Massachusetts, and London, England

First paperback printing, 1984

Copyright © 1982 by
The Institute for Architecture and
Urban Studies and
The Massachusetts Institute of
Technology

*Library of Congress Cataloguing in
Publication Data*
Rossi, Aldo, 1931-
The architecture of the city.
(Oppositions books)
Translation of: L'architettura
della citta.
"Published for the Graham
Foundation for Advanced Studies in
the Fine Arts, Chicago, Illinois, and
the Institute for Architecture and
Urban Studies, New York,
New York."
Includes index.
1. City planning. 2. Architecture.
I. Eisenman, Peter, 1932-
II. Title.
III. Series.
NA9031.R6713 711'.4 81-19382
ISBN-13: 978-0-262-18101-3 (hc. alk. paper)
           978-0-262-68043-1 (pb. alk. paper)

Typography by The Old Typosopher in
Century Expanded. Printed and bound
in the United States of America.

*Cover drawing: Wooden armature for the
construction of vaults. From* Principj di
Architettura Civile, *Francesco Milizia,
1832.*

20   19   18   17   16

Other titles in the OPPOSITIONS
BOOKS series:

**Essays in Architectural Criticism:
Modern Architecture and
Historical Change**
Alan Colquhoun
Preface by Kenneth Frampton

A Scientific Autobiography
Aldo Rossi
Postscript by Vincent Scully
Translation by Lawrence Venuti

Contents

Editor's Preface

The tradition of the architect-writer is well precedented in the history of architecture in Italy. From the Renaissance to the nineteenth century, it was characteristic of certain architects to present their ideas in a systematic treatise. Based on the model of Vitruvius, Alberti produced the Renaissance model for such writing. This was followed by treatises like those of Serlio and Palladio. Serlio produced a series of volumes which constitute a handbook of architecture, starting with ancient building and including speculations about unbuilt future work. These unbuilt designs, which were to become more important than his modest built work, are not so much significant in terms of specific projects, but are rather models which begin to elaborate many of the types to which Palladio would refer. Palladio wrote the "Quattro Libri" ten years before his death, as a kind of résumé of his career. These books contain the redrawing of his projects and buildings, thereby serving as much as a record of his intentions as of his actual work. Whether drawing Roman ruins or redrawing his own projects, Palladio was primarily interested in the derivation, invention, and ultimately the distortion of types from existing models. Thus the idea of the interrelationship of drawing and writing became part of an architectural tradition.

This tradition has continued in Italy up to the present century. The writings of Scamozzi, Milizia, and Lodoli, not to mention the more recent writings and designs of Giuseppe Pagano, certainly must be seen as its bearers, as, indeed, must Aldo Rossi's "The Architecture of the City." To understand Rossi's architecture, it is also necessary to understand his writings and his drawings. Yet "The Architecture of the City" is also a significant departure from past models. This is because, while purporting to be a scientific theory, a modern-day equivalent of the Renaissance treatise, it is on another level a unique anticipation of Rossi's subsequent architecture.

The task of this preface, then, is to locate this book for an American audience not only in its own tradition, in the context of Italian theoretical writings by architects, but also in the more contemporary context of Italy in the 1960s and 1970s. The first edition of this book, taken from Rossi's lectures and notes, appeared in 1966 during the traumatic years of student discontent as a polemical critique of the Modern Movement position on the city. A second Italian edition appeared in 1970 with a new introduction. The book was then translated into Spanish, German, and Portuguese editions. Finally, in 1978, a fourth Italian edition appeared with new illustrations. To reissue it now, in its first English-language edition, with all of the supplementary material that it has acquired during its successive publications, is to recognize the unique cultural context within which it was first produced and continued to develop; all of this material is part of the book's history. In this way, the book stands as a singular and parallel record of ideas that Rossi has been developing in both drawing and other writing over the last fifteen years. As such, it is in itself an "analogous artifact."

In its American edition, "The Architecture of the City" is not so much a literal transcription of the original as a carefully revised edition—revised so as to provide the style and flavor of the original without encumbering it with some of the rhetorical and repetitive passages which are part of the original text. The rather academic style of presentation in the Italian occasionally makes for a certain stiltedness in English, and in such cases we have preferred to opt for clarity and simplicity.

My own introduction which follows is in certain ways not only about this book, but also about the Rossi that this book anticipates. In this sense, it is a kind of analogous writing of Rossi's ideas. Like his analogous drawings, and his writings which also can be seen as analogous instruments, it attempts to collapse and dislocate the time and place of the evolution of Rossi's ideas. For this reason, it is taken from a reading of his later writings, including "A Scientific Autobiography," and from many private discussions with him, as much as from the text at hand. Like the fourth Italian edition, which brought together the preceding pieces of the book's history, all of which themselves had separate memories, this book is similarly, and to an even greater degree, a "collective" artifact. My own introduction attempts to enter into this memory and in this sense serves as a kind of analogy of an analogy, a creation of yet another artifact with its own history and memory. It seeks in this way to illustrate the analogous current which washes back and forth from drawing to drawing, and from writing to writing, in Rossi's work.

P.E.

1a

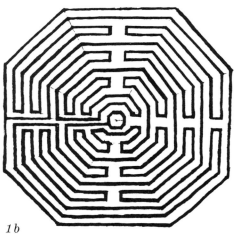

1b

1a Horizontal section of the
Mausoleum of Hadrian, built 135-139
A.D., later transformed into the
Castel Sant'Angelo.
1b Drawing of a labyrinth by Dom
Nicolas de Rély, 1611, based on the
paving pattern on the floor of Amiens
Cathedral. This design, executed in
1288, was known as the "Maison
Dédalus" or House of Daedalus.

. . . the relief and design of structures appears more clearly when content, which is the living energy of meaning, is neutralized, somewhat like the architecture of an uninhabited or deserted city, reduced to its skeleton by some catastrophe of nature or art. A city no longer inhabited, not simply left behind, but haunted by meaning and culture, this state of being haunted, which keeps the city from returning to nature . . .
Jacques Derrida
Writing and Difference

The image on the cover of the fourth Italian edition of Aldo Rossi's *L'Architettura della città* summarizes in condensed form not only the ambivalent nature of Rossi's architectural work, but also the intrinsic problem of its relationship to the idea of city which is proposed by this book. This image, a horizontal section of the Mausoleum of Hadrian in the Castel Sant'Angelo in Rome, reads as a spiral. The spiral is associated with the form of the labyrinth, a construction which, according to classical myth, was the invention of Daedalus. Daedalus, as the only architect of mythology and the supposed inventor of many "wondrous" works of architecture, has become for history the symbol par excellence of the humanist architect. As such, the labyrinth, Daedalus's creation, can be considered emblematic of a humanist condition of architecture. But this is not the spiral's only meaning. As an unfolding path or route, the spiral has also been interpreted as a psychological figure, the symbol of a process of transformation. Thus, we are obliged to interpret Rossi's use of the image on the cover of his book in two ways: first, in terms of the spiral as a mausoleum, as representing a symbolic place of death, in this case—even if unconsciously on his part—that of humanism; and at the same time, in terms of the spiral as labyrinth, as representing a place of transformation.

The spiral has a further, more personal meaning for Rossi. It symbolizes his own rite of passage, his role as part of a generation progressively more distanced from the positivism of modern architecture by the collapse of historical time and left drifting into an uncertain present. While this book in many ways is a critique of the Modern Movement, it nevertheless reflects an ambivalence with respect to modernism. It suggests Rossi's own uncertainty as much with the general ideology of modernism as with the failure of the specific aspirations of modern architecture. Rossi's anxiety with respect to modernism is thus refracted through his sympathy with its very concerns. It was, after all, modernism which focused on the city as one of architecture's central problems. Prior to modernism, cities were thought to have evolved over time through a process which was an imitation of natural law. But in the view of the polemicists of the Modern Movement, this natural time had run out, and in its place succeeded the time of historicism.

For the architects of the early twentieth century, the appropriateness of the act of intervening clinically in the city's historical and natural evolution was beyond question. Supported by the enormous moral impetus of social and technological necessity (which had replaced the model of natural evolution), they attempted from the stronghold of their "castle of purity" to storm the bastion of evils identified with the nineteenth-century city. To them the stakes appeared higher than they had ever been. In this heroic climate of modernism the city of modern architecture, supposedly born out of a rupture of history, was progressively propelled by that very history toward the vision of a sanitized utopia.

The perceived failure of modern architecture to realize this utopia—either to supersede the nineteenth-century city or to mitigate its destruction after the bombings of the Second World War—became the primary condition confronting the architects of a generation which matured in the early 1960s. Their disillusionment and anger were in direct proportion to modern architecture's failure, as much with its unrealized aspirations—its castle of purity—as with their own sense of loss and the impossibility of return; these feelings were directed at the heroic fathers of modern architecture, both for having been and also for having failed. For Rossi's generation it was no longer possible to be a hero, no longer possible to be an idealist; the potential for such memories and fantasies had been taken away forever. No other generation had to follow such a sense of expectation with such a sense of loss. Cynicism and pessimism came to fill the void created by the loss of hope.

The Texts of Analogy

Now let us . . . suppose that Rome is not a human habitation but a psychical entity with a similarly long and copious past—an entity, that is to say, in which nothing that has once come into existence will have passed away and all the earlier phases of development continue to exist alongside the latest one. . . . If we want to represent historical sequence in spatial terms we can only do it by juxtaposition in space: the same space cannot have two different contents. . . . It shows us how far we are from mastering the characteristics of mental life by representing them in pictorial terms.
Sigmund Freud
Civilization and Its Discontents

The Architecture of the City along with all of Rossi's production is an attempt to build a different kind of castle from that of the moderns. It is an elaborate scaffold erected for and by someone who can no longer climb its steps to die a hero's death. Proposing an *other* architecture, an *other* architect, and most importantly, an *other* process for their understanding, it can be seen as an attempt to break not only from the traditional humanist definition of the relationship of object and subject, but also from the more recent modernist one. Modernism proposed a new interpretation of the subject which was never fulfilled by modern architecture; in this respect modern architecture can be seen as simply an extension of nineteenth-century functionalism. Rossi's new construct begins as a critique of the city of modern architecture and from this goes on to propose an *other* object.

The *other* object, the architecture of the book's title, is now defined in two ways: as the ultimate and verifiable data within the real city, and as an autonomous structure. But this data is not gathered and applied with the reductive scientism used by the proponents of the Modern Movement city, but rather through a more complex rationalism provided by urban geography, economics, and above all history. Nor is its autonomy entirely that of modernism, of the discipline of architecture in itself. Rather, it resides in architecture's specific processes and its built reality.

This twofold idea of the city as ultimate data—an archaeological artifact—and of the city as autonomous structure not only characterizes the new city as an *object*, but more importantly, and perhaps inadvertently, redefines its *subject*—the architect himself. As opposed to the humanist architect of the sixteenth century, and the functionalist architect of the twentieth century, Rossi's architect would seem to be an unheroic, autonomous researcher—much like his psychoanalyst counterpart who is similarly distanced from the object of his analysis and who no

4

longer believes in science or progress. However, not surprisingly, this redefinition of the architect as a neutral subject is problematic.

Whereas the humanist conception attempted an integration of subject and object, the modernist conception polemically attempted their separation. The problematic nature of the practice of modern architecture with respect to the theory of modernism has to do precisely with its inability to effect this separation and thus its contamination with imperatives from the humanist conception. Rossi intuitively understands this problem; but he cannot face the consequences of taking on the unrealized program of modernism. Therefore, his new formulation focuses on a mediating element: the process of the work. If the subject and the object are to be independent, it is now the process, previously considered neutral, which must assume the forces which formerly were contained in the subject and the object. Into this new idea of process Rossi reintroduces the elements of history and typology, but not as a nostalgia for narrative or a reductive scientism. Rather, history becomes analogous to a "skeleton" whose condition serves as a measure of time and, in turn, is measured by time. It is this skeleton which bears the imprint of the actions that have taken place and will take place in the city. For Rossi, architecture's history lies in its *material*; and it is this material which becomes the object of analysis—the city. Typology, on the other hand, becomes the instrument, the "apparatus"—to borrow a term which Rossi will later use in his *Scientific Autobiography*—of time's measurement; it attempts to be both logical and scientific. The skeleton and its measuring apparatus become the process and ultimately the object of the autonomous researcher. History and type, as components parts of research, allow for transformations of themselves which are "prearranged but still unforeseeable."

The skeleton, an image which also appears in Rossi's *Scientific Autobiography*, is a particularly useful analogue for this idea of city. For the skeleton links the city to history. It is a history which is limited to the historiographical act—to a pure knowledge of the past, without the historicizing imperative to determine the future. For Rossi, historicism, the modernist critique of history, is an impediment to invention. Historicism deals in causes or imperatives while history focuses on effects or facts. The skeleton thus provides an analogue for Rossi's understanding of history, for it is at once a structure and a ruin, a record of events and a record of time, and in this sense a statement of facts and not causes. But these are not its only attributes. For it is also an object that can be used to study its own structure. This structure has two aspects: one is its own abstract significance; the other is the precise nature of its individual parts. The latter is of particular importance because the mere study of structure—of the vertebrae of the skeleton—is far too general for Rossi. Any generalized framework acts as a mesh which always allows the most important parts to pass through—in this case, the city's most singular elements and those which give it its specificity.

Thus, the skeleton, which may on one level be compared to the urban plan, while a general structure of parts, is also a material artifact in itself: a collective artifact. The skeleton's nature as a collective artifact allows us to understand Rossi's metaphor of the city as a giant man-made house, a macrocosm of the individual house of man. Here the dissolution of scale becomes central to the argument, as will be seen. This giant house comes into being through a double process. One process is that of production, in the sense of the city as a work of *manufatto* (manufacture), an object literally made by the hands of men; the second process is that of time, which ultimately produces an autonomous artifact. The first process assumes a time which is only that of manufacture—a time with no before or after; it relates the object of manufacture, which has no extensive or indeterminate history, to man. The second process is not only singular as opposed to collective, but it supersedes man in that it has its own reason and motivation and thus its own autonomous form, which, by virtue of its not being determined by the subject man, is independent of its use.

This latter process, that of time, can be seen in Rossi's concept of *permanence,* which affects collective and individual artifacts in the city in different ways. The two main permanences in the city are housing and monuments. With respect to the first, Rossi distinguishes between housing and individual houses. Housing is a permanence in the city while individual houses are not; thus, a residential district in the city may persist as such over many centuries, while individual houses within a district will tend to change. With respect to monuments, the relationship is the opposite, for here it is the individual artifact that persists in the city. Monuments are defined by Rossi as primary elements in the city which are persistent and characteristic urban artifacts. They are distinguished from housing, the other primary element in the city, by their nature as a place of symbolic function, and thus a function related to time, as opposed to a place of conventional function, which is only related to use.

As a permanence and a primary element in the city, a monument is dialectically related to the city's growth, and this dialectic of permanence and growth is characteristic of time in Rossi's skeleton-city. It implies a city which not only possesses a before and an after, but which is defined by their interrelationship. Rossi defines primary elements as "those elements which can both retard and accelerate the process of urbanization in a city." Thus they are catalytic. When a monument retards the process of urbanization, it is considered by Rossi to be "pathological." The Alhambra in Granada is an example of one such part of a city functioning as a museum piece. In the city whose analogue is the skeleton, such a museum piece is like an embalmed body: it gives only the appearance of being alive.

These preserved or pathological permanences, mummified presences in the city, often tend to owe their permanent character to their location within a specific context. In this sense, the quasi-naturalistic urbanism of the contemporary "contextualists" is dialectically opposed, in Rossi's view, to the concept of evolutionary time. For Rossi real time tends to erode and supersede the neatly circumscribed and meticulously observed imagery of a specific urban context. In light of the recent development of a so-called contextual urbanism which has come to dominate urban thought some fifteen years after the original publication of this book, Rossi's text can be seen as an anticipatory argument against the "empty formalism" of context reductively seen as a plan relationship of figure and ground.

However, permanences in the city are not only "pathological." At times they may be "propelling." They serve to bring the past into the present, providing a past that can still be experienced. Artifacts like the Theater at Arles or the Palazzo della Ragione in Padua tend to synchronize with the process of urbanization because they are not defined only by an original or previous function, nor by their context, but have survived precisely because of their form—one which is able to accommodate different functions over time. Here again, the analogue of the skeleton can be seen to be quite precise. Like the skeleton which is not living and has lost its original function, only its form remaining intact, the propelling permanence continues to function as a record of time. This argument, which in itself is a critique of "naive functionalism," contains within it Rossi's concept of specific place or *locus*.

The *locus* is a component of an individual artifact which, like permanence, is determined not just by space but also by time, by topography and form, and, most importantly, by its having been the site of a succession of both ancient and more recent events. For Rossi, the city is a theater of human events. This theater is no longer just a representation; it is a reality. It absorbs events and feelings, and every new event contains within it a memory of the past and a potential memory of the future. Thus, while the locus is a site which can accommodate a series of events, it also in itself *constitutes* an event. In this sense, it is a unique or characteristic place, a "*locus solus*." Its singularity is recognizable in signs that come to mark the occurrence of these events. Included in this idea of the *locus solus*, then, is the specific but also universal relationship between a certain site and the buildings that are on it. Buildings may be signs of events that have occurred on a specific site; and this threefold relationship of site, event, and sign becomes a characteristic of urban artifacts. Hence, the *locus* may be said to be the place on which architecture or form can be imprinted. Architecture gives form to the singularity of place, and it is in this specific form that the *locus* persists through many changes, particularly transformations of function. Rossi uses the example of the city of Split in Yugoslavia. He says:
The city of Split which grew up within the walls of Diocletian's palace gave new uses and new meanings to unchangeable forms. This is symbolic of the meaning of the architecture of the city, where the broadest adaptability to multiple functions corresponds to an extreme precision of form.

This relationship suggests a different limit to history. History exists so long as an object is in use; that is, so long as a form relates to its original function. However, when form and function are severed, and only form remains vital, history shifts into the realm of memory. When history ends, memory begins. The singular form of Split now not only signifies its own individuality, but at the same time, it is also a sign, a record of events that are part of a collective—that is, urban—memory. History comes to be known through the relationship between a collective memory of events, the singularity of place (*locus solus*), and the sign of the place as expressed in form.

Thus is can be said that the process by which the city is imprinted with form is urban history, but the succession of events constitutes its memory. The "soul of the city," an idea derived by Rossi from the French urban geographers, resides in its history; once this soul is given form, it becomes the sign of a place. Memory becomes the guide to its structure. If time in the chronological sense belonged to a classical context, and in the historicist sense to a modernist context, then once associated with memory rather than history, it moves into a *psychological* context.

The new time of architecture is thus that of memory, which replaces history. The individual artifact for the first time is understood within the psychological construct of collective memory. Time as collective memory leads Rossi to his particular transformation of the idea of type. With the introduction of memory into the object, the object comes to embody both an idea of itself and a memory of a former self. Type is no longer a neutral structure found in history but rather an analytical and experimental structure which now can be used to operate on the skeleton of history; it becomes an apparatus, an instrument for analysis and measure. As has been said, this apparatus, while purportedly scientific and logical, is not reductive, but allows urban elements to be perceived as having a meaning that is always original and authentic and, although typologically predetermined, often unforeseen. Its logic, then, exists prior to a form, but also comes to constitute the form in a new way.

Thus it can be said that the apparatus used to measure the object implies and also is implied in the object itself. This returns us to the analogue of the skeleton, which was seen to be at once instrument and object. With this recognition appears a new *object-apparatus*, an object—as opposed to a subject—that for the first time *analyzes and also invents*. This is the *other* process mediating between architect and architecture. In the past, innovations in architecture did not generally occur through the object; typology was never seen as having the potential to be the animating force of a *design process*. Rossi, however, discovers in typology the possibility of invention precisely because type is now both process and object. As a process, it contains a synthetic character which is in itself a manifestation of form. Moreover, while the alteration of certain typological elements over time is a stimulus to invention, it is also the effect of memory on type which allows for the new process of design. Memory fuses with history to give type-form a significance beyond that of an original function. Thus, typology, which previously consisted only of the classification of the known, now can serve as a catalyst for invention. It becomes the essence of design for the autonomous researcher.

Both the idea of the end of history, when a form no longer embodies its original function, and the passing of type from the realm of history into that of memory lead Rossi to his internalized, analogous design process. Analogy is Rossi's most important apparatus. It is equally useful to him in writing and in drawing. It is in this context that this book can be seen as an analogous artifact itself—a written analogue to built and drawn artifacts. The written analogue, like the drawn one, is bound up with both place and memory. Yet unlike the city, the urban skeleton, the analogue is detached from specific place and specific time, and becomes instead an abstract *locus* existing in what is a purely typological or *architectural* time-place. In this way, by displacing type from history to make a connection between place and memory, Rossi attempts through the erasure of history and transcendence of real places to reconcile the contradictions of modernist utopia—literally "no place"—and humanist reality—built "some place."

The time of analogy, a bifocal lens of history and memory, takes in and collapses chronological time—the time of events—and atmospheric time—the time of place: place and event, *locus solus* plus *time-place*. The place of analogy is thereby abstracted from the real city. Linking type-forms and specific places, it dispossesses, reassociates, and thus transforms real places and real times. It is *no place*, but a no place that is different from that of modernist utopia precisely because it is rooted in both history and memory. This suppression of the precise boundaries of time and place within the analogue produces the same kind of dialectic that exists in memory between remembering and forgetting.

Here the analogous city can be seen to subvert the real city. Where the skeleton was seen as the form and measure of specific times and places in the city, the analogous design process displaces the specifics of time and place in the city for another reality, a psychological one based on memory. While the skeleton, as a physical and analytical object embedded in a humanist and modernist context, represents verifiable data, archaeological artifact, memory and analogy bring the process of architecture into the realm of the psychological, transforming

8

both subject and object. The analogous process, when applied to the actual geography of the city, therefore acts as a corrosive agent.

The subversive analogues proposed in Rossi's work involve two kinds of transformation. One is the dislocation of place, the other the dissolution of scale. In the former, the logical geography of the skeleton is displaced through typological invention. Rossi uses the example of Canaletto's painting of three Palladian projects; here, the different places of the projects are collapsed into one place. In the latter kind of transformation, the dissolution of scale allows the individual building to refer analogically to the city as a whole. This is illustrated in Rossi's example of Diocletian's Palace at Split: "Split discovers in its typological form an entire city. From here it follows that the single building can be designed by analogy with the city." Even more importantly, this implies, the design of cities lies latent in the idea of the individual building. In Rossi's view, the city's dimensions are unimportant because its meaning and quality reside not in its different scales, but in its actual constructions and individual artifacts. Once again, it is time which connects things which belong to different scales and heterogeneous contexts. This time-place continuity opposes the discontinuity between the industrial—modernist—city and the historical—humanist—city which was proclaimed by the Modern Movement.

Rossi's denial of the importance of scale in the context of the city is thereby a direct assault on most twentieth-century urbanism. Yet precisely within this context it becomes problematic. For with the dissolution of scale in the analogous process there is a seeming return to the very same humanist position first proposed in Alberti's reciprocal metaphor of the house and the city: "the city is like a large house, and the house in turn is like a small city." Rossi's attempt to propose an *other* urban model through analogy becomes conflated with this specifically fifteenth-century model of the city as the microcosm of a harmonic and macrocosmic universe. For Rossi, the object represents a dialectic between the giant collective house of the city and its individual, specific houses, the city's artifacts. So long as this dialectic remains internal to architecture and thereby autonomous, the city as object is separate from man. Like a truly modernist object, it grows upon itself and refers to itself, acquiring its own consciousness and memory. However, once it is seen to be based on a metaphorical conception of the house of individual man, it returns again to the Albertian humanist relationship and a fifteenth-century conception of the object. Rossi never resolves this ambivalence in his work. For despite the latent humanism, there is always an overriding pessimism which undercuts this potential neo-Enlightenment position. In Rossi's own pronouncement, "the time of each man is limited; the future, therefore, must be the present."

Analogy, as has been said, allows for both memory and history. It mixes "autobiography and civic history," individual and collective. In Rossi's formulation, all great manifestations of social life and all great works of art are born in unconscious life. This leads him directly, if unwittingly, into a second contradiction. The city, a social entity, is in psychological terms a product of a collective unconscious. At the same time, as an amalgam of formal artifacts, it is a product of many individuals. That is, it is both a product *of* the collective and a design *for* the collective. In both cases the *collective subject* is the central concept. This returns us to Rossi's idea of the *locus*. Whereas the *locus solus* defines the nature of the object, *homo civilis* now defines the nature of the subject. The contradiction of the singular object and the collective subject further betrays Rossi's neo-humanism, for despite his pessimism about the power of the individual to domi-

9

nate history, still he sees the city ultimately as "the human achievement par excellence."

In the end, there is no model for a twentieth-century city in Rossi's work, no city-object which corresponds to the collective psychological subject. Rossi finally obscures the presence of a psychological context and undermines the necessity for a psychological model. To propose that the same relationship between individual subject (man) and individual object (house) which existed in the Renaissance now obtains between the collective psychological subject (the population of the modern city) and its singular object (the city, but seen as a house at a different scale) is to imply that nothing has changed, that the city of humanist man is the same place as the city of psychological man. Rossi's psychological subject—the autonomous researcher—still continues to seek his own home in the collective house of the city.

Houses of Memory

Cities are in reality great camps of the living and the dead where many elements remain like signals, symbols, cautions. When the holiday is over, what remains of the architecture is scarred, and the sand consumes the street again. There is nothing left but to resume with a certain obstinacy the reconstruction of elements and instruments in expectation of another holiday.
Aldo Rossi
A Scientific Autobiography

For Aldo Rossi the European city has become the house of the dead. Its history, its function, has ended; it has erased the specific memories of the houses of individual childhood to become a *locus* of collective memory. As a giant or collective house of memory, it has a psychological reality which arises from its being a place of fantasy and illusion, an analogue of both life and death as transitional states. For Rossi, writings and drawings are an attempt to explore this giant house of memory and all those specific places of habitation encountered between the childhood house of fantasy and hope and the house of illusion and death.

The bourgeois house of Rossi's childhood permitted fantasy, but denied the ordering of type. *The Architecture of the City* attempts, through the apparatus of type, to place the city before us in such a way that, in spite of history, memory can imagine and reconstruct a future time of fantasy. This memory is set into motion through the inventive potential of the typological apparatus, the analogous design process. Rossi's drawings of the "analogous city" can be seen to evolve directly from his writing of *The Architecture of the City*. The analogous drawing embodies a changed condition of representation; it exists as the record of its own history. Thus, Rossi's drawings of the city, giving form to their own history, become *part* of the city, not just a representation of it. They have an authenticity, a reality which is, precisely, that of illusion. This reality may then, in turn, be *represented* in actual buildings.

The architectural drawing, formerly thought of exclusively as a form of representation, now becomes the *locus* of another reality. It is not only the site of illusion, as it has been traditionally, but also a real place of the suspended time of both life and death. Its reality is neither foward time—progress—nor past time—nostalgia, for by being an autonomous object it eludes both the progressive and regressive forces of historicism. In this way it, and not its built representation, becomes architecture: the *locus* of a collective idea of death and,

10

through its autonomous invention, of a new metaphysic of life in which death is no longer a finality but only a transitional state. The analogous drawing thereby approximates this changed condition of subject—man—relative to his object—city.

Rossi's analogous drawings, like his analogous writings, deal primarily with time. Unlike the analgous writings, however, the drawings represent the suspension of two times: the one processual—where the drawn object is something moving toward but not yet arrived at its built representation; and the other atmospheric—where drawn shadows indicate the stopping of the clock, are a frozen and constant reminder of this new equation of life and death. No longer in the analogous drawing is time represented by a precisely measured aspect of light, the length of a shadow, or the aging of a thing. Rather, time is expressed as an infinite past which takes things back to the timelessness of childhood, of illusions, of fragments of possessions and autobiographical images of the author's own alienated childhood—of which history's narrative can no longer give an effective account. Yet for Rossi, this personal aspect of architecture is unsentimentalized. In his personal vision of time, the same dialectic applies as in the city: history provides the material for biography but memory provides the material for autobiography; as in the city, memory begins when history ends. It encompasses both future time and past time: a project that has to be done and one that is already completed. The images of ruin activate this unconscious memory, linking the discarded and the fragmentary with new beginnings. Here again, the apparently coherent orderliness of logic is biographical, but fragments are autobiographical. Abandonment and death—the attributes of the skeleton—are through this dialectic now seen as parts of a process of transformation; death is a new beginning associated with some unknown hope.

Ultimately, *The Architecture of the City*, notwithstanding its attempt to place itself within a certain tradition of "scientific" writing about the city, is a very private and personal text. It is the written analogue of yet another analogous process: the unconscious revelation of a potential new relationship of man to object. It anticipates the psychological subject—*homo civilis*—of the collective unconscious; but at the same time, it also nostalgically evokes the individual subject, the mythic hero-architect of humanism, the inventor of the house. The shadow of the humanist poet hovers continuously behind the figure of the autonomous researcher. The potential transformation of the individual into the collective subject is left in suspension. Ambiguously, the object of the analogous city begins to define the subject once again, not so much as a humanist-hero, nor as the psychological collective, but as a complex, divided, and shattered solitary survivor, appearing before, but not withstanding, the collective will of history.

Peter Eisenman

In the fifteen years since its first publication, this book has been published in four languages and numerous editions and has influenced a generation of young European architects. I first set forth the idea of the analogous city in the introduction to the second Italian edition and certain clarifications in the introduction to the Portuguese edition, and since then I have preferred not to make any additions to the text. Like a painting, a building, or a novel, a book becomes a collective artifact; anyone can modify it in his own way, the author notwithstanding. The figure is clear, as in Henry James's "figure in the carpet," but everyone sees it in a different way. James's image suggests that clear analysis gives rise to questions that are difficult to subject to further analysis. For this reason, when I first wrote this book, its style and literary construction were of particular concern to me, as they always are, because only the perfect clarity of a rational system allows one to confront irrational questions, forces one to consider the irrational in the only way possible: through the use of reason.

I believe that the concepts of *locus*, monument, and type have opened up a general discussion which, if at times inhibited by academicism, at other times has produced significant studies and initiated a debate that still today is far from being resolved. For reasons of chronology, I have used great discretion in altering the book, mostly modifying the illustrations and clarifying the language of the present translation.

America . . . For this country I have decided to write a special introduction. Even though I was influenced by American culture as a young man, especially its literature and film, the influence was more fantastic than scientific. My slight knowledge of the language and lack of direct experience of the country made it alien to me as a field of work. Its architecture, its people, American things were not yet precious to me. Even more seriously, I could not measure my own architecture—my ideas and my buildings—on the immeasurable body, static and dynamic, sane and feverish, that is the United States. Nonetheless, I was convinced that there was an official Italian academic ignorance of America; film directors and writers understood it far better than architects, critics, and scholars.

In the last few years, in the course of my visiting and working in America, *L'architettura della città* has returned to mind. Although eminently sensible critics have found this to be a paradox, I have discovered the American city and countryside to be the decisive confirmation of this book. Perhaps, one might say, this is because America is by now an "old" country full of monuments and traditions, or because in America the city of parts is a historic and dynamic reality; but more importantly, it is because America seems to be constructed in accordance with the arguments presented in this book.

What does this mean?

Once the pioneers arrived in this vast new country, they had to organize their cities. They followed one of two models: either cities were laid out along grid lines, as is the case in most Latin American cities, New York, and other centers, or they were established as "main street" villages, the image of which has become legendary in film westerns. In both cases, the buildings of the by now bourgeois European city had a particular relevance: church, bank, school, bar, and market. Even the American house maintained with extreme precision two fundamental European typologies: the Spanish corral and patio in Latin America, and the English country house in the United States.

2 View of Nantucket, Massachusetts.

13

3

5

4

6

7

I could offer many examples of this but I am hardly an expert on the history of American architecture and cities; I prefer to stay with my impressions, albeit ones rooted in a sense of history. The market in Providence, towns in Nantucket where the white houses of the fishermen are like fragments of ships and the church towers echo the lighthouses, seaports like Galveston—all seem to be, and are, constructed out of preexisting elements that are then deformed by their own context; just as the large American cities exalt the urban whole of stone and cement, brick and glass, from which *they* are constructed. Perhaps no urban construct in the world equals that of a city like New York. New York is a city of monuments such as I did not believe could exist.

Few Europeans understood this during the years of the Modern Movement in architecture; but certainly Adolf Loos did in his project for the *Chicago Tribune* competition. That enormous Doric column, which to many Europeans may have seemed only a game, a Viennese *divertissement*, is the synthesis of the distorting effects of scale and the application of "style" in an American framework.

This framework of the American urban context or landscape makes it as impressive to walk through Wall Street on Sunday as it would be to walk into a realization of one of Serlio's perspective drawings (or of some other Renaissance theoretician). The contributions of, and the intersection with, European experiences here have created an "analogous city" of unexpected meaning, as unexpected as the meaning of the "styles" and "orders" that have been applied to it. This meaning is completely different from what historians of modern architecture typically see: an America composed of disparate examples of good architecture, to be sought out with guides—an America of a necessarily "international style" and of the isolated masterpiece of the great artist in a sea of mediocrity and businessmen's buildings. The exact opposite is true.

American architecture is above all "the architecture of the city": primary elements, monuments, parts. Thus, if we wish to speak of "style," in the sense of Renaissance and Palladian and Gothic architecture, we cannot leave out America.

All of these architectures reemerge in my projects. After I had completed work on the *Casa dello Studente* in Chieti, an American student gave me a publication on Thomas Jefferson's Academical Village at the University of Virginia. I found a number of striking analogies to my own work, yet I had previously known nothing of this project. Carlo Aymonino, in an article entitled "Une architecture de l'optimisme," has written: "If, to make an absurd supposition, Aldo Rossi were to do a project for a new city, I am convinced that his project would resemble the plans made two hundred years ago upon which many American cities were based: a street network that permits the division of property, a church that is a church, a public building whose function would be immediately apparent, a theater, a courthouse, individual houses. Everyone would be able to judge whether the building corresponded to his ideal—a process and a structure that would give confidence as much to the designer as to those who would use it." In these terms, the American city is a new chapter of this book rather than merely an introduction.

I spoke in the introduction to the first Italian edition of a necessary chapter that I could not yet write about colonial cities. In the magnificent book *Urbanismo español en America* by Javier Rojas and Louis Moreno,[1] there are certain plans that deserve particular study, plans of incredible cities in which the churches,

3 View of Nantucket, Massachusetts.
4 Project for the Chicago Tribune Building, Adolf Loos, 1922.
5 University of Virginia, Charlottesville, Virginia, Thomas Jefferson, 1817.
6 Aerial view of the University of Virginia, Charlottesville, Virginia, Thomas Jefferson, 1817.
7 View of Wall Street, New York City.

15

8 Church of Rosário, Bahia, Brazil.
9 Sanctuary of Senhor do Bomfim,
Bahia, Brazil.
10 Aerial rendering of Cranbrook
Academy of Art, Bloomfield Hills,
Michigan, Eliel Saarinen, 1926.
11 Bellefontaine Cemetery, St. Louis,
Missouri.

8

9

10

11

courts, and gallerias of Seville and Milan are transformed into new urban design elements. In my earlier introduction, I spoke of *la fabbrica della città* and not of "urban architecture": *fabbrica* means "building" in the old Latin and Renaissance sense of man's construction as it continues over time. Still today, the Milanese call their cathedral "la fabbrica del dôm," and understand by this expression both the size and the difficulty of the church's construction, the idea of a single building whose process goes on over time. Clearly, the Cathedrals of Milan and Reggio Emilia and the Tempio Malatestiano in Rimini were—are—beautiful in their incompleteness. They were and are a kind of abandoned architecture—abandoned by time, by chance, or by the destiny of the city. The city in its growth is defined by its artifacts, leaving open many possibilities and containing unexplored potential. This has nothing to do with the concept of open form or open work; rather it suggests the idea of *interrupted* work. The analogous city is in essence the city in its diverse totality; this fact is visible in the echoes of the East and the North that one finds in Venice, in the piecemeal structure of New York, and in the memories and analogies that every city always offers.

Interrupted work cannot be foreseen by the individual. It is, so to speak, a historical accident, an occurrence, a change in the history of the city. But, as I point out later in this book with respect to the Napoleonic plan for Milan, there is ultimately a relationship between any single architectural project and the destiny of the city. When a project or a form is not utopian or abstract but evolves from the specific problems of the city, it persists and expresses these problems both through its style and form as well as through its many deformations. These deformations or alterations are of limited importance precisely because architecture, or the *fabbrica* of the city, constitutes an essentially *collective* artifact and derives from this its characteristic features.

I concluded the first edition of this book in 1966 by writing, "Thus the complex structure of the city arises from a discourse whose terms of reference are as yet inadequately developed. This discourse is perhaps exactly like the laws that regulate the life and destiny of individual men; each biography, although compressed between birth and death, contains much complexity. Clearly the architecture of the city, the human thing par excellence, is—even beyond the meaning and the feelings with which we recognize it—the real sign of this biography."

This overlapping of the individual and the collective memory, together with the invention that takes place within the *time* of the city, has led me to the concept of *analogy*. Analogy expresses itself through a process of architectural design whose elements are preexisting and formally defined, but whose true meaning is unforeseen at the beginning and unfolds only at the end of the process. Thus the meaning of the process is identified with the meaning of the city.

This, in the end, is the meaning of preexisting elements: the city, like the biography of an individual man, presents itself through certain clearly defined elements such as house, school, church, factory, monument. But this biography of the city and of its buildings, apparently so clearly defined, has in itself sufficient imagination and interest—deriving precisely from their reality—ultimately to envelop it in a fabric of artifacts and feelings that is stronger than either architecture or form, and goes beyond any utopian or formalistic vision of the city.

I think of a nameless architecture of large cities, streets, and residential blocks, of houses scattered in the countryside, of the urban cemetery in such a city as St.

Louis, of the people, living and dead, who have continued to build the city. We may look at modern cities without enthusiasm, but if we could only see with the eye of the archaeologist of Mycenae, we would find behind the facades and fragments of architecture the figures of the oldest heroes of our culture.

I have eagerly written this introduction for the first American edition of the book both because this rereading, like every experience or design, reflects my own development, and because the emerging character of the American city adds an extraordinary testimony to this book.

Perhaps, as I said at the beginning, this is the meaning of the architecture of the city; like the figure in the carpet, the figure is clear but everyone reads it in a different way. Or rather, the more clear it is, the more open it is to a complex evolution.

New York, 1978

*12 Nineteenth-century engraving of
the Ponte del Diavolo on the St.
Gotthard Pass, Switzerland, by R.
Dikenmann. Nature and man's
construction.*

Introduction
Urban Artifacts and a
Theory of the City

The city, which is the subject of this book, is to be understood here as architecture. By architecture I mean not only the visible image of the city and the sum of its different architectures, but architecture as construction, the construction of the city over time. I believe that this point of view, objectively speaking, constitutes the most comprehensive way of analyzing the city; it addresses the ultimate and definitive fact in the life of the collective, the creation of the environment in which it lives.

I use the term architecture in a positive and pragmatic sense, as a creation inseparable from civilized life and the society in which it is manifested. By nature it is collective. As the first men built houses to provide more favorable surroundings for their life, fashioning an artificial climate for themselves, so they built with aesthetic intention. Architecture came into being along with the first traces of the city; it is deeply rooted in the formation of civilization and is a permanent, universal, and necessary artifact.

Aesthetic intention and the creation of better surroundings for life are the two permanent characteristics of architecture. These aspects emerge from any significant attempt to explain the city as a human creation. But because architecture gives concrete form to society and is intimately connected with it and with nature, it differs fundamentally from every other art and science. This is the basis for an empirical study of the city as it has evolved from the earliest settlements. With time, the city grows upon itself; it acquires a consciousness and memory. In the course of its construction, its original themes persist, but at the same time it modifies and renders these themes of its own development more specific. Thus, while Florence is a real city, its memory and form come to have values that also are true and representative of other experiences. At the same time, the universality of these experiences is not sufficient to explain the precise form, the type of object which is Florence.

The contrast between particular and universal, between individual and collective, emerges from the city and from its construction, its architecture. This contrast is one of the principal viewpoints from which the city will be studied in this book. It manifests itself in different ways: in the relationship between the public and private sphere, between public and private buildings, between the rational design of urban architecture and the values of *locus* or place.

At the same time, my interest in quantitative problems and their relationship to qualitative ones was one of the reasons this book came into being. My studies of the city have always underscored the difficulties of establishing an overall synthesis and of proceeding readily to produce a quantitative evaluation of analytic material. In fact, while each urban intervention seems fated to rely on general criteria of planning, each part of the city seems to be a singular place, a *locus solus*. Although it is impossible to make decisions about such interventions in any rational manner solely on the basis of local situations, one must realize that their singularity is still what characterizes them.

Urban studies never attribute sufficient importance to research dealing with singular urban artifacts. By ignoring them—precisely those aspects of reality that are most individual, particular, irregular, and also most interesting—we end up constructing theories as artificial as they are useless. With this in mind, I have sought to establish an *analytical method* susceptible to quantitative evaluation and capable of collecting the material to be studied under unified criteria. This method, presented as a theory of urban artifacts, stems from the identifi-

21

cation of the city itself as an artifact and from its division into individual buildings and dwelling areas.* While the division of the city along these lines has been proposed many times, it has never been placed in this particular context.

Architecture, attesting to the tastes and attitudes of generations, to public events and private tragedies, to new and old facts, is the fixed stage for human events. The collective and the private, society and the individual, balance and confront one another in the city. The city is composed of many people seeking a general order that is consistent with their own particular environment.

The changes in housing and in the land on which houses leave their imprint become signs of this daily life. One need only look at the layers of the city that archaeologists show us; they appear as a primordial and eternal fabric of life, an immutable pattern. Anyone who remembers European cities after the bombings of the last war retains an image of disemboweled houses where, amid the rubble, fragments of familiar places remained standing, with their colors of faded wallpaper, laundry hanging suspended in the air, barking dogs—the untidy intimacy of places. And always we could see the house of our childhood, strangely aged, present in the flux of the city.

Images, engravings, and photographs of these disemboweled cities, record this vision. Destruction and demolition, expropriation and rapid changes in use and as a result of speculation and obsolescence, are the most recognizable signs of urban dynamics. But beyond all else, the images suggest the interrupted destiny of the individual, of his often sad and difficult participation in the destiny of the collective. This vision in its entirety seems to be reflected with a quality of permanence in urban monuments. Monuments, signs of the collective will as expressed through the principles of architecture, offer themselves as primary elements, fixed points in the urban dynamic.

The laws of reality and their modifications thus constitute the structure of human creation. It is the purpose of this study to organize and order these principal problems of urban science. The study of these problems in their totality, with all their implications, returns urban science to the broader complex of human sciences; but it is in such a framework that I believe that urban science has its own autonomy (even though in the course of this study I will often question the nature of that autonomy and its limits as a science). We can study the city from a number of points of view, but it emerges as autonomous only when we take it as a fundamental given, as a construction and as architecture; only when we analyze urban artifacts for what they are, the final constructed result of a complex operation, taking into account all of the facts of this operation which cannot be embraced by the history of architecture, by sociology, or by other sciences. Urban science, understood in this way, can be seen in its comprehensiveness to constitute one of the principal chapters in the history of culture.

Among the various methods employed in this study of the city, the most important is the comparative one. Because the city will be seen comparatively, I lay particular emphasis on the importance of the historical method; but I also maintain that we cannot study the city simply from a historical point of view. Instead we must carefully elaborate a city's enduring elements or *permanences* so as to avoid seeing the history of the city solely as a function of them. I believe that permanent elements can even be considered pathological at times. The significance of permanent elements in the study of the city can be compared to that which fixed structures have in linguistics; this is especially evident as the study of the city presents analogies with that of linguistics, above all in terms of the complexity of its processes of transformation and permanence.

The points specified by Ferdinand de Saussure[1] for the development of linguistics can be translated into a program for the development of an urban science: description and history of existing cities; research on the forces that are at play in a permanent and universal way in all urban artifacts; and naturally, delimitation and definition of the field of study. Bypassing a systematic development of a program of this type, however, I have instead sought to dwell particularly on historical problems and methods of describing urban artifacts, on the relationships between local factors and the construction of urban artifacts, and on the identification of the principal forces at play in the city—that is, the forces that are at play in a permanent and universal way.

The last part of this book attempts to set forth the political problem of the city; here the political problem is understood as a problem of choice by which a city realizes itself through its own idea of city. In fact, I am convinced that there should be many more studies devoted to the history of the idea of the city, that is, to the history of ideal cities and urban utopias. To my knowledge, undertakings in this area are scarce and fragmentary, although some partial studies exist in the fields of architectural history and the history of political ideas. In effect, there is a continuous process of influence, exchange, and often opposition among urban artifacts, and the city and ideal proposals make this process concrete. I maintain that the history of architecture and built urban artifacts is always the history of the architecture of the ruling classes; it remains to be seen within what limits and with what concrete success eras of revolution have imposed their own alternative proposals for organizing the city.

In beginning a study of the city, we find ourselves confronted with two very different positions. These are best exemplified in the Greek city, where the Aristotelian analysis of urban reality is counterposed to that of Plato's Republic. This opposition raises important methodological questions. I am inclined to believe that Aristotelian planning, insofar as it was a study of artifacts, decisively opened the road to the study of the city and also to urban geography and urban architecture. Yet doubtless we cannot explain certain experiences without availing ourselves of both these levels of analysis. Certainly ideas of a purely spatial type have at times notably modified, in form and through direct or indirect interventions, the times and modes of the urban dynamic.

There exists a mass of impressive studies to refer to in the elaboration of an urban theory, but it is necessary to gather these studies from the most disparate places, then to avail ourselves of what they suggest about the construction of a general frame of reference, and finally to apply this knowledge to a specific urban theory. Without here outlining such an overall frame of reference for the history of the study of the city, we can note that two major systems exist: one that considers the city as the product of the generative-functional systems of its architecture and thus of urban space, and one that considers it as a spatial structure. In the first, the city is derived from an analysis of political, social, and economic systems and is treated from the viewpoint of these disciplines; the second belongs more to architecture and geography. Although I begin with this second viewpoint, I also draw on those facts from the first which raise significant questions.

In this work, then, I will refer to writers from diverse fields who have elaborated theses that I consider fundamental (not, of course, without certain qualifications). However, there are not a great many works which I find valuable, considering the mass of material available; and in any case let me observe generally that if an author or a book does not play an important part in an analysis, or if a point of view does not constitute an essential contribution to a work of research, it is meaningless to cite it. Therefore I prefer to discuss only the works of those authors who seem to be fundamental for a study of this kind. The theories of some of these scholars, in fact, constitute the hypotheses of my study. Wherever one chooses to lay the groundwork for an autonomous urban theory, it is impossible to avoid their contributions.

There are also certain fundamental contributions that I would have liked to consider except that they are naturally beyond the scope of this discussion, for example the profound intuitions of Fustel de Coulanges and Theodor Mommsen.[2] In the case of the first of these writers I refer in particular to the importance he ascribes to institutions as truly constant elements of historical life and to the relationship between myth and institution. Myths come and go, passing slowly from one place to another; every generation recounts them differently and adds new elements to the patrimony received from the past; but behind this changing reality, there is a permanent reality that in some way manages to elude the action of time. We must recognize the true foundation of this reality in religious tradition. The relationships which man found with the gods in the ancient city, the cults that he consecrated to them, the names under which he invoked them, the gifts and the sacrifices made to them were all tied to inviolable laws. The individual man had no power over them.

I believe that the importance of ritual in its collective nature and its essential character as an element for preserving myth constitutes a key to understanding the meaning of monuments and, moreover, the implications of the founding of the city and of the transmission of ideas in an urban context. I attribute an especial importance to monuments, although their significance in the urban dynamic may at times be elusive. This work must be carried forward; I am convinced that in order to do so, it will be necessary to probe into the relationship between monument, ritual, and mythological elements along the lines indicated by Fustel de Coulanges. For if the ritual is the permanent and conserving element of myth, then so too is the monument, since, in the very moment that it testifies to myth, it renders ritual forms possible.

Such a study should, once again, begin with the Greek city, which offers many significant insights concerning the meaning of the urban structure, and which at its origins had an inseparable relationship with the mode of being and behavior of human beings. The researches of modern anthropology on the social structure of primitive villages also raise new issues relative to the study of urban planning; they demand a study of urban artifacts according to their essential themes. The existence of such essential themes implies a foundation for the study of urban artifacts, and requires a knowledge of a larger number of artifacts and an integration of these artifacts in time and space—more precisely, a clarifying of those forces that are at work in a permanent and universal way in all urban artifacts.

Let us consider the relationship between an actual urban artifact and the utopian idea of the city. Generally this relationship is studied within a limited period of history, within a modest framework, and with results that are usually questionable. What are the limits within which we can integrate such limited analyses into the larger framework of the permanent and universal forces at play in the city? I am convinced that the polemics that arose between utopian socialism and

24

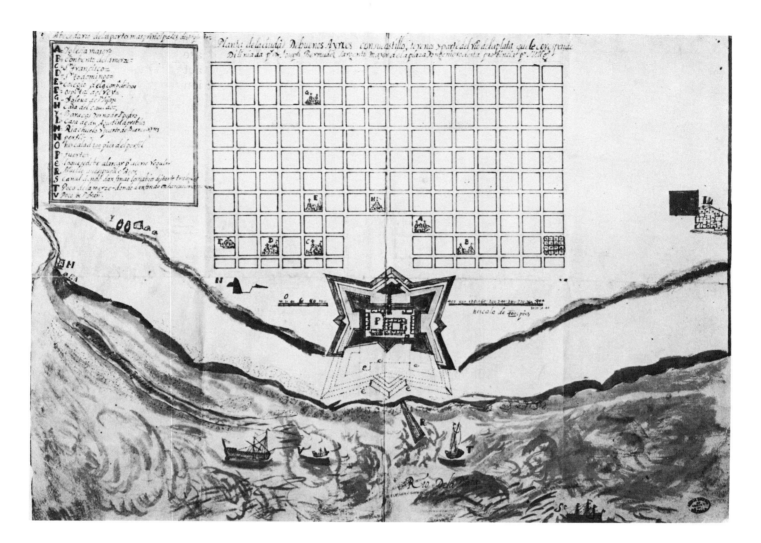

*13 Plan of the city and castle of
Buenos Aires on Rio de la Plata,
1708.*

14 Santiago de Compostela, Spain.
The "rueiro" or rural road leading
from the city into the country.

scientific socialism during the second half of the nineteenth century constitute important scholarly material, but we cannot consider only their purely political aspects; these must be measured against the reality of urban artifacts or else we will perpetuate serious distortions. And this must be done for the full range of urban artifacts. What we see in actuality are the application and extension of only partial conclusions to the history of the city. Generally, the most difficult historical problems of the city are resolved by dividing history into periods and hence ignoring or misunderstanding the universal and permanent character of the forces of the urban dynamic; and here the importance of a comparative method becomes evident.

Thus, in their obsession with certain sociological characteristics of the industrial city, urban scholars have obscured a series of extremely important artifacts which can enrich urban science with a contribution as original as it is necessary. I am thinking, for example, of the settlements and colonial cities founded by Europeans particularly after the discovery of America. Little exists on this topic; Gilberto Freyre, for example, discusses the influence of certain urban and building typologies that the Portuguese brought to Brazil and how these were structurally linked to the type of society established in Brazil.[3] The relationship between the rural and latifundist families in the Portuguese colonization of Brazil was associated with the theocracy conceived by the Jesuits and, together with the Spanish and French influence, was enormously important in the formation of the South American city. I consider such research to be very important for the study of urban utopias and the construction of the city.

This book is divided into four parts: in the first I will consider problems of description and classification and thus of typology; in the second, the structure of the city in terms of its different elements; in the third, the architecture of the city and the *locus* on which it is imprinted and thus urban history; and in the fourth, the basic questions of urban dynamics and the problem of politics as choice.

The urban image, its architecture, pervades all of these problems and invests all of man's inhabited and constructed realm with value. It arises inevitably because it is so deeply rooted in the human condition. As Pierre Vidal de la Blache wrote, "the heath, the woods, the cultivated fields, the uncultivated zones, are related in an inseparable whole, the memory of which man carries with him."[4] This inseparable whole is at once the *natural* and the *artificial* homeland of man, and suggests a definition of natural which also applies to architecture. I am thinking of Francesco Milizia's definition of the essence of architecture as the imitation of nature: "Although architecture in reality lacks a model in nature, it has another model derived from man's natural labor in constructing his first house."[5]

With this definition in mind, I believe that the urban theoretical scheme presented in this book can give rise to many kinds of development, and that these developments can in turn take unexpected emphases and directions. For I am convinced that progress concerning knowledge of the city can be real and efficacious only if we do not try to reduce the city to any one of its partial aspects, thereby losing sight of its broader significance. My outline for the establishment of an urban theory should be evaluated within this framework. It is the result of long research and is intended to initiate a discourse on its own development and research rather than simply to act as a confirmation of results.

27

Our description of the city will be concerned primarily with its form. This form depends on real facts, which in turn refer to real experiences: Athens, Rome, Paris. The architecture of the city summarizes the city's form, and from this form we can consider the city's problems.

By architecture of the city we mean two different things: first, the city seen as a gigantic man-made object, a work of engineering and architecture that is large and complex and growing over time; second, certain more limited but still crucial aspects of the city, namely urban artifacts, which like the city itself are characterized by their own history and thus by their own form. In both cases architecture clearly represents only one aspect of a more complex reality, of a larger structure; but at the same time, as the ultimate verifiable fact of this reality, it constitutes the most concrete possible position from which to address the problem.

We can understand this more readily by looking at specific urban artifacts, for immediately a series of obvious problems opens up for us. We are also able to perceive certain problems that are less obvious: these involve the quality and the uniqueness of each urban artifact.

In almost all European cities there are large palaces, building complexes, or agglomerations that constitute whole pieces of the city and whose function now is no longer the original one. When one visits a monument of this type, for example the Palazzo della Ragione in Padua, one is always surprised by a series of questions intimately associated with it. In particular, one is struck by the multiplicity of functions that a building of this type can contain over time and how these functions are entirely independent of the form. At the same time, it is precisely the form that impresses us; we live it and experience it, and in turn it structures the city.

Where does the individuality of such a building begin and on what does it depend? Clearly it depends more on its form than on its material, even if the latter plays a substantial role; but it also depends on being a complicated entity which has developed in both space and time. We realize, for example, that if the architectural construction we are examining had been built recently, it would not have the same value. In that case the architecture in itself would be subject to judgment, and we could discuss its style and its form; but it would not yet present us with that richness of its own history which is characteristic of an urban artifact.

In an urban artifact, certain original values and functions remain, others are totally altered; about some stylistic aspects of the form we are certain, others are less obvious. We contemplate the values that remain—I am also referring to spiritual values—and try to ascertain whether they have some connection with the building's materiality, and whether they constitute the only empirical facts that pertain to the problem. At this point, we might discuss what our idea of the building is, our most general memory of it as a product of the collective, and what relationship it affords us with this collective.

It also happens that when we visit a palazzo like the one in Padua or travel through a particular city, we are subjected to different experiences, different impressions. There are people who do not like a place because it is associated with some ominous moment in their lives; others attribute an auspicious character to a place. All these experiences, their sum, constitute the city. It is in this

15 Palazzo della Ragione, Padua, Italy.

29

16

16 Palazzo della Ragione, Padua, Italy.

17 Palazzo della Ragione, Padua, Italy.

18 Palazzo della Ragione, Padua, Italy. Above: "Drawing of the remains of the Salone della Ragione ruined by a hurricane on August 17, 1956," by Giorgio Fossati. Below: Ground floor plan as it has existed from 1425 up to today, according to the reconstruction by A. Moschetti. Thirteenth-century walls in black.

17

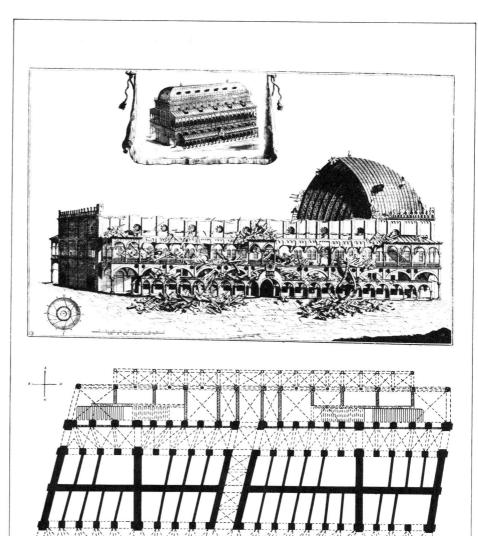

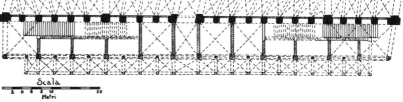

18

sense that we must judge the *quality* of a space—a notion that may be extremely difficult for our modern sensibility. This was the sense in which the ancients consecrated a place, and it presupposes a type of analysis far more profound than the simplistic sort offered by certain psychological interpretations that rely only on the legibility of form.

We need, as I have said, only consider one specific urban artifact for a whole string of questions to present themselves; for it is a general characteristic of urban artifacts that they return us to certain major themes: individuality, *locus*, design, memory. A particular type of knowledge is delineated along with each artifact, a knowledge that is more complete and different from that with which we are familiar. It remains for us to investigate how much is real in this complex of knowledge.

I repeat that the reality I am concerned with here is that of the architecture of the city—that is, its form, which seems to summarize the total character of urban artifacts, including their origins. Moreover, a description of form takes into account all of the empirical facts we have already alluded to and can be quantified through rigorous observation. This is in part what we mean by urban morphology: a description of the forms of an urban artifact. On the other hand, this description is nothing but one moment, one instrument. It draws us closer to a knowledge of structure, but it is not identical with it.

Although all of the students of the city have stopped short of a consideration of the structure of urban artifacts, many have recognized that beyond the elements they had enumerated there remained the *âme de la cité*, in other words, the *quality* of urban artifacts. French geographers, for example, concentrated on the development of an important descriptive system, but they failed to exploit it to conquer this ultimate stronghold; thus, after indicating that the city is constituted as a totality and that this totality is its raison d'être, they left the significance of the structure they had glimpsed unexamined. Nor could they do otherwise with the premises from which they had set out: all of these studies failed to make an analysis of the actual quality of specific urban artifacts.

The Urban Artifact as a Work of Art

I will later examine the main outlines of these studies, but first it is necessary to introduce one fundamental consideration and several authors whose work guides this investigation.

As soon as we address questions about the individuality and structure of a specific urban artifact, a series of issues is raised which, in its totality, seems to constitute a system that enables us to analyze a work of art. As the present investigation is intended to establish and identify the nature of urban artifacts, we should initially state that there is *something in the nature of urban artifacts that renders them very similar—and not only metaphorically—to a work of art*. They are material constructions, but notwithstanding the material, something different: although they are conditioned, they also condition.[1]

This aspect of "art" in urban artifacts is closely linked to their quality, their uniqueness, and thus also to their analysis and definition. This is an extremely complex subject, for even beyond their psychological aspects, urban artifacts are complex in themselves, and while it may be possible to analyze them, it is difficult to define them. The nature of this problem has always been of particular

32

interest to me, and I am convinced that it directly concerns the architecture of the city.

If one takes any urban artifact—a building, a street, a district—and attempts to describe it, the same difficulties arise which we encountered earlier with respect to the Palazzo della Ragione in Padua. Some of these difficulties derive from the ambiguity of language, and in part these difficulties can be overcome, but there will always be a type of experience recognizable only to those who have walked through the particular building, street, or district.

Thus, the concept that one person has of an urban artifact will always differ from that of someone who "lives" that same artifact. These considerations, however, can delimit our task; it is possible that our task consists principally in defining an urban artifact from the standpoint of its manufacture: in other words, to define and classify a street, a city, a street in a city; then the location of this street, its function, its architecture; then the street systems possible in the city and many other things.

We must therefore concern ourselves with urban geography, urban topography, architecture, and several other disciplines. The problem is far from easy, but not impossible, and in the following paragraphs we will attempt an analysis along these lines. This means that, in a very general way, we can establish a logical geography of any city; this logical geography will be applied essentially to the problems of language, description, and classification. Thus, we can address such fundamental questions as those of typology, which have not yet been the object of serious systematic work in the domain of the urban sciences. At the base of the existing classifications there are too many unverified hypotheses, which necessarily lead to meaningless generalizations.

By using those disciplines to which I have just referred, we are working toward a broader, more concrete, and more complete analysis of urban artifacts. The city is seen as the human achievement par excellence; perhaps, too, it has to do with those things that can only be grasped by actually experiencing a given urban artifact. This conception of the city, or better, urban artifacts, as a work of art has, in fact, always appeared in studies of the city; we can also discover it in the form of greatly varying intuitions and descriptions in artists of all eras and in many manifestations of social and religious life. In the latter case it has always been tied to a specific place, event, and form in the city.

The question of the city as a work of art, however, presents itself explicitly and scientifically above all in relation to the conception of the nature of collective artifacts, and I maintain that no urban research can ignore this aspect of the problem. How are collective urban artifacts related to works of art? All great manifestations of social life have in common with the work of art the fact that they are born in unconscious life. This life is collective in the former, individual in the latter; but this is only a secondary difference because one is a product of the public and the other is for the public: the public provides the common denominator.

Setting forth the problem in this manner, Claude Lévi-Strauss[2] brought the study of the city into a realm rich with unexpected developments. He noted how, more than other works of art, the city achieves a balance between natural and artificial elements; it is an object of nature and a subject of culture. Maurice Halbwachs[3] advanced this analysis further when he postulated that imagination and collective memory are the typical characteristics of urban artifacts.

These studies of the city which embrace its structural complexity have an unexpected and little-known precedent in the work of Carlo Cattaneo. Cattaneo never explicitly considered the question of the artistic nature of urban artifacts, but the close connection in his thinking between art and science as two concrete aspects of the development of the human mind anticipates this approach. Later I will discuss how his concept of the city as the ideal principle of history, the connection between country and city, and other issues that he raised relate to urban artifacts. While at this point I am mostly interested in how he approaches the city, in fact Cattaneo never makes any distinction between city and country since he considers that all inhabited places are the work of man: " . . . every region is distinguished from the wilderness in this respect: that it is an immense repository of labor . . . . This land is thus not a work of nature; it is the work of our hands, our artificial homeland."[4]

City and region, agricultural land and forest become human works because they are an immense repository of the labor of our hands. But to the extent that they are our "artificial homeland" and objects that have been constructed, they also testify to values; they constitute memory and permanence. The city *is* in its history. Hence, the relationship between place and man and the work of art—which is the ultimate, decisive fact shaping and directing urban evolution according to an aesthetic finality—affords us a complex mode of studying the city.

Naturally we must also take into account how people orient themselves within the city, the evolution and formation of their sense of space. This aspect constitutes, in my opinion, the most important feature of some recent American work, notably that of Kevin Lynch.[5] It relates to the conceptualization of space, and can be based in large measure on anthropological studies and urban characteristics. Observations of this type were also made by Maximilien Sorre using such material, particularly the work of Marcel Mauss on the correspondence between group names and place names among Eskimos.[6] For now, this argument will merely serve as an introduction to our study; it will be more useful to return to it after we have considered several other aspects of the urban artifact—of the city, that is, as a great, comprehensive representation of the human condition.

I will interpret this representation against the background of its most fixed and significant stage: architecture. Sometimes I ask myself why architecture is not analyzed in these terms, that is, in terms of its profound value as a human thing that shapes reality and adapts material according to an aesthetic conception. It is in this sense not only the place of the human condition, but itself a part of that condition, and is represented in the city and its monuments, in districts, dwellings, and all urban artifacts that emerge from inhabited space. It is from this point of view that a few theorists have tried to analyze the urban structure, to sense the fixed points, the true structural junctions of the city, those points from which the activity of reason proceeds.

I will now take up the *hypothesis of the city as a man-made object*, as a work of architecture or engineering that grows over time; this is one of the most substantial hypotheses from which to work.[7]

It seems that useful answers to many ambiguities are still provided by the work of Camillo Sitte, who in his search for laws of the construction of the city that were not limited to purely technical considerations took full account of the

34

"beauty" of the urban scheme, of its form: "We have at our disposal three major methods of city planning, and several subsidiary types. The major ones are the gridiron system, the radial system, and the triangular system. The sub-types are mostly hybrids of these three. Artistically speaking, not one of them is of any interest, for in their veins pulses not a single drop of artistic blood. All three are concerned exclusively with the arrangement of street patterns, and hence their intention is from the start a purely technical one. A network of streets always serves only the purposes of communication, never of art, since it can never be comprehended sensorily, can never be grasped as a whole except in a plan of it. In our discussions so far street networks have not been mentioned for just that reason; neither those of ancient Athens, of Rome, of Nuremberg, or of Venice. They are of no concern artistically, because they are inapprehensible in their entirety. Only that which a spectator can hold in view, what can be seen, is of artistic importance: for instance, the single street or the individual plaza."[8]

Sitte's admonition is important for its empiricism, and it seems to me that this takes us back to certain American experiences which we mentioned above, where artistic quality can be seen as a function of the ability to give concrete form to a symbol. Sitte's lesson beyond question helps to prevent many confusions. It refers us to the technique of urban construction, where there is still the actual moment of designing a square and then a principle which provides for its logical transmission, for the teaching of its design. But the models are always, somehow, the single street, the specific square.

On the other hand, Sitte's lesson also contains a gross misconception in that it reduces the city as a work of art to one artistic episode having more or less legibility rather than to a concrete, overall experience. We believe the reverse to be true, that the whole is more important than the single parts, and that only the urban artifact in its totality, from street system and urban topography down to the things that can be perceived in strolling up and down a street, constitutes this totality. Naturally we must examine this total architecture in terms of its parts.

We must begin with a question that opens the way to the problem of classification—that of the typology of buildings and their relationship to the city. This relationship constitutes a basic hypothesis of this work, and one that I will analyze from various viewpoints, always considering buildings as moments and parts of the whole that is the city. This position was clear to the architectural theorists of the Enlightenment. In his lessons at the Ecole Polytechnique, Durand wrote, "Just as the walls, the columns, &c., are the elements which compose buildings, so buildings are the elements which compose cities."[9]

Typological Questions

The city as above all else a human thing is constituted of its architecture and of all those works that constitute the true means of transforming nature. Bronze Age men adapted the landscape to social needs by constructing artificial islands of brick, by digging wells, drainage canals, and watercourses. The first houses sheltered their inhabitants from the external environment and furnished a climate that man could begin to control; the development of an urban nucleus expanded this type of control to the creation and extension of a microclimate. Neolithic villages already offered the first transformations of the world according to man's needs. The "artificial homeland" is as old as man.

35

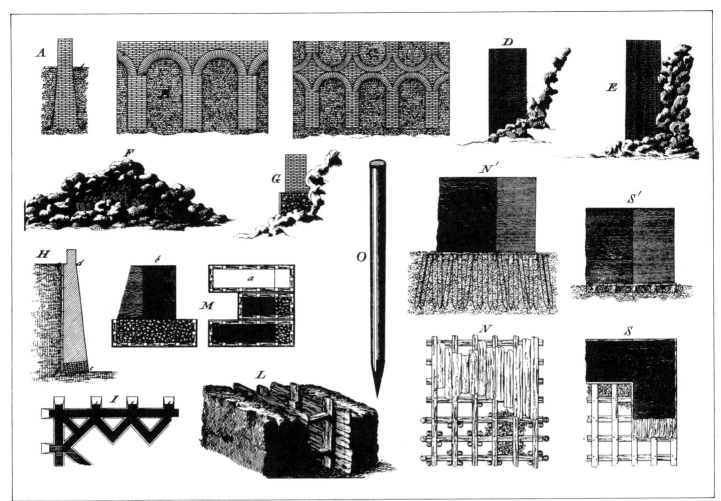

19

19 Various types of foundations. From "Principj di Architettura Civile," Francesco Milizia, 1832.

20 Courtyard housing and walled marketplace. A) Plan of a Greek house. B) Plan of a Roman house. C) Plan by Scipione Maffei showing half of the marketplace of Verona. D) View of the shops of the marketplace (marked "c" in the plan). E) External view of the wall encircling the marketplace. From "Principj di Architettura Civile," Francesco Milizia, 1832.

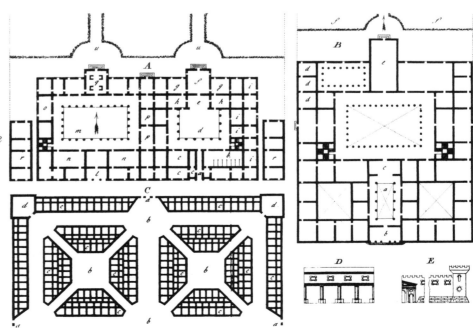

20

21

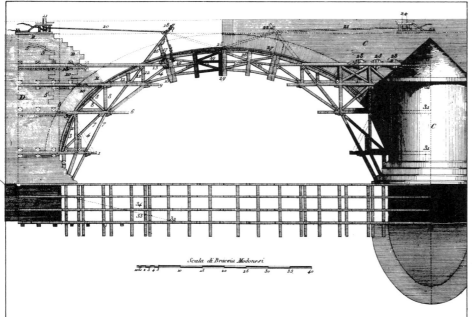

21 The Doric order. From "Principj di Architettura Civile," Francesco Milizia, 1832.
22 Wooden armature for the construction of vaults. From "Principj di Architettura Civile," Francesco Milizia, 1832.

22

23

24

23 Corral of Valvanera, Seville,
Spain.
24 Corral of Valvanera, Seville,
Spain.
25 Calle Pais Vasco, parallel to the
main street of the town of Viana in
Spain.
26 "Alley of the Washerwomen"
between Corso San Gottardo and the
Naviglio canal, Milan.

25

26

In precisely this sense of transformation the first forms and types of habitation, as well as temples and more complex buildings, were constituted. The *type* developed according to both needs and aspirations to beauty; a particular type was associated with a form and a way of life, although its specific shape varied widely from society to society. The concept of type thus became the basis of architecture, a fact attested to both by practice and by the treatises.

It therefore seems clear that typological questions are important. They have always entered into the history of architecture, and arise naturally whenever urban problems are confronted. Theoreticians such as Francesco Milizia never defined type as such, but statements like the following seem to be anticipatory: "The comfort of any building consists of three principal items: its site, its form, and the organization of its parts."[10] I would define the concept of type as something that is permanent and complex, a logical principle that is prior to form and that constitutes it.

One of the major theoreticians of architecture, Quatremère de Quincy, understood the importance of these problems and gave a masterly definition of type and model:
"The word 'type' represents not so much the image of a thing to be copied or perfectly imitated as the idea of an element that must itself serve as a rule for the model . . . . The model, understood in terms of the practical execution of art, is an object that must be repeated such as it is; type, on the contrary, is an object. according to which one can conceive works that do not resemble one another at all. Everything is precise and given in the model; everything is more or less vague in the type. Thus we see that the imitation of types involves nothing that feelings or spirit cannot recognize. . . .

"We also see that all inventions, notwithstanding subsequent changes, always retain their elementary principle in a way that is clear and manifest to the senses and to reason. It is similar to a kind of nucleus around which the developments and variations of forms to which the object was susceptible gather and mesh. Therefore a thousand things of every kind have come down to us, and one of the principal tasks of science and philosophy is to seek their origins and primary causes so as to grasp their purposes. Here is what must be called 'type' in architecture, as in every other branch of human inventions and institutions. . . . We have engaged in this discussion in order to render the value of the word *type*—taken metaphorically in a great number of works—clearly comprehensible, and to show the error of those who either disregard it because it is not a model, or misrepresent it by imposing on it the rigor of a model that would imply the conditions of an identical copy."[11]

In the first part of this passage, the author rejects the possibility of type as something to be imitated or copied because in this case there would be, as he asserts in the second part, no "creation of the model"—that is, there would be no making of architecture. The second part states that in architecture (whether model or form) there is an element that plays its own role, not something to which the architectonic object conforms but something that is nevertheless present in the model. This is the *rule*, the structuring principle of architecture.

In fact, it can be said that this principle is a constant. Such an argument presupposes that the architectural artifact is conceived as a structure and that this structure is revealed and can be recognized in the artifact itself. As a constant, this principle, which we can call the typical element, or simply the type, is to be found in all architectural artifacts. It is also then a cultural element and as such can be investigated in different architectural artifacts; typology becomes in this way the analytical moment of architecture, and it becomes readily identifiable at the level of urban artifacts.

Thus typology presents itself as the study of types of elements that cannot be further reduced, elements of a city as well as of an architecture. The question of monocentric cities or of buildings that are or are not centralized, for example, is specifically typological; no type can be identified with only one form, even if all architectural forms are reducible to types. The process of reduction is a necessary, logical operation, and it is impossible to talk about problems of form without this presupposition. In this sense all architectural theories are also theories of typology, and in an actual design it is difficult to distinguish the two moments.

Type is thus a constant and manifests itself with a character of necessity; but even though it is predetermined, it reacts dialectically with technique, function, and style, as well as with both the collective character and the individual moment of the architectural artifact. It is clear, for example, that the central plan is a fixed and constant type in religious architecture; but even so, each time a central plan is chosen, dialectical themes are put into play with the architecture of the church, with its functions, with its constructional technique, and with the collective that participates in the life of that church. I tend to believe that housing types have not changed from antiquity up to today, but this is not to say that the actual way of living has not changed, nor that new ways of living are not always possible. The house with a loggia is an old scheme; a corridor that gives access to rooms is necessary in plan and present in any number of urban houses. But there are a great many variations on this theme among individual houses at different times.

Ultimately, we can say that type is the very idea of architecture, that which is closest to its essence. In spite of changes, it has always imposed itself on the "feelings and reason" as the principle of architecture and of the city.

While the problem of typology has never been treated in a systematic way and with the necessary breadth, today its study is beginning to emerge in architecture schools and seems quite promising. I am convinced that architects themselves, if they wish to enlarge and establish their own work, must again be concerned with arguments of this nature.[12] Typology is an element that plays its own role in constituting form; it is a constant. The problem is to discern the modalities within which it operates and, moreover, its effective value.

Certainly, of the many past studies in this field, with a few exceptions and save for some honest attempts to redress the omission, few have addressed this problem with much attention. They have always avoided or displaced it, suddenly pursuing something else—namely *function*. Since this problem of function is of absolutely primary importance in the domain of our inquiry, I will try to see how it emerges in studies of the city and urban artifacts in general and how it has evolved. Let us say immediately that the problem can be addressed only when we have first considered the related problems of description and classification. For the most part, existing classifications have failed to go beyond the problem of function.

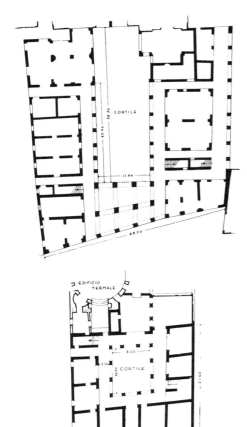

EDIFICIO
TERMALE

CORTILE

CORTILE

27

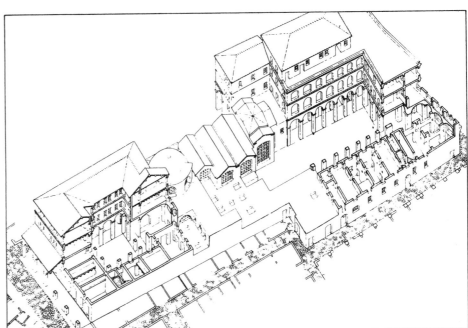

28

CASE GIARDINO

29

30

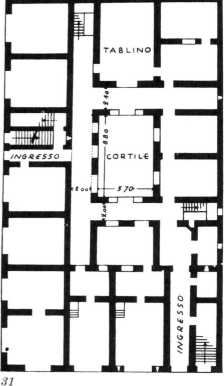

31

27 Plan of the House of Aurighi, above, and Serapide, below, Ostia Antica, Rome, as reconstructed by Italo Gismondi, 1940.

28 Insula with the Houses of Aurighi and Serapide and bathhouse in the middle, Ostia Antica, Rome. Axonometric drawing by Italo Gismondi.

29 The zone of Ostia Antica, Rome, including the Houses of Aurighi and Serapide, as reconstructed by Italo Gismondi, 1940.

30 Internal courtyard of House of Diana, Ostia Antica, Rome. Rendering by Italo Gismondi.

31 House of Diana, Ostia Antica, Rome. Plan as reconstructed by Italo Gismondi, 1940.

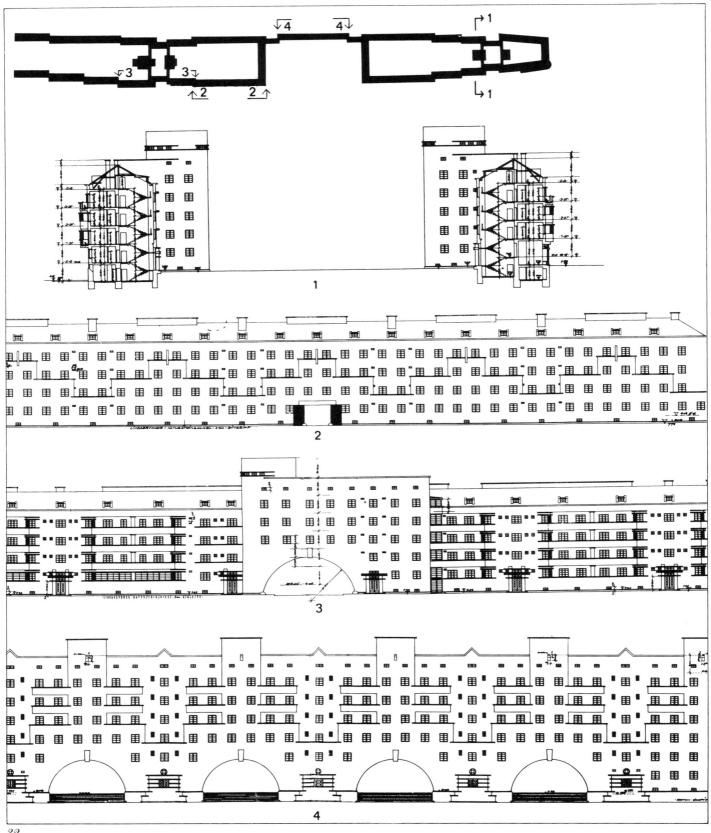

1

2

3

4

33

32 Section and elevations from
various orientations of
Heiligenstädter Strasse Nos. 82–90,
Karl Marx-Hof, Vienna, Karl Ehn.
33 Karl Marx-Hof, Vienna, begun
1927.

Critique of Naive Functionalism

We have indicated the principal questions that arise in relation to an urban artifact—among them, individuality, *locus*, memory, design itself. Function was not mentioned. I believe that any explanation of urban artifacts in terms of function must be rejected if the issue is to elucidate their structure and formation. We will later give some examples of important urban artifacts whose function has changed over time or for which a specific function does not even exist. Thus, one thesis of this study, in its effort to affirm the value of architecture in the analysis of the city, is the denial of the explanation of urban artifacts in terms of function. I maintain, on the contrary, that far from being illuminating, this explanation is regressive because it impedes us from studying forms and knowing the world of architecture according to its true laws.

We hasten to say that this does not entail the rejection of the concept of function in its most proper sense, however, that is, as an algebra of values that can be known as functions of one another, nor does it deny that between functions and form one may seek to establish more complex ties than the linear ones of cause and effect (which are belied by reality itself). More specifically, we reject that conception of functionalism dictated by an ingenuous empiricism which holds that *functions bring form together* and in themselves constitute urban artifacts and architecture.

So conceived, function, physiological in nature, can be likened to a bodily organ whose function justifies its formation and development and whose alterations of function imply an alteration of form. In this light, functionalism and organicism, the two principal currents which have pervaded modern architecture, reveal their common roots and the reason for their weakness and fundamental ambiguity. Through them form is divested of its most complex derivations: type is reduced to a simple scheme of organization, a diagram of circulation routes, and architecture is seen as possessing no autonomous value. Thus the aesthetic intentionality and necessity that characterize urban artifacts and establish their complex ties cannot be further analyzed.

Although the doctrine of functionalism has earlier origins, it was enunciated and applied clearly by Bronislaw Malinowski, who refers explicitly to that which is man-made, to the object, the house: "Take the human habitation . . . here again the integral function of the object must be taken into account when the various phases of its technological construction and the elements of its structure are studied."[13] From a beginning of this sort one quickly descends to a consideration solely of the purposes which man-made items, the object and the house, serve. The question "for what purpose?" ends up as a simple justification that prevents an analysis of what is real.

This concept of function comes to be assumed as a given in all architectural and urbanistic thinking and, particularly in the field of geography, leads to a functionalist and organicist characterization of a large part of modern architecture. In studies of the classification of cities, it overwhelms and takes priority over the urban landscape and form; and although many writers express doubts as to the validity and exactitude of this type of classification, they argue that there is no other viable classification to offer as an alternative. Thus Georges Chabot,[14] after declaring the impossibility of giving the city a precise definition because there is always a "residue" that is impossible to describe in a precise way, then turns to function, even if he immediately admits its inadequacy.

In such formulations, the city as an agglomeration is explained precisely on the basis of what functions its citizens seek to exercise; the function of a city becomes its raison d'être, and in this form reveals itself. In many cases the study of morphology is reduced to a simple study of function. Once the concept of function is established, in fact, one immediately arrives at obvious classifications: commercial cities, cultural cities, industrial cities, military cities, etc.

Morever, even in the context of a somewhat general critique of the concept of function, it must be pointed out that there is already within this system of assigning functions a difficulty in establishing the role of the *commercial function*. In fact, as proposed, the concept of classification according to function is far too superficial; it assumes an identical value for all types of functions, which simply is not the case. Actually, the fact that the commercial function is predominant is increasingly evident.

This commercial function is the basis, in terms of production, of an "economic" explanation of the city that, beginning with the classical formulation offered by Max Weber,[15] has undergone a specific development, one to which we shall have to return later. Given a function-based classification of the city, it is only logical that the commercial function in both the city's formation and its development presents itself as the most convincing explanation for the multiplicity of urban artifacts and is tied to economic theories of the city.

Once we attribute different values to different functions, we deny the validity of naive functonalism; in fact, using this line of reasoning, we see that naive functionalism ends up contradicting its own initial hypothesis. Furthermore, if urban artifacts were constantly able to reform and renew themselves simply by establishing new functions, the values of the urban structure, as revealed through its architecture, would be continuous and easily available. The permanence of buildings and forms would have no significance, and the very idea of the transmission of a culture, of which the city is an element, would be questionable. None of this corresponds to reality.

Naive functionalist theory is quite convenient for elementary classifications, however, and it is difficult to see what can substitute for it at this level. It serves, that is, to maintain a certain order, and to provide us with a simple instrumental fact—just so long as it does not pretend that an explanation for more complex facts can be extracted from this same order.

On the other hand, the definition of type that we have tried to propose for urban artifacts and architecture, a definition which was first enunciated in the Enlightenment, allows us to proceed to an accurate classification of urban artifacts, and ultimately also to a classification based on function wherever the latter constitutes an aspect of the general definition. If, alternatively, we begin with a classification based on function, type would have to be treated in a very different way; indeed, if we insist on the primacy of function we must then understand type as the organizing model of this function. But this understanding of type, and consequently urban artifacts and architecture, as the organizing principle of certain functions, almost totally denies us an adequate knowledge of reality. Even if a classification of buildings and cities according to their function is permissible as a generalization of certain kinds of data, it is inconceivable to reduce the structure of urban artifacts to a problem of organizing some more or less important function. Precisely this serious distortion has impeded and in large measure continues to impede any real progress in studies of the city.

For if urban artifacts present nothing but a problem of organization and classification, then they have neither continuity nor individuality. Monuments and architecture have no reason to exist; they do not "say" anything to us. Such positions clearly take on an ideological character when they pretend to objectify and quantify urban artifacts; utilitarian in nature, these views are adopted as if they were products for consumption. Later we will see the more specifically architectural implications of this notion.

To conclude, we are willing to accept functional classification as a practical and contingent criterion, the equivalent of a number of other criteria—for example, social make-up, constructional system, development of the area, and so on—since such classifications have a certain utility; nonetheless it is clear that they are more useful for telling us something about the point of view adopted for classification than about an element itself. With these provisos in mind, they can be accepted.

Problems of Classification

In my summary of functionalist theory I have deliberately emphasized those aspects that have made it so predominant and widely accepted. This is in part because functionalism has had great success in the world of architecture, and those who have been educated in this discipline over the past fifty years can detach themselves from it only with difficulty. One ought to inquire into how it has actually determined modern architecture, and still inhibits its progressive evolution today; but this is not an issue I wish to pursue here.

Instead, I wish to concentrate on the importance of other interpretations within the domain of architecture and the city which constitute the foundations of the thesis that I am advancing. These include the social geography of Jean Tricart, the theory of persistence of Marcel Poète, and Enlightenment theory, particularly that of Milizia. All of these interest me primarily because they are based on a continuous reading of the city and its architecture and have implications for a general theory of urban artifacts.

For Tricart,[16] the *social content* of the city is the basis for reading it; the study of social content must precede the description of the geographical artifacts that ultimately give the urban landscape its meaning. Social facts, to the extent that they present themselves as a specific content, precede forms and function and, one might say, embrace them.

The task of human geography is to study the structures of the city in connection with the form of the place where they appear; this necessitates a sociological study of place. But before proceeding to an analysis of place, it is necessary to establish *a priori* the limits within which place can be defined. Tricart thus establishes three different orders or scales:
1. the scale of the street, including the built areas and empty spaces that surround it;
2. the scale of the district, consisting of a group of blocks with common characteristics;
3. the scale of the entire city, considered as a group of districts.
The principle that renders these quantities homogeneous and relates them is social content.

48

On the basis of Tricart's thesis, I will develop one particular type of urban analysis which is consistent with his premises and takes a topographical point of view that seems quite important to me. But before doing so, I wish to register a fundamental objection to the scale of his study, or the three parts into which he divides the city. That urban artifacts should be studied solely in terms of place we can certainly admit, but what we cannot agree with is that places can somehow be explained on the basis of different scales. Moreover, even if we admit that the notion is useful either didactically or for practical research, it implies something unacceptable. This has to do with the *quality* of urban artifacts.

Therefore while we do not wholly deny that there are different scales of study, we believe that it is inconceivable to think that urban artifacts change in some way as a result of their size. The contrary thesis implies accepting, as do many, the principle that the city is modified as it extends, or that urban artifacts in themselves are different because of the size at which they are produced. As was stated by Richard Ratcliff, "To consider the problems of locational maldistribution only in the metropolitan context is to encourage the popular but false assumption that these are the problems of size. We shall see that the problems to be viewed crop up in varying degrees of intensity in villages, towns, cities, and metropolises, for the dynamic forces of urbanism are vital wherever men and things are found compacted, and the urban organism is subject to the same natural and social laws regardless of size. To ascribe the problems of the city to size is to imply that solutions lie in reversing the growth process, that is, in deconcentration; both the assumption and the implication are questionable."[17]

At the scale of the street, one of the fundamental elements in the urban landscape is the inhabited real estate and thus the structure of urban real property. I speak of inhabited real estate and not the house because the definition is far more precise in the various European languages. Real estate has to do with the deed registry of land parcels in which the principal use of the ground is for construction. The usage of inhabited land in large measure tends to be residential, but one could also speak of specialized real estate and mixed real estate, although this classification, while useful, is not sufficient.

To classify this land, we can begin with some considerations that are apparent from plans. Thus we have the following:
1. a block of houses surrounded by open space;
2. a block of houses connected to each other and facing the street, constituting a continuous wall parallel to the street itself;
3. a deep block of houses that almost totally occupies the available space;
4. houses with closed courts and small interior structures.

A classification of this type can be considered descriptive, geometric, or topographic. We can carry it further and accumulate other classificatory data relative to technical equipment, stylistic phenomena, the relationship between green and occupied spaces, etc. The questions this information gives rise to can lead us back to the principal issues which are, roughly speaking, those that deal with
1. objective facts;
2. the influence of the real-estate structure and economic data;
3. historical-social influences.
The real-estate structure and economic questions are of particular importance and are intimately bound up with what we call historical-social influences. In order to demonstrate the advantages of an analysis of this type, in the second

chapter of this book we will examine the problems of housing and the residential district. For now, we will continue with the subject of real-estate structure and economic data, even if the second is given summary treatment.

The shape of the plots of land in a city, their formation and their evolution, represents a long history of urban property and of the classes intimately associated with the city. Tricart has stated very clearly that an analysis of the contrasts in the form of plots confirms the existence of a class struggle. Modifications of the real-estate structure, which we can follow with absolute precision through historical registry maps, indicate the emergence of an urban bourgeoisie and the phenomenon of the progressive concentration of capital.

A criterion of this type applied to a city with as extraordinary a life cycle as ancient Rome offers information of paradigmatic clarity. It allows us to trace the evolution from the agricultural city to the formation of the great public spaces of the Imperial age and the subsequent transition from the courtyard houses of the Republic to the formation of the great plebeian *insulae*. The enormous lots that constituted the *insulae*, an extraordinary conception of the house-district, anticipate the concepts of the modern capitalist city and its spatial divison. They also help to explain its dysfunction and contradictions.

Real estate, which we considered earlier from a topographic point of view, also offers other possibilities of classification when seen in a socio-economic context. We can distinguish the following:
1. the "pre-capitalist" house, which is established by a proprietor without exploitative ends;
2. the "capitalist" house, which is meant for rental and in which everything is subordinated to the production of revenue. Initially it might be intended either for the rich or the poor, but in the first case, following the usual evolution of needs, the house drops rapidly in class status in response to social changes. These changes in status create blighted zones, one of the most typical problems of the modern capitalist city and as such the object of particular study in the United States, where they are more evident than in Italy;
3. the "para-capitalist" house, built for one family with one floor rented out;
4. the "socialist" house, which is a new type of construction appearing in socialist countries where there is no longer private land ownership and also in advanced democratic countries. Among the earliest European examples are the houses constructed by the city of Vienna after the First World War.

When this analysis of social content is applied with particular attention to urban topography, it becomes capable of providing us with a fairly complete knowledge of the city; such an analysis proceeds by means of successive syntheses, causing certain elementary facts to come to light which ultimately encompass more general facts. In addition, through the analysis of social content, the formal aspect of urban artifacts takes on a reasonably convincing interpretation, and a number of themes emerge that play an important role in the urban structure.

From the scientific point of view, the work of Marcel Poète[18] is without doubt one of the most modern studies of the city. Poète concerns himself with urban artifacts to the extent that they are indicative of the conditions of the urban organism; they provide precise information which is verifiable in the existing city. Their raison d'être is their continuity: while geographic, economic, and statistical information must also be taken into consideration along with historical facts, it is knowledge of the past that constitutes the terms of the present and the measure of the future.

Such knowledge can be derived from a study of city plans; these possess precise formal characteristics: for example, the form of a city's streets can be straight, sinuous, or curved. But the general form of the city also has a meaning of its own, and its needs naturally tend to be expressed in its built works, which beyond certain obvious differences present undeniable similarities. Thus in urban architecture a more or less clearly articulated bond is established between the shapes of things throughout history. Against a background of the differences between historical periods and civilizations, it therefore becomes possible to verify a certain constancy of themes, and this constancy assures a relative unity to the urban expression. From this develop the relationships between the city and the geographic region, which can be analyzed effectively in terms of the role of the street. Thus in Poète's analysis, the street acquires major significance; the city is born in a fixed place but the street gives it life. The association of the destiny of the city with communication arteries becomes a fundamental principle of development.

In his study of the relationship between the street and the city, Poète arrives at important conclusions. For any given city it should be possible to establish a classification of streets which should then be reflected in the map of the geographic area. Streets, whether cultural or commercial, should also be able to be characterized according to the nature of the changes that are effected because of them. Thus Poète repeats the Greek geographer Strabo's observation about the "shadow cities" along the Flaminian Way, whose development is explained as occurring "more because they were found situated along that road than for any inherent importance."[19]

From the street, Poète's analysis passes to the urban land, which contains natural artifacts as well as civic ones and becomes associated with the composition of the city. In the urban composition, everything must express as faithfully as possible the particular life of the collective organism. At the basis of this organism that is the city is the *persistence of the plan*.

This concept of persistence is fundamental to the theory of Poète; it also informs the analysis of Pierre Lavedan,[20] one of the most complete analyses available to us, with its interposing of elements drawn from geography and the history of architecture. In Lavedan, persistence is the generator of the plan, and this generator becomes the principal object of urban research because through an understanding of it one can rediscover the spatial formation of the city. The generator embodies a concept of persistence which is reflected in a city's physical structures, streets, and urban monuments.

The contributions of Poète and Lavedan, together with those of the geographers Chabot and Tricart, are among the most significant offerings of the French school to urban theory.

The contribution of Enlightenment thought to a comprehensive theory of urban artifacts would merit a separate study. One objective of the treatise writers of the eighteenth century was to establish principles of architecture that could be

34 Karl Marx-Hof, Vienna.

developed from logical bases, in a certain sense independently of design; thus the treatise took shape as a series of propositions derived serially from one another. Second, they conceived of the single element always as part of a system, the system of the city; therefore it was the city that conferred criteria of necessity and reality on single buildings. Third, they distinguished form, as the final manifestation of structure, from the analytical aspect of structure; thus form had a "classical" persistence of its own which could not be reduced to the logic of the moment.

One could discuss the second argument at length, but more substantial knowledge would certainly be necessary; clearly, while this argument applies to the existing city, it also postulates the future city and the inseparable relationship between the constitution of an artifact and its surroundings. Yet Voltaire had already indicated, in his analysis of the *grand siècle*, the limits of such architectures, how uninteresting a city would be if the task of every constructed work was to establish a direct relationship with the city itself.[21] The manifestation of these concepts is found in the Napoleonic plans and projects, which represent one of the moments of major equilibrium in urban history.

On the basis of these three arguments developed in the Enlightenment, we can examine the theory of Milizia.[22] The classification proposed by Milizia, an architectural essayist concerned with theories of urban artifacts, deals with both individual buildings and the city as a whole. He classified urban buildings as either private or public, the former meaning housing and the latter referring to certain "principal elements" which I will call *primary*. In addition, he presents these groupings as classes, which permits him to make distinctions within classes, distinguishing each principal element as a building type within a general function, or better, a general idea of the city. For example, villas and houses are in the first class, while in the second are police buildings, public utilities, storage facilities, etc. Buildings for public use are further distinguished as universities, libraries, and so on.

Milizia's analysis refers in the first place, then, to classes (public and private), in the second to the location of elements in the city, and in the third to the form and organization of individual buildings. "Greater public convenience demands that these buildings [for public use] be situated near the center of the city and organized around a large community square."[23] The general system is the city; the development of its elements is then bound up with the development of the system adopted.

What kind of city does Milizia have in mind? It is a city that is conceived together with its architecture. "Even without extravagant buildings, cities can appear beautiful and breathe desire. But to speak of a beautiful city is also to speak of good architecture."[24] This assertion seems definitive for all Enlightenment treatises on architecture; a beautiful city means good architecture, and vice versa.

It is unlikely that Enlightenment thinkers paused over this statement, so ingrained was it in their way of thinking; we know that their lack of understanding of the Gothic city was a result of their inability to accept the validity of single elements that constituted an urban landscape without seeing these elements relative to some larger system. If in their failure to understand the meaning and thus the beauty of the Gothic city they were shortsighted, this of course does not make their own system incorrect. However, to us today the beauty of the Gothic city appears precisely in that it is an extraordinary urban artifact whose unique-

53

ness is clearly recognizable in its components. Through our investigation of the parts of this city we grasp its beauty: it too participates in a system. There is nothing more false than an organic or spontaneous definition of the Gothic city.

There is yet another aspect of modernity in Milizia's position. After establishing his concept of classes, he goes on to classify each building type within the overall framework and to characterize it according to its function. This notion of function, which is treated independently of general considerations of form, is understood more as the building's purpose than as its function *per se*. Thus buildings for practical uses and those that are constructed for functions that are not equally tangible or pragmatic are put in the same class; for example, buildings for public health or safety are found in the same class as structures built for their magnificence or grandeur.

There are at least three arguments in favor of this position. Most important is the recognition of the city as a complex structure in which parts can be found that function as works of art. The second has to do with the value ascribed to a general typological discourse on urban artifacts or, in other words, the realization that one can give a technical explanation for those aspects of the city that by nature demand a more complex explanation by reducing them to their typological essence. The third argument relates to the fact that this typological essence plays "its own role" in the constitution of the model.

For example, in analyzing the monument, Milizia arrives at three criteria: "that it is directed toward the public good; that it is appropriately located; and that it is constituted according to laws of fitness."[25] "With respect to the customs governing the construction of monuments, no more can be said here generally than that they should be meaningful and expressive, of a simple structure, and with a clear and short inscription, so that the briefest glance reveals the effect for which they were constructed."[26] In other words, insofar as the nature of the monument is concerned, even if we cannot offer more than a tautology—a monument is a monument—we can still establish conditions around it which illustrate its typological and compositional characteristics, whether these precisely elucidate its nature or not. Again, these characteristics are for the most part of an urban nature; but they are equally conditions of architecture, that is, of composition.

This is a basic issue to which we will return later: namely, the way in which principles and classifications in the Enlightenment conception were a general aspect of architecture, but that in its realization and evaluation, architecture involved primarily the individual work and the individual architect. Milizia himself scorned the builders who mixed architectural and social orders as well as the proponents of objective models of functional organization such as were later produced by Romanticism, asserting that "to derive functional organization from beehives is to go insect-hunting . . . ."[27] Here again we find within a single formulation the two themes which were to be fundamental in the subsequent development of architectural thought, and which already indicated in their dual aspects of organicism and functionalism their anticipation of the Romantic sensibility: the abstract order of organization and the reference to nature.

With respect to function itself, Milizia writes, ". . . because of its enormous variety functional organization cannot always be regulated by fixed and constant laws, and as a result must always resist generalization. For the most part, the most renowned architects, when they wish to concern themselves with functional organization, mainly produced drawings and descriptions of their buildings rather than rules that could then be learned."[28] This passage clearly shows how function is understood here as a relationship and not a scheme of organization; in fact, as such it is rejected. But this attitude did not preclude a contemporaneous search for rules that might transmit principles of architecture.

I am now going to consider some of the questions underlying the various theories just outlined, emphasizing certain points which are crucial for the present study. The first theory referred to was drawn from the French school of geographers; I noted that although it provided a good descriptive system, it stopped short of an analysis of the structure of the city. In particular I mentioned the work of Chabot, for whom the city is a totality that constructs itself and in which all the elements participate in forming the *âme de la cité*. How is this latter perception to be reconciled with Chabot's study of function? The answer, already implicit in some of what has been said so far, is partially suggested by Sorre's critique of Chabot's book. Sorre wrote that for Chabot, in essence, *"la vie seule explique la vie."* This means that if the city explains itself, then a classification by functions is not an explanation but rather a descriptive system. This can be rephrased in the following manner: a description of function is easy to verify; like any study of urban morphology, it is an instrument. Furthermore, since it does not posit any element of continuity between the *genre de vie* and the urban structure, as the naive functionalists would like, it seems to be as useful an element of analysis as any other. We will retain from Chabot's studies his concept of the city as a totality and his approach to an understanding of this totality through the study of its various manifestations, its behavior.

In presenting the work of Tricart I tried to indicate the importance of a study of the city that takes social content as its point of departure; I believe that the study of social content has the capacity to illuminate the meaning of urban evolution in a concrete way. I especially emphasized the aspects of this research that relate to urban topography and therefore the formation of boundaries and the value of urban land as basic elements of the city; later we will look at these aspects from the standpoint of economic theory.

With respect to Lavedan's work, we can pose the following question: if the structure Lavedan proposes is a real structure, formed of streets, monuments, and the like, how does it relate to the present study? Structure, as Lavedan understands it, means the structure of urban artifacts, and in this way it resembles Poète's concept of the persistence of the plan and the plan as a generator. As this generator is by nature both real and abstract, it cannot be catalogued like a function. Moreover, since every function can be articulated through a form, and forms in turn contain the potential to exist as urban artifacts, one can say that forms tend to allow themselves to be articulated as urban elements; thus if a form is articulated at all, one can assume that a specific urban artifact persists together with it, and that it is precisely a form that persists through a set of transformations which constitutes an urban artifact par excellence.

I have already made a critique of naive functionalist classifications; I repeat, at times they are acceptable, so long as they remain within the handbooks of architecture to which they are appropriate. Such classifications presuppose that all urban artifacts are created to serve particular functions in a static way and that their structure precisely coincides with the function they perform at a certain moment. I maintain, on the contrary, that the city is something that persists

55

through its transformations, and that the complex or simple transformations of functions that it gradually undergoes are moments in the reality of its structure. Function here is meant only in the sense of complex relationships between many orders of facts. I reject linear interpretations of cause and effect because they are belied by reality itself. This interpretation certainly differs from that of "use" or of "functional organization."

I also wish to emphasize my reservations about a certain language and reading of the city and urban artifacts which present a serious obstacle to urban research. In many ways, this language is linked with naive functionalism on the one hand and a form of architectural romanticism on the other. I refer to the two terms *organic* and *rational*, which have been borrowed by the architectural language and which, although they possess an indubitable historical validity for making distinctions between one style or type of architecture and another, certainly do not help us to clarify concepts or somehow to comprehend urban artifacts.

The term *organic* is derived from biology; I have elsewhere noted that the basis of Friedrich Ratzel's functionalism was a hypothesis that likened the city to an organism, the form of which was constituted by function itself.[29] This physiological hypothesis is as brilliant as it is inapplicable to the structure of urban artifacts and to architectural design (although the application to the problem of design is a subject in itself and requires a separate treatment). Among the most prominent terms of this organic language are *organism, organic growth, urban fabric*. Similarly, in some of the more serious ecological studies, parallels between the city and the human organism and the processes of the biological world have been suggested, although quickly abandoned. The terminology, in fact, is so pervasive among those in the field that at first sight it seems intimately tied to the material under consideration, and only with some difficulty is it possible to avoid the use of a term like *architectural organism* and substitute for it a more appropriate word like *building*. The same can be said for *fabric*. It even seems that some authors define modern architecture *tout court* as organic, and by virtue of its powerful appeal this terminology has passed rapidly from serious studies[30] to the profession and to journalism.

The terminology of the so-called rationalist variety is no less imprecise. To speak of rational urbanism is simply a tautology, since the rationalization of spatial choices is by definition a condition of urbanism. "Rationalist" definitions have the undoubted merit, however, of always referring to urbanism as a discipline (precisely because of its character of rationality) and thus offer a terminology of clearly superior usefulness. To say that the medieval city is organic reveals an absolute ignorance of the political, religious, and economic structures of the medieval city, not to mention its spatial structure. To say, on the other hand, that the plan of Miletus is rational is true even if it is so general as to be generic and fails to offer us any real idea of Miletus's layout (beyond the ambiguity of confounding rationality with what is a simple geometric scheme).

Both of these aspects are aptly characterized in Milizia's comment cited earlier about functional organization and beehives.[31] Thus, even though this terminology undoubtedly possesses a certain poetic expressiveness; and as such might be of interest to us, it has nothing to do with a theory of urban artifacts. It is really a vehicle of confusion, and it would be useful to drop it altogether.

Urban artifacts, as we have said, are complex; this means that they have components and that each component has a different value. Thus, in speaking of the typological essence in architecture we said that it "has its own role to play in the model"; in other words, the typological essence is a component element. However, before attempting a typological reading of the city based on a theory of urban artifacts and their structure, it is necessary to proceed slowly to some precise definitions.

Exactly how are urban artifacts complex? A partial answer has already been given with respect to the theories of Chabot and Poète. One can agree that their statements relative to the soul of the city and the concept of permanence go beyond naive functionalism and approach an understanding of the quality of urban artifacts. On the other hand, little attention has really been given to this problem of quality, a problem which surfaces mainly in historical research, although there is already some progress in the recognition that the nature of urban artifacts is in many ways like that of a work of art and, most important, that a key element for understanding urban artifacts is their collective character.

On the basis of these considerations it is possible to delineate a type of reading for urban structures. But we must begin by posing two general sets of questions: First, from what points of view is it possible to read the city; how many ways are there for understanding its structure? Is it possible to say, and what does it mean to say, that a reading is interdisciplinary; do some disciplines take precedence over others? Obviously, these questions are closely linked. Second, what are the possibilities for an autonomous urban science?

Of the two questions, the second is clearly decisive. In fact, if there is an urban science, the first group of questions ends up having little meaning; that which today is often defined as interdisciplinary is nothing other than a problem of specialization and occurs in any field of knowledge. But the response to this second question depends on a recognition that the city is constructed in its totality, that all of its components participate in its constitution as an artifact. In other words, on the most general level, it must be understood that the city represents the progress of human reason, is a human creation par excellence; and this statement has meaning only when the fundamental point is emphasized that the city and every urban artifact are by nature collective. I am often asked why only historians give us a complete picture of the city. I believe the answer is that historians are concerned with the urban artifact in its totality.

Clearly, to think of urban science as a historical science is a mistake, for in this case we would be obliged to speak only of urban history. What I mean to suggest, however, is that from the point of view of urban structure, urban history seems more useful than any other form of research on the city. Later I will address the contribution of history to urban science in a more detailed way, but since this problem is particularly important it would be useful to make a few specific observations right away.

Monuments and the Theory of Permanences

These concern the theory of *permanences* as posited by both Poète and Lavedan. This theory is in some respects related to my initial hypothesis of the city as a man-made object. One must remember that the difference between past and future, from the point of view of the theory of knowledge, in large measure reflects the fact that the past is partly being experienced now, and this may be the

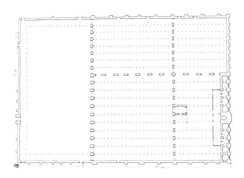

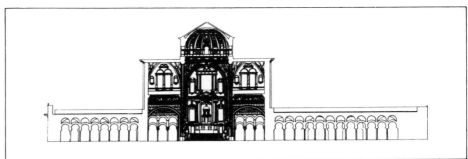

36

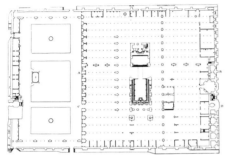

35

35 The Mezquita or Arab mosque
Medjid-al-Djamia, eighth to tenth
century, Córdoba, Spain, and its
transformation into a cathedral,
1599. Above: Plan during Arab
period. Below: Plan of cathedral.
36 Section of cathedral, formerly
Arab mosque, Córdoba, Spain.
37 Aerial view of cathedral, formerly
Arab mosque, Córdoba, Spain.
38 Plan of the Alhambra, Granada,
Spain.

37

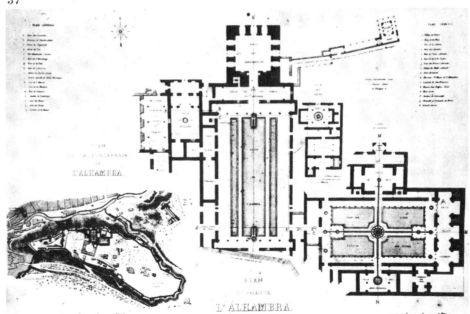

38

meaning to give permanences: they are a past that we are still experiencing.

Poète's theory is not very explicit on this point, but I will try to summarize it briefly. Although he presents a number of hypotheses among which are economic considerations that relate to the evolution of the city, it is in substance a historical theory centered on the phenomenon of "persistences." These persistences are revealed through monuments, the physical signs of the past, as well as through the persistence of a city's basic layout and plans. This last point is Poète's most important discovery. Cities tend to remain on their axes of development, maintaining the position of their original layout and growing according to the direction and meaning of their older artifacts, which often appear remote from present-day ones. Sometimes these artifacts persist virtually unchanged, endowed with a continuous vitality; other times they exhaust themselves, and then only the permanence of their form, their physical sign, their *locus* remains. The most meaningful permanences are those provided by the street and the plan. The plan persists at different levels; it becomes differentiated in its attributes, often deformed, but in substance it is not displaced. This is the most valid part of Poète's theory; even if it cannot be said to be completely a historical theory, it is essentially born from the study of history.

At first sight it may seem that permanences absorb all of the continuity of urban artifacts, but in reality this is not so, because not all things in the city survive, or if they do, their modalities are so diverse as often to resist comparison. In this sense, according to the theory of permanences, in order to explain an urban artifact, one is forced to look beyond it to the present-day actions that modify it. In substance, the historical method is one that isolates. It tends not only to differentiate permanences but to focus entirely on them, since they alone can show what a city once was by indicating the way its past differs from its present. Thus permanences may appear with respect to the city as isolated and aberrant artifacts which characterize a system only as the form of a past that we are still experiencing.

In this respect, permanences present two aspects: on the one hand, they can be considered as propelling elements; on the other, as pathological elements. Artifacts either enable us to understand the city in its totality, or they appear as a series of isolated elements that we can link only tenuously to an urban system. To illustrate the distinction between permanent elements that are vital and those that are pathological, we can again take the Palazzo della Ragione in Padua as an example. I remarked on its permanent character before, but now by permanence I mean not only that one can still experience the form of the past in this monument but that the physical form of the past has assumed different functions and has continued to function, conditioning the urban area in which it stands and continuing to constitute an important urban focus. In part this building is still in use; even if everyone is convinced that it is a work of art, it still functions quite readily at ground level as a retail market. This proves its vitality.

An example of a pathological permanence can be seen in the Alhambra in Granada. It no longer houses either Moorish or Castilian kings, and if we accepted functionalist classifications, we would have to say that this building once represented the major function of Granada. It is evident that at Granada we experience the form of the past in a way that is quite different from at Padua. In the first instance, the form of the past has assumed a different function but it is still intimately tied to the city; it has been modified and we can imagine future modifications. In the second, it stands virtually isolated in the city; nothing can be

59

added. It constitutes, in fact, an experience so *essential* that it cannot be modified (in this sense, the palace of Charles V in Granada must be counted an exception, since precisely because it lacked this quality it could so easily be destroyed). But in both cases the urban artifacts are a part of the city that cannot be suppressed because they constitute it.

In choosing these two examples, I have defined a persistent urban artifact as something very similar to a monument. I could in fact have spoken of the Doge's Palace in Venice or the Theater at Nîmes or the Mezquita of Córdoba, and the argument would not change. In fact, I am inclined to believe that persistence in an urban artifact often causes it to become identified as a monument, and that a monument persists in the city both symbolically and physically. A monument's persistence or permanence is a result of its capacity to constitute the city, its history and art, its being and memory.

We have just distinguished between a historical or propelling permanence as a form of a past that we still experience and a pathological permanence as something that is isolated and aberrant. In large measure the pathological form is identifiable because of a particular *context*, since context itself can be seen either as the persistence of a function over time or as something isolated from the urban structure, that is, as something which stands outside of technological and social evolution. Context is commonly understood as referring primarily to residential sections of the city, and in this sense, its preservation is counter to the real dynamic of the city; so-called contextual preservation is related to the city in time like the embalmed corpse of a saint to the image of his historical personality. In contextual preservation there is a sort of urban naturalism at work which admittedly can give rise to suggestive images—for example, a visit to a dead city is always a memorable experience—but in such cases we are well outside the realm of a past that we still experience. Naturally, then, I am referring mainly to living cities which have an uninterrupted span of development. The problems of dead cities only tangentially concern urban science; they are matters for the historian and the archaeologist. It is at best an abstraction to seek to reduce urban artifacts to archaeological ones.

So far we have spoken only of monuments, inasmuch as they are fixed elements of the urban structure, as having a true aesthetic intentionality, but this can be a simplification. The hypothesis of the city as a man-made object and a work of art attributes as much legitimacy of expression to a house or any other minor work as to a monument. But perhaps this carries us too far afield; I mainly want to establish at this point that the dynamic process of the city tends more to evolution than preservation, and that in evolution monuments are not only preserved but continuously presented as propelling elements of development. This is a fact that can be verified.

Moreover, I have already attempted to demonstrate how function alone is insufficient to explain the continuity of urban artifacts; if the origin of the typology of urban artifacts is simply function, this hardly accounts for the phenomenon of survival. A function must always be defined in time and in society: that which closely depends on it is always bound up with its development. An urban artifact determined by one function only cannot be seen as anything other than an explication of that function. In reality, we frequently continue to appreciate elements whose function has been lost over time; the value of these artifacts often resides solely in their form, which is integral to the general form of the city; it is, so to speak, an invariant of it. Often, too, these artifacts are closely bound up with the
60

constitutive elements, with the origins of the city, and are included among its monuments. Thus we see the importance of the parameter of time in the study of urban artifacts; to think of a persistent urban artifact as something tied to a single period of history constitutes one of the greatest fallacies of urban science.

The form of the city is always the form of a particular time of the city; but there are many times in the formation of the city, and a city may change its face even in the course of one man's life, its original references ceasing to exist. As Baudelaire wrote, "The old Paris is no more; the form of a city changes more quickly, alas, than the heart of a mortal."[32] We look upon the houses of our childhood as unbelievably old, and often the city erases our memories as it changes.

The various considerations we have put forward in this chapter now permit us to attempt a specific reading of the city. The city will be seen as an architecture of different parts or components, these being principally the *dwelling* and *primary elements*. It is this reading that I will develop in the following pages, beginning with the concept of the *study area*. Since dwellings cover the major portion of the urban surface and rarely have a character of permanence, their evolution should be studied together with the area upon which they are found; thus I will speak of the *dwelling area*.

I will also consider the decisive role played by primary elements in the formation and constitution of the city. This role tends to be revealed through their character of permanence in the case of the monuments, which, as we will see, have a very particular relationship to primary elements. Farther on we will investigate what effective role primary elements have in the structure of urban artifacts, and for what reasons urban artifacts can be said to be works of art or, at least, how the overall structure of the city is similar to a work of art. Our previous analysis should enable us to recognize this overall composition of the city and the reasons for its architecture.

There is nothing new in all of this. Yet in attempting to formulate a theory of urban artifacts that is consistent with reality, I have benefited from highly diverse sources. From these I consider some of the themes I have discussed—function, permanence, classification, and typology—to be particularly significant.

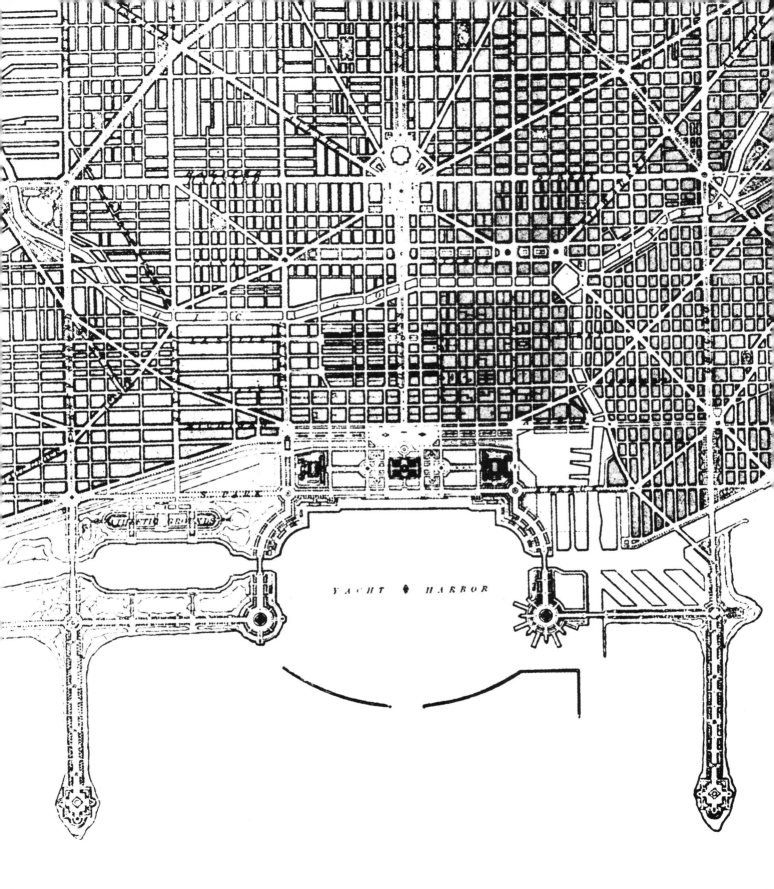

YACHT ✦ HARBOR

In our hypothesis of the city as a man-made object—as a total architecture—we have put forward three distinct propositions. The first of these is that urban development has a temporal dimension, that the city has a before and an after. This suggests that we can connect comparable phenomena which are not by nature homogeneous along temporal coordinates. The idea of permanence derives from this proposition. The second proposition concerns the spatial continuity of the city. To accept this continuity means to assume that all those elements which we find in a certain region or within a certain urban area are artifacts of a homogeneous nature, without discontinuities. This is a very controversial assumption, and we must continually return to it and its implications. (For example, it would deny that there is a qualitative leap from the historical city to the city of the Industrial Revolution. It would also deny that the open city and the closed city are different kinds of artifacts.) Finally, as a third proposition, we have acknowledged that within the urban structure there are some primary elements of a particular nature which have the power to retard or accelerate the urban process.

I will now concern myself specifically with the place in which urban artifacts are manifested, that is, the area in which they can be seen, the physical ground they occupy. This area is to some extent determined by natural factors, but it is also a public object and a substantial part of the architecture of the city. We can consider this area as a whole, as the projection of the city's form on a horizontal plane, or else we can look at individual parts. Geographers call this the *site*—the area on which a city rises, the surface that it actually occupies. From this geographical perspective it is essential for describing the city and, along with location and situation, an important element for classifying different cities.

This brings us to the concept of the *study area*. Since we assume that between any urban element and any urban artifact there exists an interrelationship whose particularity is related to a specific city, it is necessary to elaborate the nature of the immediate urban context. Such a minimum urban context constitutes the study area, by which we mean a portion of the urban area that can be defined or described by comparison to other larger elements of the overall urban area, for example, the street system.

The study area, then, is an abstraction with respect to the space of the city, and as such, it serves to define specific elements more clearly. For example, in order to define the characteristics of a certain plot of land and its influence on a housing type, it is useful to examine the contiguous lots, those elements which demarcate a particular context, to see if their form is entirely anomalous or whether they arise from more general conditions in the city. But the study area can also be defined by historical elements which may coincide with a particular urban artifact. Just to consider this area in itself means to recognize that there are both specific and disparate qualities within parts of the more general urban whole. This aspect of urban artifacts is extremely important; the recognition of their specificity allows us to understand their structure better.

Several other aspects of the study area should be mentioned. For example, there is a relationship between the spatial idea of the study area and the sociological one of "natural area," and this leads us to the concept of the residential district. Another aspect of the study area is its character as a *recinto* or vertical slice of the city. In all these cases, it is necessary to define the limits of the urban whole with which we are concerned; this is the best defense against the serious distortions that are so common in those studies where the growth of the city and the

39 Plan of the street system of Chicago, Daniel Burnham, 1909.

63

evolution of urban artifacts are taken to be continuous natural processes and where the real differences within them disappear. The reality of the structure of urban artifacts is such that cities are distinct in time and space, *per genus et differentiam*. Each modification of an urban artifact presupposes a qualitative as well as a quantitative change.

We will attempt to show that between the two facts of building typology and urban morphology a revealing binary relationship exists; and further, that the study of this relationship is extremely useful for understanding the structure of urban artifacts. Even though this structure is not part of that relationship, it can for the most part be clarified by a knowledge of it.

The a priori importance that I attach to the study area implies my conviction of the following:
1. With respect to urban intervention today one should operate on a limited part of the city, although this does not preclude an abstract plan of the city's development and the possibility of an altogether different point of view. Such a self-imposed limitation is a more realistic approach from the standpoint of both knowledge and program.

2. The city is not by nature a creation that can be reduced to a single basic idea. This is true both for the modern metropolis and for the concept of the city as the sum of many parts,'of quarters and districts that are highly diverse and differentiated in their sociological and formal characteristics. In fact, this differentiation constitutes one of the typical characteristics of the city. To reduce these diverse aspects to one kind of explanation, and thus to one formal law, is a mistake. The city in its totality and beauty is made up of numerous different moments of formation; the unity of these moments is the urban unity as a whole. The possibility for reading the city with any continuity resides in its dominant formal and spatial characteristics.[1]

The form of the study area, seen as a constituent part of the city, is thus useful for analyzing the form of the city itself. This type of analysis does not involve a communitarian idea of the area nor any of the implications in the idea of community which relate to neighborhood; these questions are largely sociological in nature. In the present context the study area always involves a notion of the unity both of the urban whole as it has emerged through a process of diverse growth and differentiation, and of those individual areas or parts of the city that have acquired their own characteristics. The city comes to be seen as a "masterpiece," something that is substantiated in form and space but understood in time, in its different moments (which cannot be predicted with certainty). The unity of these parts is fundamentally supplied by history, by the city's memory of itself.

These areas, these parts, are defined essentially by their location, their imprint on the ground, their topographical limits, and their physical presence; and in this way they can be distinguished within the urban whole. Thus, we arrive at a more general and conceptual development of the problem: the study area can be defined as a concept that takes in a series of spatial and social factors which act as determining influences on the inhabitants of a sufficiently circumscribed cultural and geographical area.

From the standpoint of urban morphology the definition is simpler. Here the study area would include all of those urban areas that have a physical and social homogeneity. (Even if defining what constitutes homogeneity in things is not

64

easy, especially from a formal point of view, it is still possible to define a typological homogeneity: that is, all those areas where consistent modes and types of living are realized in similar buildings; thus the homogeneity of residential districts, *Siedlungen*, etc.) The study of these characteristics ends up by becoming
specific to social morphology or social geography (and in this sense homogeneity
can also be defined sociologically), so that the activities of social groups are
analyzed with respect to how they are continuously manifested in fixed territorial characteristics.

The study area thus becomes a particular moment in the study of the city and as
such gives rise to a true and proper urban ecology, which is a necesary pre-
requisite for studies of the city. The two distinctive features that take shape in
this relationship are mass and density, and these are manifested in the
homogeneity of the occupation of space in both plan and section. The study area
is a surface that relates to the specific mass and density of a part of the city and
also becomes a dynamic moment within the life of the city itself.

The concept of area just developed is closely bound up with that of the residential
district. I have already introduced this notion in speaking of Tricart's theory,
but at this point I think it would be appropriate to return to the idea of the part or
segment of the city, and to view the city as a spatial system formed of parts, each
with its own characteristics. Fritz Schumacher has also developed a theory of
this type and it seems to have much validity. As we have suggested, the study of
the urban residential district is simply an extension of the concept of the study
area.*

Residential Districts as Study Areas

*The Italian *quartiere*, the equivalent of
the French *quartier*, has been translated
here and throughout as "district," but this
does not do full justice to the original. The
intended meaning of the word is more or
less retained in an expression like
"working class quarters," where it
suggests a residential area which has
evolved in the city rather than been
superimposed upon it (by zoning, for
example).—*Ed.*

The residential district is thus a moment, a piece of the city's form. It is intimately bound up with the city's evolution and nature, and is itself constituted of
parts, which in turn summarize the city's image. We actually experience these
parts. In social terms, it is a morphological and structural unit characterized by a
certain urban landscape, a certain social content, and its function; thus a change
in any one of these elements is enough to define its limits. We should also bear in
mind that an analysis of the residential district as a social artifact based on the division of social or economic classes as well as on economic functions corresponds
in an essential way to the process of formation of the modern metropolis; this
process is the same for ancient Rome as for the large cities of today. Moreover, I
would maintain that these residential districts are not so much subordinated to
one another as relatively autonomous parts; their relationships cannot be
explained as a simple function of dependence but seemingly respond to the entire
urban structure.

To state that a part of the larger city constitutes a smaller city within it is to chal-
lenge another aspect of functionalist theory. This aspect is *zoning*. I am referring here not to zoning as a technical practice, which is somewhat acceptable and
has another meaning, but rather to the theory of zoning as it was first advanced
scientifically in 1923 by Robert Park and Ernest Burgess with respect to the city
of Chicago. In Burgess's study of Chicago,[2] zoning came to be defined as the tendency of the city to be disposed in concentric residential districts around either a
central business district or a governmental core. In his description of that city,
Burgess indicated a series of concentric zones which corresponded to well-defined functions: the business and governmental zones which absorbed the commercial, social, administrative, and transportation life; the transitional zones

which encircled the center and represented a kind of aureole of decay, formed of poor residences where blacks and recent immigrants lived and where small offices were found; the working-class residential zone for workers who wanted to live near their factories; the zone of wealthier residences, including single-family dwellings and multi-story houses; and finally an external zone where the daily commuters were clustered at the intersections of roads which converged on the cities.

Among the critiques made of this theory, which seemed overly schematic even as applied to Chicago, that of Homer Hoyt[3] gained a certain acceptance. It attempted to establish, if also in an overly schematic way, a principle of growth according to certain axes of traffic or transportation, in this way superimposing on the concentric sectors radial vectors which emanated out from the center of the city. Such a theory is related to that of Schumacher, especially to his proposals for the plan of Hamburg.

It is appropriate to note that although the term *zoning* appeared in the form of a theory with Burgess, it had made its first appearance in Reinhard Baumeister's studies in 1870[4] and also was applied to the plan of 1925 for the city of Berlin. But in Berlin it was used in an entirely different way; it indicated five zones in the city (residential, parkland, commercial, industrial, mixed), but the disposition of these zones was not radiocentric. Although the business center coincided with the historical center, there was an alternation of industrial, residential, and open land zones which contradicted Burgess's formulation.[5]

I do not wish to contest Burgess's theory; this has already been done by many. I only mention it here to emphasize the fundamental weakness of considering the various parts of the city merely as embodiments of functions, and so narrowly as to describe the entire city as if no other considerations existed. This theory is limiting in that it conceives of the city as a series of moments which can be compared in a simple way and which can be resolved on the basis of a simple rule of functional differentiation; such a theory results in suppressing the most important values implicit in the structure of urban artifacts. In contrast to this approach is the possibility we have suggested of considering urban artifacts in their entirety, of resolving one part of the city completely, determining all of the relationships that can be established within it.

In this context Baumeister's formulation is as useful as any, for beyond a doubt, specialized zones do exist. We may say these zones are *characteristic*: that is, they have a particular physiognomy and are autonomous parts. Their distribution in the city does not depend—at least not only—on the various interdependent functions which the city requires, but rather relies mainly on the entire historical process of the city through which they come to be exactly as they are, according to their particular make-up. Thus, in studying Vienna, Hugo Hassinger described the city in 1910 as comprised of the *Altstadt* which was encircled by the *Ring*, which was in turn surrounded by the *Gürtel*, with the *Grossstädtischer Vorstadtgürtel*, the section of highest density, between the *Ring* and the *Gürtel*. In addition to these zones, he distinguished the *Grossstadtkern*, the nucleus of the city, and spoke of the *Grossstädtischer Weichbild*, the zone constituted partly by the city proper and partly by the countryside which American scholars later defined as the urban fringes. Despite his rigid plans and parceling of lots in a checkerboard plan superimposed on the city, Hassinger grasped a basic characteristic that is still valid today and is intimately part of the form of Vienna. Here already the issue is not one of the merely functional division of the

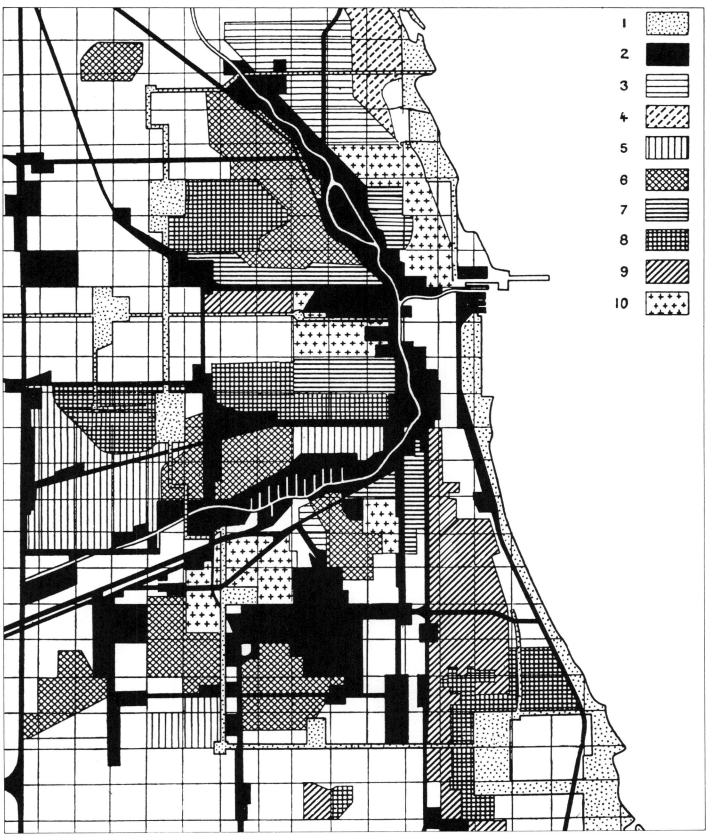

41 *Plan of Frankfurt am Main, West Germany. 1) Old center. 2) Fifteenth-century city. 3) Modern districts. 4) Railroad lines. 5) Parks. 6) Woods.*

42 *Plan of Vienna. Schematic plan at upper right indicates the different phases of urban development. 1) Vienna in 1683. 2) Old districts of the eighteenth and beginning of the nineteenth century within the walls of 1703. 3) The Ring. 4) Districts of 1860. 5) Development from the end of the nineteenth and beginning of the twentieth century.*

41

42

city, but rather of a *definition by parts and by forms, by characteristics*; these characteristics are a synthesis of functions and values.[6]

In general, every city possesses a center. This center is either more or less complex and has different characteristics, and it plays a particular role in the urban life. Tertiary activities are in part concentrated in this center, mostly along the axes of external communications, and in part within large residential complexes. What characterizes the city from a general standpoint of the relationships between zones is the existence of a complex and polynuclear tertiary network. But its center as well as other subcenters can only be studied in terms of primary urban artifacts. Only by knowing their structure and location can we know their particular role.

As we have said, the city is distinguished by its various parts, and these, from the formal and historical standpoint, constitute complex urban artifacts. As is consistent with a theory of urban artifacts that emphasizes the structures of artifacts rather than their functions, we can say that individual parts of the city are distinguishable as characteristic; they are *characteristic parts*. Since the residential district is predominant and undergoes noticeable environmental changes over time which characterize its site far more than its buildings, I propose to use the term *residential* or *dwelling area* (the term *area* once again being derived from sociological literature).

It is universally acknowledged that residential districts in ancient cities, with their centers, their monuments, and their way of life, were well demarcated from one another; this is verifiable in urban history as much as in the physical reality of the architecture itself. These characteristics are no less apparent in the modern city, above all in the great European cities, whether there has been an effort to subsume the city in a grand overall design, as in Paris, or there is an absolutely emerging urban form that is typically shaped by different places and situations, as in London.

This latter phenomenon is also predominant in American cities, and its many components develop, often dramatically, as a major urban problem. Without even touching here on the social aspects of the problem, we find in the very formation and evolution of the American city a confirmation of the "city of parts."

Kevin Lynch writes, "Many persons interviewed took care to point out that Boston, while confusing in its path pattern even to the experienced inhabitant, has, in the number and vividness of its differentiated districts, a quality that quite makes up for it. As one person put it: 'Each part of Boston is different from the other. You can tell pretty much what area you're in . . .' [New York] was cited . . . because it has a number of well-defined characteristic districts set in an ordered frame of rivers and streets."[7] In his constant concern with the residential district, Lynch speaks of "areas of reference" as having "little perceptual content, but they are useful as organizing concepts . . . " and distinguishes between introverted districts "turned in upon themselves with little reference to the surrounding area" and isolated districts that arise independently of their zone.[8] This aspect of Lynch's work supports the thesis of the city as constituted of differentiated parts.

Along with Lynch's psychological analyses it should also be possible to carry out *linguistic* research that would produce evidence of the deepest layers of the urban structure. One thinks of the Viennese expression *Heimatbezirk*, which identifies the residential district with both one's homeland and one's living space. Willy Hellpach rightly spoke of the metropolis as the "homeland" of modern man. *Heimatbezirk* especially expresses the morphological and historical structure of Vienna, a city that is both international and at the same time the only real place in the monolithic conception of the Hapsburg state. In Milan, to take another example, the division of the areas outside of the Spanish walls into *borghi* can be understood only by close morphological-historical study; here a phenomenon of persistence has so much remained alive in the language that the principal zone of San Gottardo is still called *el burg* by the Milanese.

This type of linguistic research, like psychological research, is capable of producing useful information concerning the formation of cities. Toponymy, for example, frequently provides important contributions to the study of urban development; it is apparent that all cities contain numerous examples of significant physical modifications of the land which are recorded in the names of their older streets and roads. In Milan, streets named Bottonuto, Poslaghetto, Pantano, and San Giovanni in Conca, instantly recall a zone of swamps and ancient hydraulic works. A similar phenomenon can be found in the Marais quarter in Paris. Such studies confirm what we know about how a city is structured according to characteristic parts.

The Individual Dwelling

To take the dwelling as a category in itself does not mean to adopt a functional criterion of urban land-use division but simply to treat an urban artifact in such a way that it is in itself primary in the composition of the city. To this end, the use of the term *dwelling area* in the sense illustrated in the preceding pages can bring the study of the individual dwelling within the general theory of urban artifacts.

The city has always been characterized largely by the individual dwelling. It can be said that cities in which the residential aspect was not present do not exist or have not existed; and where the residential function was initially subordinated to other urban artifacts (the castle, the military encampment), a modification of the city's structure soon occurred to confer importance on the individual dwelling.

One cannot argue either by historical analysis or by description of actual sites that a dwelling is something amorphous or easily and quickly transformable. The form in which residential building types are realized, the typological aspect that characterizes them, is closely bound up with the urban form, and the house, which materially represents a people's way of life, the precise manifestation of a culture, is modified very slowly. Viollet-le-Duc, in the great panorama of French architecture contained in his *Dictionnaire raisonné de l'architecture française du XIᵉ au XVIᵉ siècle*, says, "In the art of architecture, the house is certainly that which best characterizes the customs, tastes, and usages of a people; its order, like its organization, changes only over very long periods of time."[9]

In ancient Rome individual dwellings were classified quite rigidly into the *domus* type and the *insula* type; these two types characterized the city and the fourteen regions of Augustus. In its own divisions and evolution, the *insula* was virtually a microcosm of the city. There was more social mixing in it than is commonly thought, and as with houses built in Paris after 1850, social differentiation

70

was signified by changes in height. Of extremely poor and temporary construction, these *insulae* constantly renewed themselves; they constituted the urban substratum, the material out of which the city was molded. Already in the *insula*, as in any other form of mass housing, one of the most important forces of urban growth could be felt: speculation. The mechanism of speculation as applied to the residential landscape was responsible for the most characteristic moments of growth in the Imperial city. Without acknowledging this fact, we cannot understand the system of public buildings, their dislocation, and the logic of city growth. An analogous situation, even if not characterized by such high density, existed in the ancient Greek cities.

The form of Vienna also is derived from the problem of housing. The application of the *Hofquartierspflicht*[10] greatly increased the density of the center, specifically influenced the building typology of multi-story housing, and decisively stimulated the development of the suburbs. An effort to reinstate the dwelling as a determining influence on the form of the city and as a typical urban artifact is seen in the conception of the workers' *Siedlungen* in the years following the First World War. The program of the city of Vienna was intended above all to realize typical complexes whose form would be intimately linked to the form of the city. On this point Peter Behrens wrote, "To criticize their construction on the basis of principles contrived at the drawing table is to take the wrong path, because nothing appears so changeable and heterogenous as the needs, habits, and multiplicity of situations of a population that resides in a particular region."[11] The relationship between the dwelling and its area thus became primary.

In America, the vast surface areas of cities cannot be explained without acknowledging the tendency toward a type of sparse, single-family housing. Jean Gottman's study of "megalopolis" is very precise in this respect.[12]

The location of the individual dwelling depends upon many factors: geographic, morphological, historical, economic. Once again, the geographic factors seem to be determined by the economic ones. The alternation of residential zones, as well as their specialized structure from a typological standpoint, seems largely dependent on economic patterns, and the mechanisms of speculation encourage this alternation. This is also true in the most contemporary examples, apparently even in the socialist city, which, owing to difficulties that are hard to identify, at the present time does not seem to offer a basic alternative to this economic-based process of urban growth. Evidently, even where the mechanism of speculation does not exist, there always tends to be an expression of preferences which are difficult to resolve in the choice of where one lives. Such problems are played out within the overall framework of choices in the urban dynamic.

It is logical and important to understand that the success of residential complexes is also related to the existence of public services and collective facilities. These make for the dispersal of dwelling areas; certainly residential concentration in the ancient cities and in Imperial Rome can be plausibly explained by the almost total absence of public transportation and the uncommonness of private transportation. But there are some exceptions to this—for example, the ancient Greek city and the morphology of some northern cities.

43 *Reconstruction of thirteenth-century house, Burgundy, France, Viollet-le-Duc. Above: Facade. Below: Plan of ground floor.*

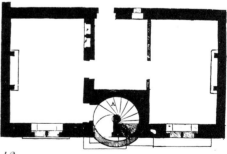

43

Yet it is difficult to prove that this relationship is the determining factor. This is to say that the form of a city has not yet been determined by a particular system of public transportation; nor in general can such a system be expected to produce a certain urban form or to follow it. In other words, I do not believe that the subway of any large city can be an object of controversy except with respect to its technical efficiency, but the same can hardly be said of residential settlements, which are the object of constant controversy in terms of their structure as urban artifacts. Thus there exists a specific aspect of the housing issue that is intimately bound up with the problem of the city, its way of life, its physical form and image—that is, with its structure. This specific element has nothing to do with any kind of technical services, for the latter do not constitute urban artifacts.

The result is that the study of the individual dwelling offers one of the best means of studying the city and vice versa. Perhaps nothing so illustrates the structural differences between a Mediterranean city such as Taranto and a northern one such as Zurich as the different aspects of their housing; I refer particularly to the morphological and structural aspects. Considerations of this type also obtain with respect to Alpine villages and all those aggregations where the residential artifact is in itself dominant, if not unique. Each of these examples illustrates Viollet-le-Duc's assertion that the house—its order and its organization—is not modified except over long periods of time.

Naturally one must remember that among the typological issues of housing are included many elements that do not concern only the spatial aspects of the problem. At this point, however, I do not wish to discuss them; it is only necessary to recognize that they exist. Thus it is clear that a good amount of interesting information can be obtained by relating the preceding discussion to certain sociological positions and, better, political ones concerning the significance of housing as a moment in the life of the city. It would be possible, for example, to extract much useful data from a study of the relationship that exists between information of this kind and specific solutions by architects.

I will now attempt to explore the relationship between the individual dwelling and architects by taking the example of Berlin, where much documentation exists not only on housing, as is the case for many other cities, but also on the modern districts. Since housing is one of the most important issues in the thematics of modern architecture in Germany on the level of both theory and practice, it will be useful to see what relationships actually exist between the theoretical formulations and what has been realized. Many outstanding contributions were made during the interwar period relative to this problem in Germany, among them those of Werner Hegemann, Walter Gropius, Alexander Klein, and Henry van de Velde.

The Typological Problem of Housing in Berlin

Since housing, like many other urban issues, concerns cities and, for better or worse, cities are something we can describe, it is useful to approach this issue in the context of a specific city. In speaking of housing in a specific city, then, it is necessary to try to make as few generalizations as possible. Clearly all cities will always have something in common relative to this issue, and by inquiring how much one artifact has in common with others, we will come closer to elaborating a general theory.

The problem of housing typology in Berlin is extremely interesting, especially

*44 Rural community of Appenzell-
am-Rhein, Switzerland, in 1814.
Drawing by J. Jakob Mock von
Herisau.*

45 *Plan of Berlin. 1) Gardens and parks. 2) Forests.*
Inset plan, lower right, showing phases of urban development:
1) The old center. 2) Dorotheenstadt.
3) Eighteenth-century walls.

with respect to other cities, and I will attempt to indicate the patterns that enable us to recognize a certain uniformity or continuity in this issue in Berlin, ultimately showing the capacity of a few typical residential models, past and present, to shed light on a series of questions concerning housing which in turn relate to the urban condition and a theory of urban development. The particular interest of Berlin housing becomes apparent on an examination of the city's plan.[13]

In 1936, the geographer Louis Herbert distinguished four major types of structures in Berlin; these distinctions related to four zones defined by their distance from the historical center:

1. a zone of uniform and continuous structures, such as buildings of the "large city" type, possessing at least four stories;

2. a zone of diversified urban structures, which could be divided into two classes: in the center of the city, new buildings mixed with very old and low buildings of no more than three floors; and along the edges of the center, a continuous interspersion of high and low housing, open spaces, fields, and parceled land;

3. large areas for industry;

4. residential areas open at the outer edges of the city, comprised of villas and single-family dwellings principally constructed after 1918.

Between the fourth zone and the periphery there was a continuous blending of industrial zones, residential zones, and villages in transformation. These external zones differed greatly from one another, and ranged from the working-class and industrial districts of Henningsdorf and Pankow to the upper-class district of Grünewald. On the basis of this already existing organization of Berlin, Reinhard Baumeister in 1870 formulated the concept of zoning which later was incorporated in the Prussian building code.

In Greater Berlin the morphology of the residential complexes was thus quite varied; the different complexes not directly linked to one another were characterized by precise building types: multi-story housing, speculative housing, and single-family housing. This typological variety represents a very modern type of urban structure also produced subsequently in other European cities, even though it never achieved such definitive articulation as in Berlin. Considered in its dual aspect of urban structure and typological structure, it is one of the principal characteristics of the German metropolis. The *Siedlungen* are a product of these conditions and must be so judged.

The structure of the residential complexes can be classified according to the following fundamental types:

1. residential blocks;

2. semi-detached houses;

3. single-family houses.

These different types present themselves in Berlin with greater frequency than in any other European city for historical-cultural and geographical reasons. The Gothic building, preserved for a long time in other German cities where it constituted the primary image up until the devastations of the last war, in Berlin had disappeared almost completely by the end of the nineteenth century.

Block structures, derived from the police regulations of 1851, constitute one of the most integral forms of exploitation of the urban land; these were normally designed around a series of courtyards facing the interior facades of the blocks. Buildings of this type were also characteristic of such cities as Hamburg and Vienna. The very large presence in Berlin of this type of housing, known as *Mietkasernen* or "rental barracks," led to its characterization as a "barracks city."

74

Courtyard housing represents one typical solution in central Europe, and as such was adopted by many modern architects, in Vienna as in Berlin. The courtyards were transformed into large gardens, which came to include nursery schools and vendors' kiosks. Some of the best examples of housing in the German Rationalist period are associated with this form.

The *Siedlungen* of the Rationalists are characterized by *detached structures*, and these represent a highly polemical and scientific position; their layout, which demands a totally free division of the land, depends on solar orientation rather than on the general form of the district. The structure of these detached buildings is completely disengaged from the street, and precisely for this reason totally alters the nineteenth-century type of urban development. In these examples, public green spaces are particularly important.

The study of the cell, of the individual habitable unit, is fundamental with respect to the *Siedlungen*. All the architects who worked on shaping these residential districts and engaged in the formulation of economical building types sought to find the exact form of *Existenzminimum*, the optimum dimensional unit from the point of view of organization and economy. This is one of the most important aspects of the work of the Rationalists on the problem of housing.

We can only suggest that the formulation of *Existenzminimum* presupposed a static relationship between a certain style of life—hypothetical even if statistically verifiable—and a certain type of lodging, and this resulted in the rapid obsolescence of the *Siedlung*. It revealed itself to be a spatial conception that was too particular, too tied to specific solutions to function as a general element available for wide use in housing. *Existenzminimum* is only one aspect of a far more complex problem in which many variables participate.

There is a strong tradition of the *single-family house* in Berlin residential typology. Although this is one of the most interesting aspects of Rationalist residential typology, I will only mention it briefly since it demands a type of study that is parallel to but outside the bounds of our present task. In this context, Schinkel's projects for the Babelsberg castle for Wilhelm I and the castle and *Römische Bäder* of Charlottenhof take on particular importance. The plan of the Babelsberg castle presents an ordered structure, almost rigid in the organization of its rooms, while its external form is an attempt to relate to the surrounding context, especially the landscape. In this project one can see how the concept of the villa was borrowed and used as a typological model suitable for a city like Berlin. In this sense, Schinkel's work, constituting the transition from neoclassical models to romantic ones, mainly by way of the English country house, offers the basis for the early twentieth-century type of bourgeois villa.

With the spread of the villa as an urban element in the nineteenth century and the disappearance of Gothic and seventeenth-century houses, with the substitution of ministries at the center and *Mietkasernen* in the peripheral zones, the urban morphology of Berlin was profoundly modified. The changing image of Unter den Linden over the centuries is a typical case. The seventeenth-century street is truly a "promenade" under the lime trees: although of different heights, the wall of houses has a total architectural unity. They are bourgeois houses, characteristic of central Europe, constructed on narrow and deep lots and revealing formal elements from Gothic building. Houses of this type were characteristic of Vienna, Prague, Zurich, and many other cities; their origins, often mercantile, were linked to the earliest form of the modern city. With the trans-

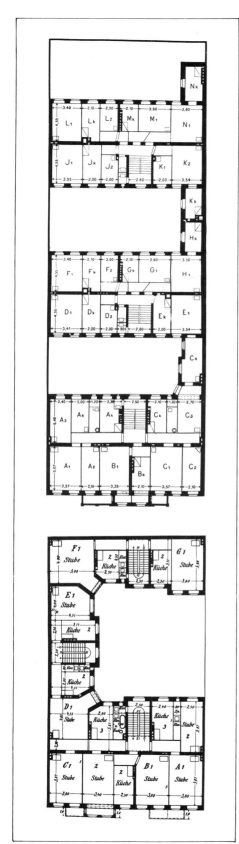

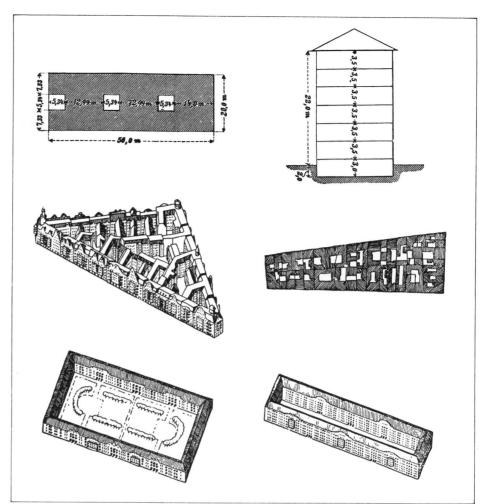

46

47

48

48 Rendering of a country estate for
Prince Wilhelm at Babelsberg, near
Potsdam, Germany, Karl Friedrich
Schinkel. Project dates from 1834;
construction began 1835.
49 Plan of country estate for Prince
Wilhelm at Babelsberg, Karl
Friedrich Schinkel, 1834.

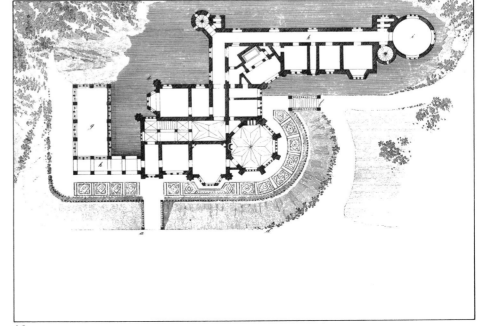

49

formation of the cities in the second half of the nineteenth century, these houses disappeared fairly rapidly, either because of building renewal or because of alterations in the use of areas. With their replacement came a profound modification of the urban landscape, often a rigid monumentalization, as in the case of Unter den Linden. For the older type of house was substituted rental housing and the villa.

To Schumacher, the separation between villas and rental barrack zones in the second half of the nineteenth century represented the crisis of urban unity in the central European city. The villa was sited to provide a closer relationship to nature, to further both social representation and social division. It refused to be, or was incapable of being, inserted into a continuous urban image. Rental housing, on the other hand, in becoming speculative housing, was degraded and never recovered the value of civic architecture.

Nonetheless, even if Schumacher's vision is correct, it must be acknowledged that the villa played a large role in the typological transformations that led to the modern house. The Berlin rental barracks have little to do with the single-family English house, whose definition is that of a particular urban type and a continuously developing residential type. The villa was initially a reduction of the palazzo (as in the case of Schinkel's Babelsberg castle), and it became increasingly elaborated in its internal organization and the rationalization and distribution of its circulation. The work of Hermann Muthesius is important for Berlin; by focusing on the function and the freedom of internal spaces, he developed the principles of the English country house in a rational way and in the context of building.

It is significant that these typological innovations did not also lead to sensitive architectural modifications, and that the greater internal freedom—a response to the bourgeois way of life—was only accompanied by a more monumental image of building and an ossification of the Schinkelesque models, wherein the difference between residential architecture and public buildings became marked. In this sense the buildings of Muthesius, one of the most typical builders of urban Berlin around 1900, are illustrative. His preoccupations with the modern house, as also expressed in his theoretical writings, concerned its typological structure independent of its formal aspects. For the latter he accepted a sort of Germanic neoclassicism with the addition of typical elements from the local traditions. This was in direct contrast to Schinkel's models, in which the house was less dependent on representational elements and classical typological schemes were not in conflict with the architecture.

But the introduction of representational elements into residential architecture in the late nineteenth century is typical of all the architecture of the period; it probably corresponds to changed social conditions and the desire to endow the house with an emblematic significance. Certainly it corresponds to the crisis of urban unity of which Schumacher spoke, and thus to the need for differentiation within a structure where increasingly diverse and antagonistic social classes lived. The villas built by the most famous architects of the Modern Movement in Berlin—Gropius, Erich Mendelsohn, Hugo Häring, etc.—developed these typological models in a fairly orthodox way; there was clearly no sense of rupture with their previous eclectic housing models, even if the image of these villas was transformed profoundly. Sociologists will have to establish the way in which this representational or emblematic element was transformed, but it is obviously a question of different aspects of the same phenomenon. These modern houses

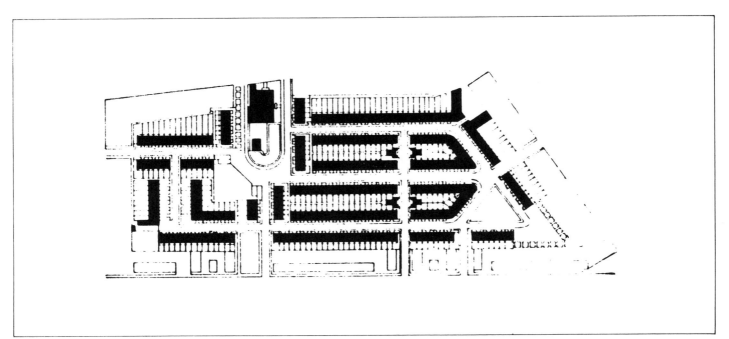

50

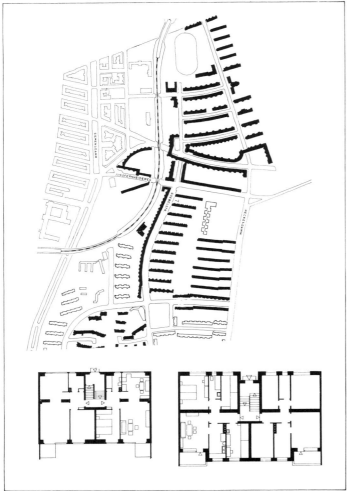

51

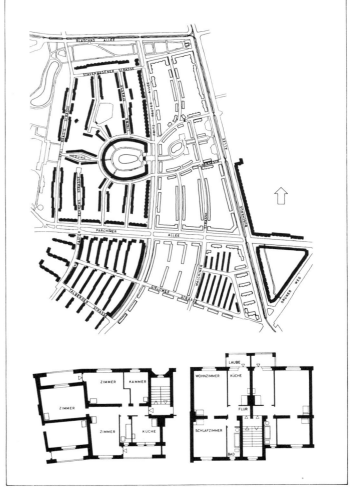

52

carry the premises of the eclectic villa to its ultimate consequences, and from this standpoint one can understand why architects like Muthesius and Van de Velde were looked upon as masters: precisely because they established a general model, even if only by translating English or Flemish experiences.

All these themes of the single-family house are represented in the *Siedlung*, which by virtue of its composite character seems to have been suited best to accepting them and to giving certain tendencies a new definition. Without lingering too long on the housing problem as interpreted by the Rationalist architects, I would like to illustrate some examples realized in Berlin during the 1920s. These are prototypical, although one could look to the equally famous examples in Frankfurt and Stuttgart.

Clearly Rationalist urban theory is epitomized, at least with respect to the residential aspect of the problem, in the *Siedlung*, which is probably a sociological model even before it is a spatial one; certainly when we speak of Rationalist urbanism we are thinking of the urbanism of the residential district. This attitude, however, particularly in view of its methodological implications, immediately reveals its insufficiency. To see the urbanism of Rationalism only as the urbanism of the residential district means to limit the magnitude of this experience to German urbanism of the 1920s. In fact, there are so many and such varied solutions that the definition is not even valid for the history of German urbanism. Moreover, the term *residential district*, which as a translation of the German *Siedlung* is as imprecise as it is useful, means so many different things that it is preferable not to use it until we have first examined it carefully.[14]

It is therefore necessary to study actual conditions and artifacts; and given the morphology of Berlin, its richness and the particularity of its urban landscape, the importance of its villas, and so on, it is possible to conclude that here the *Siedlung* has its own special coherence. The close similarity between such *Siedlungen* as Tempelhofer Felde and Britz, or anywhere that the transformation from the English model is evident, renders our primary reference to the urban site more apparent. While such examples as the Friedrich Ebert are closely linked to Rationalist theoretical formulations, in all cases it is difficult to go back from these actual images to an ideology of the *Siedlung*.

Thus, while we have so far considered the *Siedlung* in itself without referring to, indeed ignoring, the context in which it was produced, an analysis of the urbanism of the *Siedlung*, which essentially means the housing problem in Berlin during the 1920s, can only be undertaken with reference to the 1920 plan of Greater Berlin. What was the basis of this plan? It is far closer to certain recent models than one might imagine. In general, the choice of housing was more or less independent of location; it manifests itself as a moment in an urban system which depended on the evolution of a transportation system that in itself embodied the pulse of the city. Through zoning, it encouraged the self-formation of the center as a governmental and administrative district, while the centers for leisure activities, sports facilities, and the like were pushed to outlying areas.

This model is a basic reference even today, especially where the residential district is a more or less defined zone. Thus in the plan for Greater Berlin we find the following:
1. that the *Siedlungen* were not planned as autonomous districts within a city

50 Site plan of Kiefhoek district, Rotterdam, J. J. P. Oud, 1925.
51 Gross-Siedlung Siemensstadt, Berlin, 1929-1931. Above: General plan. Below: Typical apartment plan by Otto Bartning for no. 4, Goebelstrasse, left, and by Walter Gropius for no. 6, Jungfernheideweg, right.
52 Gross-Siedlung Britz, Berlin, 1925-1931. Above: General plan. Below: Typical apartment plans for the curvilinear and the rectilinear buildings on Fritz Reuter Allee, both by Bruno Taut.

made up of different sectors—a formulation of this type would have been more revolutionary than was the reality;

2. that the German Rationalists in fact recognized the problem of the large city and its metropolitan image—one has only to think of the various projects for the Friedrichstrasse, in particular those of Mies van der Rohe and Bruno Taut;

3. that the solution to the housing problem in Berlin was not entirely different from the fundamental models of housing up to that time, but represented as, well a synthesis of the new and the old, which is certainly a significant fact.

Garden City and Ville Radieuse

When I speak of fundamental models I am referrring to the English Garden City and Le Corbusier's Ville Radieuse. Steen Eiler Rasmussen made this distinction when he said that the "Garden City and the Ville Radieuse represent the two great contemporary styles of modern architecture."[15] Even though this statement refers to all of modern architecture, it will be used here to refer to two specific formulations of the housing problem. It is interesting that Rasmussen indicates in his statement that the typological question is clearer and more explicit than the ideological one, even if the former has sometimes been seen as unvarying. His statement not only has a historiographic meaning, but it also concerns the value of housing within the urban structure—something which is still a general problem today. The two models of the Garden City and the Ville Radieuse are seemingly the most explicit in this regard, and they are also the clearest in terms of the image of the city.

With this in mind, one could say that the Berlin *Siedlungen* in general—and this is equally true for other contemporary examples like those of Frankfurt—represented an attempt to set the problem of housing within the larger urban system, which was itself a product of the actual structure of the existing city and an ideal vision of the new city. This ideal vision was based upon remembered models: that is, the *Siedlung* which we are able to recognize and describe in the Berlin examples did not represent an original model; however, this does not negate the fact that it had its own particular significance among housing models. Thus, in an urban situation such as that of Berlin and other European cities, the *Siedlung* represents an attempt to mediate, more or less consciously, between two different spatial conceptions of the city. We cannot appreciate the *Siedlung* as an autonomous element in the city without also concerning ourselves with the relationships that existed between it and the city.

With respect to the Garden City and the Ville Radieuse, it is necessary to investigate the relationship between these two fundamental housing models and certain political and social theories. One work of this type is Carlo Doglio's essay on the Garden City.[16] Without trying to summarize Doglio's essay—one of the most beautifully written works on urbanism in Italy—I would like to quote from the opening paragraphs where he outlines his precise subject as well as the difficulty and complexity of the problem:

"The situation is particularly complex in the case under study because of the conformist and substantially reactionary overlay of positivistic opinions, because of an ambiguity that undermines not only the formal aspect of the problem but extends to its most hidden roots. When Osborn, to mention the most noted Howardian activist, proposed the Garden City with his pioneering examples of a truly modern and human reconstruction of centers of habitation (and thus of society, let us add), and disdainfully condemned the low-income quarters of Vienna and Stockholm, he was pitting them against the greater validity, both aesthetic

82

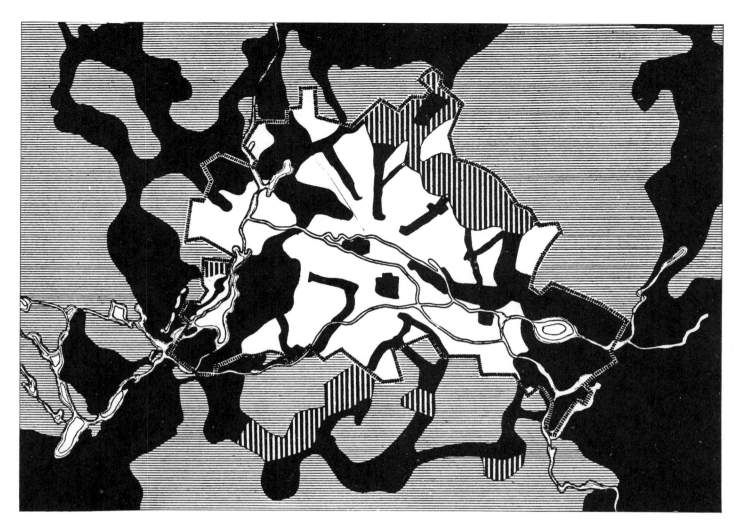

*53 Berlin, scheme of the unbuilt
areas within the city limits and the
surrounding zone, 1929, after Werner
Hegemann. In black, general unbuilt
areas; vertical stripes, fields;
horizontal stripes, agricultural
territory of other communities; dotted
line, territorial limits of Berlin.*

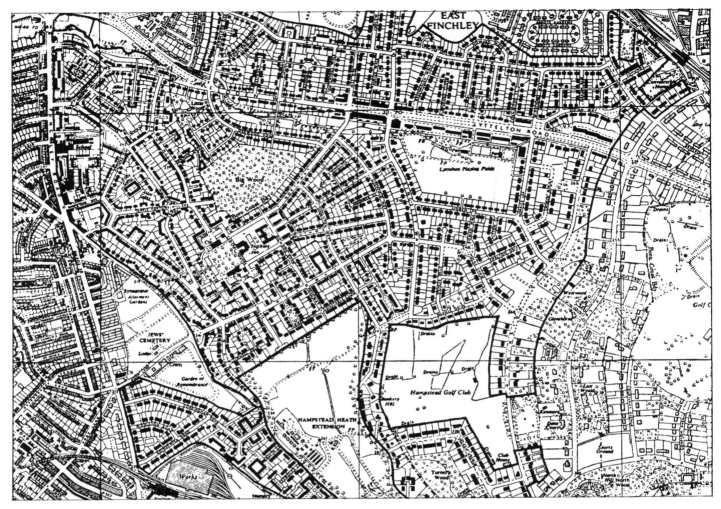

54 *General plan of Hampstead
Garden Suburb, London, Raymond
Unwin and Barry Parker, 1906.
Central zone in collaboration with
Edwin Lutyens.*

and social, that those quarters had historically . . . but when such solutions as Letchworth and Welwyn are dismissed with Marxist formulas not only because of their *form* (and the practically immovable content that derived from it) but also because of the type of structural proposal they implied (city and country, decentralization, etc.), then one can only say that in spite of everything, those solutions were more alive, more loaded with ferment and future than so many others that have been offered ever since."[17]

Since this subject would take us too far afield, I only note in passing how the study of the relationship between housing and family, with all of its cultural and political implications, found interesting application in so-called communitarian ideology. Here, the relationship between the local community and a form of democracy, between the spatial dimension as a moment in the social life of the community and its political life, is well illustrated. The problem of housing obviously emerges as a central theme in a relationship of this type.

On the other hand, where the city as a whole seems to be of primary importance, where density and size are predominant, the housing problem seems to be of less importance, or at least becomes less focused with respect to the other functions of urban life. For example, the great works of beautification and enlargement undertaken in the nineteenth-century city, although often arising out of widespread speculation, could be enjoyed by all of the population and were a positive element in their way of life. Few definitions so clearly recognize this "urban effect" as that of Hellpach, who, in contrast to his times, affirmed the validity of life in the great metropolis: "For the generation shaped by the large cities, it means not only existential space, place for living, market; but it can also become biologically and sociologically that which most profoundly represents the scene where one's life unfolds: one's native land."[18]

There is a parallel between these theories and the residential districts built in the last sixty years. Sometimes, as in the case of the German *Siedlungen* and the Italian and English examples, the translations have been quite clear. We can think of many Italian residential districts where communities that were nonurban, detached, almost untouched by the city, turning inward on themselves and their neighbors, were proposed again and again, only to be superseded by ones where a strongly plastic architectural image which was intended to change the urban image violently was preferred. We could also cite the low-density schemes, later repudiated, of the first new towns; and finally, the experiments with new kinds of residential complexes, such as those proposed by Alison and Peter Smithson and Denys Lasdun and exemplified by the blocks of Sheffield.

The English architects rediscovered a constant theme in residential typological models when they realized that the breaking up of slums brought with it a simultaneous breakup of communities which had traditionally lived in high-density areas and which, without undergoing substantial changes, were unable to establish new roots automatically in the low-density, suburban areas to which they were reassigned. The Smithsons rediscovered the concept of the street, and in their Golden Lane project proposed horizontal passageways on three levels, constituting pedestrian access routed to each individual dwelling.

Formulations of this type are expressed clearly in the Sheffield residential complex, where giant slabs are placed in an elevated position over the city, thereby obliging any future development to relate to them. The very genesis of this work testifies to its relationship with social theory, for example the necessity of recov-

85

ering the street as a stage set for the community: "The street [is a] rectangular stage set where encounters, gossip, games, fights, jealousies, courtship, and displays of pride occur."[19] At the same time, the large blocks at Sheffield recall in a new way the great Corbusian image of the Unité d'Habitation in Marseille.

Primary Elements

The concept of the study area and the dwelling area proposed in the preceding pages is insufficient by itself to characterize the formation and evolution of the city; to the concept of area must be added the totality of specific urban elements that have functioned as nuclei of aggregation. We have called these urban elements, which are of a dominant nature, primary elements because they participate in the evolution of the city over time in a permanent way, often becoming identified with the major artifacts constituting the city. The union of these primary elements with an area, in terms of location and construction, permanence of plan and permanence of building, natural artifacts and constructed artifacts, constitutes a whole which is the physical structure of the city.

To define primary elements is by no means easy. When we study a city, we find that the urban whole tends to be divided according to three principal functions: housing, fixed activities, and circulation. "Fixed activities" include stores, public and commercial buildings, universities, hospitals, and schools. In addition, the urban literature also speaks of urban equipment, urban standards, services, and infrastructures. Some of these terms are defined or definable, others less so, but for the most part each author uses them in a particular context to provide the necessary clarity. To simplify matters I will consider fixed activities as included within primary elements; I would say that the relationship of the house to the residential area is like that of fixed activities to primary elements.

I use the term fixed activities because this notion is generally accepted. But even if in speaking of fixed activities and primary elements we partly refer to the same thing, the two terms presuppose entirely different ways of conceptualizing the urban structure. What they have in common is that both refer to the public, collective character of urban elements, to the characteristic fact of public things that they are made by the collective for the collective and are by nature essentially urban. Whatever reduction of urban reality we make, we always arrive at the collective aspect; it seems to constitute the beginning and end point of the city.

On the other hand, the relationship between primary elements and residential areas corresponds, in the architectural sense, to the operative distinction made by sociologists between the public sphere and the private sphere as characteristic elements of the formation of the city. The definition given by Hans Paul Bahrdt in his *Die moderne Grossstadt* best illustrates the meaning of primary elements: "Our thesis goes like this: a city is a system in which all life, including daily life, reveals a tendency to polarize, to unfold in terms of social aggregations which are either public or private. The public sphere and the private sphere develop in a close relationship without losing their polarization, while sectors of life that cannot be characterized either as 'public' or 'private' lose their meaning. The more strongly the polarization is exerted and the closer the interchange between the public and private spheres, the more 'urban' the life of an urban aggregate is from the sociological viewpoint. In the opposite case, an aggregate will develop the character of a city to a lesser degree."[20]

86

When we consider the spatial aspect of primary elements and their role independent of their function, we realize how closely they are identified with their presence in the city. They possess a value "in themselves," but also a value dependent on their place in the city. In this sense a historical building can be understood as a primary urban artifact; it may be disconnected from its original function, or over time take on functions different from those for which it was designed, but its quality as an urban artifact, as a generator of a form of the city, remains constant. In this sense, monuments are always primary elements.

But primary elements are not only monuments, just as they are not only fixed activities; in a general sense they are *those elements capable of accelerating the process of urbanization* in a city, and they also characterize the processes of spatial transformation in an area larger than the city. Often they act as catalysts. At first their presence can be identified only by their function (and in this respect they coincide with fixed activities), but they rapidly take on a more significant value. Frequently they are not even physical, constructed, measurable artifacts; for example, sometimes the importance of an event itself "gives place" to spatial transformations of a site. I will take up this problem later in terms of the theme of *locus*.

Thus primary elements play an effective role in the dynamic of the city, and as a result of them and the way they are ordered, the urban artifact acquires its own quality, which is principally a function of its placement, its unfolding of a precise action, and its individuality. Architecture is the ultimate moment in this process and also what emerges from this complex structure.

In this way, the urban artifact and its architecture are one and the same, together constituting a work of art. "To speak of a beautiful city is to speak of good architecture"[21] because it is the latter which makes real the aesthetic intentionality of urban artifacts. But the analysis of what is real in this context can only be carried out by examining specific artifacts. To reach an understanding of urban artifacts that is verifiable in a historical context, it will now be instructive to look at two examples drawn from urban history.

The Roman or Gallo-Roman cities of the West developed according to a continuous dynamic that exists in urban elements. This dynamic is still present today in their form. When at the end of the Pax Romana the cities marked their boundaries by erecting walls, they enclosed a smaller surface area than the Roman cities had. Monuments and even well-populated areas were abandoned outside of these walls; the city enclosed only its nucleus. At Nîmes the Visigoths transformed an amphitheater into a fortress, which became a little city of two thousand inhabitants; four gates corresponding to the four cardinal directions gave access to the city, and inside there were two churches. Subsequently the city began to develop again around this monument. A similar phenomenon occurred in the city of Arles.

The vicissitudes of these cities are extraordinary. They immediately lead us to considerations about scale and suggest that the quality of artifacts is independent of their dimensions. The amphitheater at Nîmes had a precise and unequivocal form as well as function. It was not thought of as an indifferent container, but rather was highly precise in its structure, its architecture, and its form. But a succession of external events at a dramatic moment in history re-

The Dynamic of Urban Elements

versed its function, and a theater became a city. This theater-city functioned like a fortress and was adapted to enclose and defend its inhabitants.

In another example, that of Vila Viçosa in Portugal, a city developed between the walls of a castle. These walls comprised its exact boundaries as well as its landscape. The presence of this city—its meaning, its architecture, and the actual way it came to be defined—is a record of its transformations. Only the preexisting condition of a closed and stable form permitted continuity and the production of successive actions and forms. In this way, form, the architecture of urban artifacts, emerges in the dynamic of the city.

It is in this sense that I speak of the Roman cities and the forms left by them: for example, the aqueduct at Segovia that crosses the city like a geographic artifact, the Merida bridge in Estremadura, the Pantheon, the Forum, the theaters. Over time these elements of the Roman city became transformed and their functions altered, and when looked at from the point of view of urban artifacts, they suggest many typological considerations. Another outstanding example is Sixtus V's project for the transformation of the Coliseum into a wool mill; here too the extraordinary form of the amphitheater is involved. On the ground floor laboratories were planned, and on the upper levels there was to have been housing for the workers; the Coliseum would have become a huge workers' quarter and a rationally organized building. Domenico Fontana had this to say about it: "Already they have begun to remove the earth surrounding it, & to level the street that comes from Torre dei Conti & goes to the Coliseum, so that it would all be flat, as today one can still see the vestiges of this removal; & they worked there with sixty horse carriages, & a hundred men, so that [if] the Pope had lived one [more] year, the Coliseum would have been reduced to housing."[22]

How does the city grow? The original nucleus, enclosed within the walls, extends itself according to its own specific nature; and to this formal individuation corresponds a political individuation. On the outskirts of the city develop the *borghi* of the Italian city, the *faubourgs* of the French city.

Milan, whose monocentric structure is wrongly attributed to a kind of spreading out of the historical center, was defined clearly throughout the medieval period by the continued presence of the Gallo-Roman center as well as by convents and religious buildings. The persistence of the *borghi* is so strong that the principal one, San Gottardo, came to be called in dialect simply *el burg*, and still is, with no other name.

In Paris, outside the Cité, monasteries, mercantile centers, and the university grew up on the two banks of the Seine. Around these elements, centers of urban life took form; within the abbatial districts the *bourgs* formed. The abbacy of St. Germain-des-Prés, of Merovingian origin, dates to the sixth century, although it appears in documents only around the twelfth century. This *bourg* represents such a strong urban artifact within the city that it is still recognizable today in the plan of Paris. It sits at the convergence of five streets looking toward the intersection of the Croix-Rouge; there the entrance to the *bourg* of St. Germain-des-Prés was located, and the place was called *le chef de la ville* or *le bout de la ville*.[23]

55 Roman monuments, Arles, France. Aerial view of the theater and amphitheater.
56 Plan of the Santa Croce district, Florence, indicating buildings constructed on the site of the Roman amphitheater.

57a, 57b Two registry maps of the amphitheater, Nîmes, France, 1782, above, and 1809, below, indicating proprietors and trades.

55

56

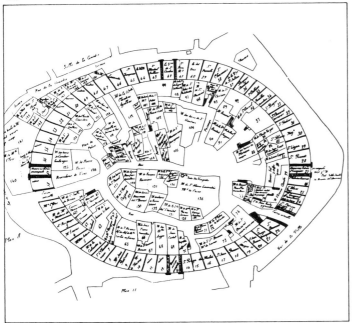

57a

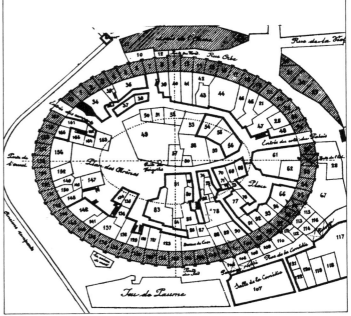

57b

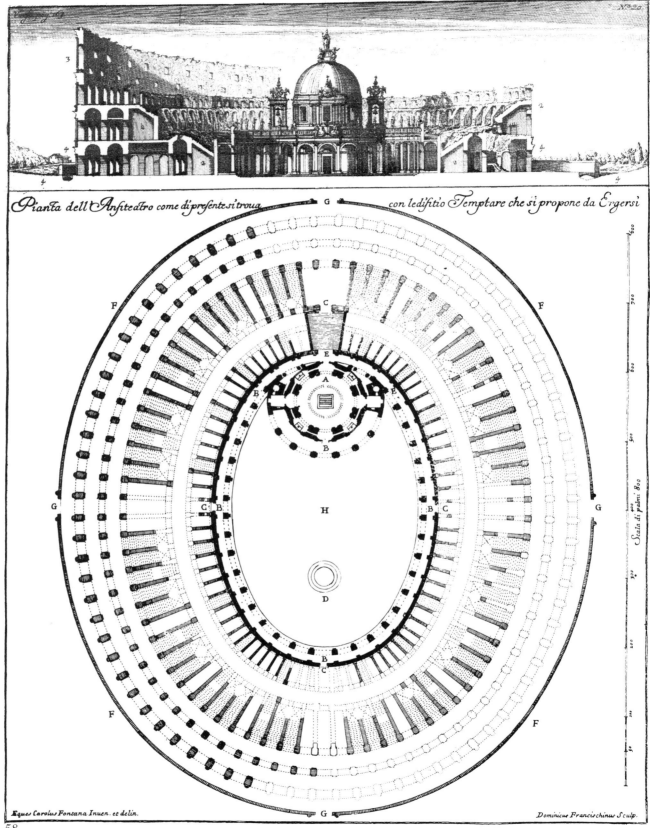

Pianta dell'Anfiteatro come di presente si troua   G   con l'edifitio Templare che si propone da Ergersi

Scala di palmi 800

Eques Carolus Fontana Inuen. et delin.   Dominicus Francischinus Sculp.

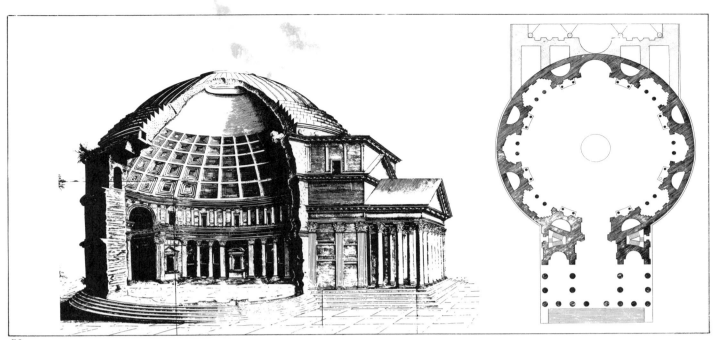

59

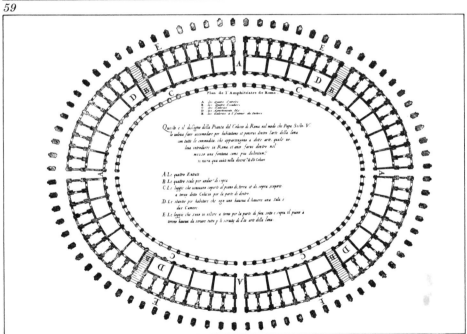

60

58 *Project for the transformation of
the Coliseum in Rome into a forum
for a centrally planned church, Carlo
Fontana, 1707.*
59 *Pantheon, Rome. Left: Sectional
rendering. Right: Plan. Both
engravings from the early eighteenth
century.*
60 *Pope Sixtus V's project for the
transformation of the Coliseum in
Rome into a wool factory, with
workers' apartments (marked "D"),
1590.*

A monument stands at a center. It is usually surrounded by buildings and becomes a place of attraction. We have said that it is a primary element, but of a special type: that is, it is typical in that it summarizes all of the questions posed by the city, but it is special because by virtue of its form its value goes beyond economics and function.

Thus, even if all the monumental structures of the city have a meta-economic character, they are also outstanding works of art, and they are characterized above all by this aspect. They constitute a value that is stronger than environment and stronger than memory. It is significant a city has never intentionally destroyed its own greatest works of architecture; the Pazzi Chapel or St. Peter's has never needed defending.

It is also significant that this value is the predominant characteristic of the city and the unique instance where the entire structure of the urban artifact is summarized in its form. The monument has permanence because it already exists in a dialectical position within urban development; it is understood in the city as something that arises either at a single point in the city or in an area of the city. In the first case, that of primary elements, the ultimate form is most important; in the second, that of the residential district, the nature of the land seems to be most important. We must remember that a theory of this type takes into account not only a knowledge of the city in terms of its parts but also its growth, and while it attributes maximum value to the precise empirical experience of primary elements and their urban surroundings, it increasingly diminishes the importance of the plan and the overall pattern of the city, which must be studied from other points of view.

The Ancient City

As we have just seen, the significance of primary elements in the evolution of the ancient city demonstrates the importance of the form of urban artifacts, that is to say, of the architecture of the city. The permanence of this form or its value as a reference is entirely independent of both the specific function for which it was designed and its coincidence with the continuity of urban institutions. For this reason, I am deliberately emphasizing the form and the architecture of the city rather than its institutions. It is a distortion of history to imagine that institutions are maintained and transmitted without interruption or alteration; a position of this sort ends up glossing over the real trauma of the city's moments of transformation.

The enormous contribution that Henri Pirenne[24] made to the study of the city and in particular the relationships between the city and civic institutions attests to the value that comes to be attributed to monuments and places, to the physical reality of the city as a permanent moment of political and institutional coming into being. Monuments and all urban constructions are reference signs which over time acquire different meanings. "Large towns and boroughs . . . have played an essential role in the history of cities. They have been, so to speak, stones of anticipation. It was around their walls that cities took shape, from the earliest appearance of the economic renaissance, the first symptoms of which could be detected at the beginning of the tenth century."[25] Even if the city did not exist in a social, economic, or legal sense, it is a significant fact that its rebirth began around the walls of the boroughs and the ancient Roman cities. Pirenne demonstrates how the classical city knew nothing analogous to the local and particularistic bourgeois city of the Middle Ages. In the classical world, urban life was the same as national life; the municipal system in antiquity thus was identical to the constitutional one. Rome, extending her domination to the Mediterranean world, made her colonized cities outposts of the Imperial system; this system survived the Germanic and Arab invasions, but over time the cities completely changed their function. This change is essential for comprehending their subsequent evolution.

At first the Church established its dioceses according to the existing districts of the Roman cities; the city in this way became the bishop's seat, and thereby caused the exodus of merchants, the decrease of commerce, and the end of interurban relationships which, having no influence on the ecclesiastical organization, also had no impact on the urban structure. Cities identified themselves with the prestige of the Church and were enriched by donations while maintaining their alignment with the Carolingians in matters of administration; so that on the one hand their wealth increased and on the other their moral prestige grew. With the fall of the Carolingian empire, feudal princes continued to respect the authority of the Church, and even during the anarchy of the tenth and eleventh centuries, the dominance of the bishops was so absolute that it extended naturally to the residential districts as well, that is, to the ancient Roman cities.

Pirenne indicates how this transfer of power actually saved the cities from ruin even when tenth-century economic conditions gave them no reason to exist, since with the disappearance of the merchants they no longer had any value to lay society. Around them the great agricultural domains existed autonomously, and the State, constituted on a purely agricultural basis, was not interested in their survival. Thus, although the castles of the princes and counts were in the countryside, the bishops were tied to the city precisely through the immobile nature of the ecclesiastical office, and this ultimately saved the city from ruin. In this way the city survived—as the physical place of the bishop's seat, not as a matter of the continuity of urban institutions.

In Pirenne's analysis, the example of Rome becomes extraordinarily revealing: "The imperial city became the pontifical city. Its historic prestige enhanced that of St. Peter's successor. Isolated, he appeared larger and at once became more powerful. One saw only him . . . and continuing to live in Rome, one made it *his* Rome, as each bishop also made the city in which he lived his city."[26]

In what way did the ancient city become the origin of the modern city? For Pirenne, it is entirely wrong to attribute the formation of the medieval city to the activities of the abbey, the castle, or the market. The cities along with their bourgeois institutions were born out of the economic and industrial reawakening of Europe. Why and how were they installed, so to speak, in the old Roman cities? Because the Roman cities, Pirenne argues, were not artificial creations; on the contrary, they reunited all the conditions of geographic order without which an urban agglomeration cannot live and prosper. Situated at the intersection of the indestructible "roads of Caesar," for centuries the roads of mankind, they were destined to become the seats of municipal life again. "The cities which from the tenth to the eleventh century had been hardly more than the center of large ecclesiastical domains began to recover, in a rapid and inevitable transformation, their long-lost original character."[27] Such a transformation could not have occurred except within or around the ancient cities, since these represented a man-made complex, a halfway point between artifice and nature,

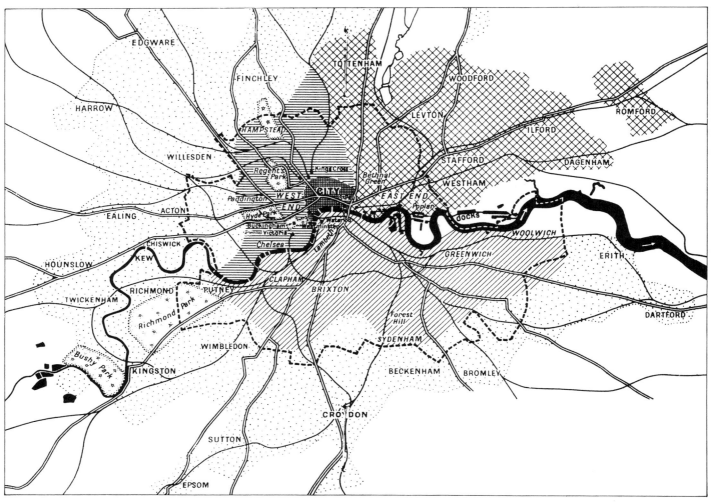

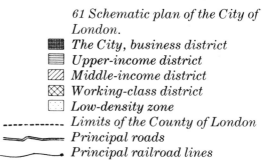

61 Schematic plan of the City of London.

▓ The City, business district
▤ Upper-income district
▨ Middle-income district
▧ Working-class district
░ Low-density zone
----------- Limits of the County of London
〜〜〜 Principal roads
⎯⎯• Principal railroad lines

which, as Pirenne affirms in reference to the Roman cities, man could not easily disregard in the course of his development. In the utilization of the bodies of the old cities, there is at once an economic and a psychological rationale. They become both a positive value and a point of reference.

This subject of the transformation of the ancient cities is also relevant with respect to the modern question of the evolution from the bourgeois city to the socialist one; here too it already seems certain that moments of institutional change cannot necessarily be related to the evolution of form. Thus to postulate a simple relationship between the two, as some would like, is an abstraction that is not responsive to the reality of urban processes. What is clear is that primary elements and monuments, because they directly represent the public sphere, acquire an increasingly necessary and complex character which is not so easily modified. The residential quarter, being an area, has a more dynamic character, but it nevertheless depends on the life of these primary elements and monuments and participates in the system constituted by the city as a whole.

Processes of Transformation

The relationship between the dwelling areas and the primary elements of a city is responsible for configurating that city in a specific way. If this can be demonstrated in cities in which historical events have always acted to unify disparate elements, it is even more apparent in the case of cities that have never managed to integrate in an overall form the urban artifacts that constitute them: thus London, Berlin, Vienna, Rome, Bari, and many other cities.

In Bari,[28] for example, the ancient city and the walled city constitute two extremely different, almost unrelated artifacts. The ancient city has never been enlarged; its nucleus is completely defined as a form. Only its principal street, which served to link it to the surrounding region, emerges intact and permanent in the texture of the walled city. In cases of this type there is always a close connection between primary elements and the area; often this connection becomes an urban artifact so absolutely predominant that it constitutes a characteristic of the city, for the city is invariably the sum of its artifacts.

Morphological analysis, one of the most important instruments for studying the city, brings these aspects into full view. Amorphous zones do not exist in the city, or where they do, they are moments of a process of transformation; they represent inconclusive times in the urban dynamic. Where phenomena of this type appear very frequently, as in the suburbs of the American city, the processes of transformation have usually been accelerated, since high density puts greater pressure on land usage. These transformations are realized through the definition of a precise area, and this is when the process of *redevelopment* occurs.

This process today characterizes a great city like London: "The idea of the precinct," writes Peter Hall, "has been instinctively applied by builders and architects for centuries, in the Oxford and Cambridge Colleges, in London's Inns of Court, in the original plans for Bloomsbury where through-traffic was kept out by gates."[29] Politics of this type constituted the basis for Patrick Abercrombie's famous precincts for Westminster and Bloomsbury; the road system was to have been readapted so that the principal streets would encircle the blocks and prevent through-traffic from penetrating.

A distinctive characteristic of all cities, and thus also of the urban aesthetic, is the tension that has been, and still is, created between areas and primary elements and between one sector of the city and another. This tension arises from the differences between urban artifacts existing in the same place and must be measured not only in terms of space but also of time. By time I mean both the historical process, in which phenomena of a permanent kind are present with all their implications, and a purely chronological process, in which such phenomena can be measured against urban artifacts of successive periods.

In this way, formerly peripheral parts of large cities in transformation often appear beautiful: London, Berlin, Milan, and Moscow reveal entirely unexpected perspectives, aspects, and images. The different *times* more than the immense spaces of the Moscow periphery, by virtue of an aesthetic pleasure that resides in the very nature of the artifacts, give us the real image of a culture in transformation, of a modification taking place in the social structure itself.

Of course, we cannot so easily entrust the values of today's cities to the natural succession of artifacts. Nothing guarantees an effective continuity. It is important to know the mechanism of transformation and above all to establish how we can act in this situation—not, I believe, through the total control of this process of change in urban artifacts, but through the control of the principal artifacts emerging in a certain period. Here the question of scale, and of the scale of intervention, comes to the fore.

The transformation of particular parts of the city over time is very closely linked to the objective phenomenon of the decay of certain zones. This phenomenon, generally referred to in the English and American literature as "obsolescence," is increasingly evident in large modern cities, and it has special characteristics in the large American cities, where it has been closely studied. For our purposes, we will define this phenomenon as characterized by a group of buildings—which may be in the neighborhood of a certain street or may constitute an entire district—that has outlived the dynamics of land use in the surrounding area (this definition has a much broader scope than some others). Such areas of the city do not follow life; often they remain islands for a long time with respect to the general development, bearing witness to different periods in the city and at the same time configurating large areas of "reserve." This phenomenon of obsolescence illustrates the validity of studying areas of the city as urban artifacts; we can then relate the transformations of such areas to the study of specific events, as we will see later in the theories of Halbwachs.

The hypothesis of the city as an entity constituted of many parts which are complete in themselves is, it seems to me, one which truly permits *freedom of choice*; and freedom of choice becomes a fundamental issue because of its implications. For example, we do not believe that questions concerning values can be decided in terms of abstract architectural and typological formulations—for example, high-rise or low-rise housing. Such questions can only be resolved at the concrete level of urban architecture. We are fully convinced that in a society where choices are free, the real freedom of the citizen rests in being able to choose one solution rather than another.

Geography or history
according to what we see
or when we think.
Carlos Barral[30]

**Geography and History;
the Human Creation**

In the preceding pages we have been primarily concerned with two issues: first, the dwelling area and primary elements, and second the city as a structure of parts. I have also dealt with monuments, with the various uses of urban elements, and with ways of reading the city. Many of these concerns were methodological in that they were aimed at defining a system of classification. Perhaps I have not always chosen the most direct approach; but I have tried to remain faithful to the studies I consider most valid and, in part, to order them. I have already remarked that there is nothing new in any of this. What is important is that behind these considerations are real artifacts which testify to the relationship of man to the city.

I have also put forward the hypothesis of the city as a man-made object and a work of art; we can observe and describe this man-made object and seek to understand its structural values. The history of the city is always inseparable from its geography; without both we cannot understand the architecture that is the physical sign of this "human thing." "The art of architecture," wrote Viollet-le-Duc, "is a human creation," and again, "Architecture, this *human* creation, is, in fact, only an application of principles born outside us and which we appropriate to ourselves by observation."[31] These principles are *in* the city; the stone landscape of building—of "brick and mortar," in C.B. Fawcett's expression—symbolizes the continuity of a community.[32] Sociologists have studied collective knowledge and urban psychology; geography and ecology have opened broad vistas. But is not architecture essential for understanding the city as a work of art?

More precise studies of specific important moments in urban history are needed to clarify the question of the architecture of the city as a total work of art. As Bernard Berenson recognized, even without developing the idea, Venetian art is explained completely by the city itself: "There was nothing the Venetians would not do to add to its [the State's] greatness, glory, and splendor. It was this which led them to make of the city itself that wondrous monument to the love and awe they felt for their Republic, which still rouses more admiration and gives more pleasure than any other one achievement of the art-impulse in man. They were not content to make their city the most beautiful in the world; they performed ceremonies in its honor partaking of all the solemnity of religious rites."[33] Such an observation is true for all cities; it refers to artifacts, and while these are manifested in different ways and with different consequences, they can still be compared. No city ever lacked a sense of its own individuality.

In distinguishing between the two principal artifacts found in the city, the dwelling area and the primary elements, we have strongly denied that housing is something amorphous and transitory. Thus, instead of focusing on the single house, in which material decay and a necessary accommodation to different social classes and modes of life are empirically observable over time, we have substituted the concept of the characteristic area. Entire parts of the city manifest concrete signs of their way of life, their own form, and their memory, and these areas may be distinguished from one another for the purpose of investigating

97

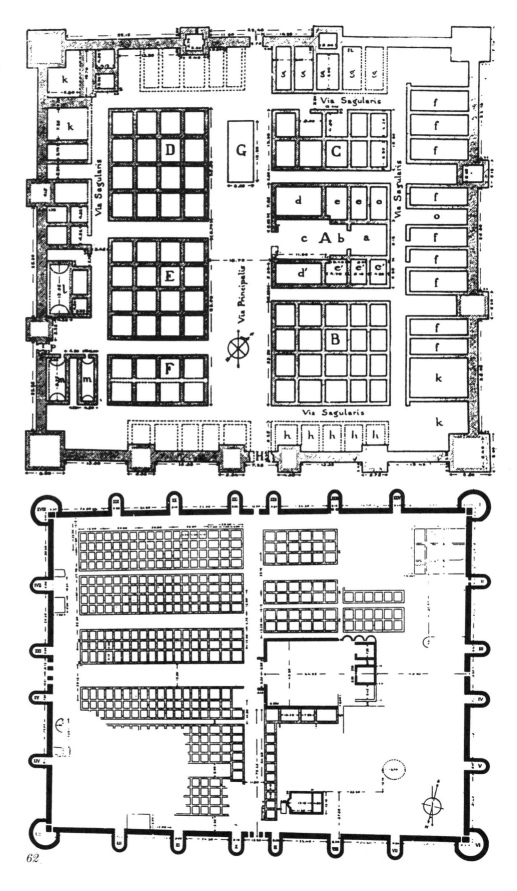

62 Plans of two Roman fortified settlements which became a type of urban formation. Above: Daganiya, Jordan. Below: El-Leggùn, Jordan.

their characteristics morphologically and possibly also historically and linguistically. In this context, the study of areas in the city raises the issues of *locus* and scale.

In contrast to the area, the primary element evolves and should be studied as an element whose presence accelerates the process of the urban dynamic. Such an element can be interpreted solely from a functional point of view as a fixed activity of the collective and for the collective, but more importantly it can be seen as an actual urban artifact, identifiable with an event or an architecture that is capable of "summarizing" the city. As such it is already the history and the idea of the city in the process of constructing itself—a "state of mind," according to Park's definition.

As the core of the hypothesis of the city as a man-made object, primary elements have an absolute clarity; they are distinguishable on the basis of their form and in a certain sense their exceptional nature within the urban fabric; they are characteristic, or better, *that which characterizes* a city. If one looks at the plan of any city, these immediately identifiable forms leap out as black spots. The same is true from a volumetric point of view.

Although I stated earlier that monuments are not the only primary elements, I seem always to end up using them as examples. For instance, I spoke of the theater at Arles, the Palazzo della Ragione in Padua, and so on. I am not sure that I can fully clarify this point but let me introduce a different argument. We know that many geographical or urbanistic texts classify cities into two large families: planned and unplanned. "In urban studies it is usual to emphasize as primary the difference between planned and unplanned towns. The former have been conceived and founded as towns, whereas the latter have emerged without conscious planning. They are settlements that have grown and been adapted to discharge urban functions. Their urban character has appeared in the course of their growth, and their layout is essentially the product of accretion of buildings about some pre-urban nucleus."[34] Thus writes Arthur E. Smailes in his text on urban geography, as have many others.

Presuming that the theoretical scheme propounded in this statement is securely founded on genuine facts, we can agree that it has a relative concreteness; it involves an elementary type of classification, and can be debated from many points of view. In fact we would say with regard to the genesis of urban artifacts that in all cases the issue is "the aggregation of buildings around some pre-urban nucleus," to use Smailes's terms. This nucleus represents a beginning of the process of urbanization during which the city is constituted together with all of its values.

Consequently, I consider the *plan* to be a primary element, the equal of a monument like a temple or a fortress. The nucleus of a planned city is itself also a primary element; it does not matter whether it initiates an urban process or characterizes it, as in Leningrad or in Ferrara. The notion that the existence of a plan makes for a rigidly defined spatial solution of a city from an overall perspective is very much debatable; the plan is always but one moment of the city in the same way that any other primary element is.

Whether the city grows around an ordered or disordered nucleus or around a single artifact, then, does not make much difference (although it surely raises different morphological issues); both these conditions tend to constitute characteristic artifacts. This is what happened in Leningrad, and this is what is happening in Brasilia, two examples which merit further study.

Scholars like Chabot and Poète never attempted to draw any distinction between the plan and single artifacts, although Chabot rightly considered the plan to be the theoretical foundation of all urban operations. However, Lavedan attached greater importance to such a distinction, as was only logical after his long work on the architecture of the city and on the urban structure of French cities. If the enormous efforts of the French school had been accompanied more often by attempts at a synthesis like Lavedan's, we would today have marvelous material at our disposal; however, that Albert Demangeon's studies on the city and its housing did not take into account the material gathered by Viollet-le-Duc is a problem that goes beyond the lack of an interdisciplinary relationship—it has to do with an attitude toward reality.

However, Lavedan should not be reproached for insisting on the *architectural aspect* since this is precisely the greatest merit of his work, and I do not think I am distorting his thinking in saying that when he speaks of the "plan" of a city, he means the architecture. In discussing the origins of the city, he wrote, "whether it is a matter of a spontaneous city or a planned city, the trace of its plan, the design of its streets, is not due to chance. There is an obedience to rules, whether unconscious in the first case or conscious and open in the second. There always exists the generating element of the plan."[35] With this formulation Lavedan restores to the plan its value as an originating element or component.

It might appear that in attempting to explain the difference between a primary element and a monument I have introduced another argument concerning the plan, which rather than making my thesis more precise has ultimately enlarged it. In fact, this enlargement permits us to return to our opening hypothesis, which we have analyzed from different viewpoints: the city is not by its nature a creation that can be reduced to a single basic idea; its processes of formation are many and varied.

The city is constituted of parts, and each one of these parts is characteristic; it also possesses primary elements around which buildings aggregate. Monuments are fixed points in the urban dynamic, and as such are stronger than economic laws. However, primary elements, in their immediate form, are not necessarily so. In this sense, the essence of monuments is their destiny, although it is obviously hard to say at what point this destiny can be predicted. In other words, it is necessary to consider both permanent urban artifacts and primary elements which may as yet have less permanence as essential to the constitution of the city, and this has to do with both architecture and politics. Thus, when primary elements assume the value of monuments either because of their intrinsic value or because of their particular historical situation, it is possible to relate this fact precisely to the history and the life of the city.

Once again, all these considerations are important only because behind them are artifacts that show their direct connection to man. For the elements constituting the city—these urban artifacts which are by nature characteristic and characterizing and as much a product of human activity as a collective artifact—are among the most authentic human testimonies. Naturally when we speak of these artifacts we are speaking of their architecture, their meaning as a human creation in itself. A French scholar recently wrote of the crisis of the French university that it seemed to him that nothing could more tangibly express this crisis than the absence of a building that "was" the French university. That Paris, although the cradle of the great European universities, never managed to "construct" such a place, signaled an internal weakness of the system. "The confrontation with this prodigious architectural phenomenon shocked me. A disquietude was born, as well as a suspicion which had to be confirmed, when I subsequently visited Coimbra, Salamanca, Göttingen, and Padua again. . . . It is the architectural nothingness of the French university which made me understand its intellectual and spiritual nothingness."[36]

Could one not say that the cathedrals and churches scattered throughout the world together with St. Peter's *constitute* the universality of the Catholic Church? I am not speaking of the monumental character of these works of architecture, nor of their stylistic aspects: I refer to their presence, their construction, their history, in other words, to the nature of urban artifacts. *Urban artifacts have their own life, their own destiny.* When one goes to a charitable institution, the sadness is almost something concrete. It is in the walls, the courtyards, the rooms. When the Parisians destroyed the Bastille, they were erasing the centuries of abuse and sadness of which the Bastille was the physical form.

At the beginning of this chapter, I spoke of the *quality* of urban artifacts. Of the authors who have proposed this type of study, Lévi-Strauss has gone further than anyone in defining the idea of quality and in stating that however rebellious our Euclidean spirit has become to a qualitative conception of space, its existence does not depend on us. "Space has values peculiar to itself, just as sounds and scents have their colors and feelings their weight. The search for correspondences of this sort is not a poet's game or an act of mystification . . . These correspondences offer the scholar an entirely new terrain, and one which may still have rich yields."[37] This concept of quality in urban artifacts has already emerged from actual research, from the concreteness of the real. The quality of architecture—the quality of the human creation—is the meaning of the city. Thus, after investigating a number of possible modes of understanding the city, we must return to the most intimate, the most private characteristics of urban artifacts; and with these aspects, those most closely bound up with architecture, I will begin the next chapter.

To conclude, I wish to emphasize that it is *quality* and *destiny* which distinguish monuments, in the geographical sense, from primary elements. With these two parameters as guides, studies on both the behavior of human groups and the individual in the city can be much enriched. I have mentioned the efforts of the American Lynch, although along different lines; it is to be hoped that such experimental research will be taken further and will yield important material for all aspects of urban psychology.

This concept of quality can also cast light on the concepts of area and boundaries, of political territory and frontier—concepts for which neither the myth of race nor the community of languages or religions sufficiently accounts. I am only suggesting here a possible guideline for research; many contributions are bound to emerge from psychology, sociology, and urban ecology. However, I am convinced that they will take on new meaning once they pay more attention to physical realities and to the architecture of our cities. We can no longer concern ourselves with the architecture of the city—in other words, architecture itself—without a general framework in which to relate urban artifacts. It is in this sense that I have spoken of the need for a new treatment.

I have already used the term *locus* several times in this book. The *locus* is a relationship between a certain specific location and the buildings that are in it. It is at once singular and universal.

The selection of the location for any building, as also for any city, was of primary importance in the classical world. The "situation"—the site—was governed by the *genius loci*, the local divinity, an intermediary who presided over all that was to unfold in it. The concept of *locus* was also present at all times for the theoretician of the Renaissance, even if by the time of Palladio and later Milizia its treatment took on an increasingly topographical and functional aspect. In the writings of Palladio, one can still sense the living presence of the classical world, the vital secret of a relationship between old and new. More than just a function of a specific architectural culture, this relationship is manifest in works like the Villa Malcontenta and the Villa Rotonda, in which it is precisely their "situation" which conditions our understanding. Viollet-le-Duc, too, in his efforts to interpret architecture as a series of logical operations based on a few rational principles, admitted the difficulty of transposing a work of architecture from one place to another. In his general theory of architecture, the *locus* participates as a unique and physical place.

More recently, a geographer like Sorre could suggest the possibility of a theory of spatial division[1] and, based on this, postulate the existence of "singular points." The *locus*, so conceived, emphasizes the conditions and qualities within undifferentiated space which are necessary for understanding an urban artifact. Along similar lines, Halbwachs, in the last years of his life, concerned himself with the topography of legendary places. He argued that during different periods holy places have presented different physiognomies, and in these can be found the images of the various Christian groups who constructed and situated them according to their aspirations and their needs.

Let us consider for a moment the space of the Catholic religion. Since the Church is indivisible this space covers the whole earth. In such a universe the concept of the individual location becomes secondary, as does that of the boundary or frontier. Space is determined with respect to a single center, the seat of the Pope; but this same earthly space is nothing but a moment, a small part of the universal space which is the place of the communion of saints. (This idea is similar to that of the transcendence of space as it is understood by the mystics.) Even in this total and undifferentiated framework, where the idea of space itself is nullified and transcended, "singular points" exist; these are the places of pilgrimage, the sanctuaries where the faithful enter into more direct communication with God. In this way the sacraments become signs of grace in the Christian doctrine. Through their visible parts they signify or indicate the invisible grace which they confer; and because in signifying it they actually confer it, they are potent signs.

It is possible to identify such a singular point by a particular event that occurred there at some time or an infinite variety of other causes, both rational and irrational. Even within the universal space of the Church, there is still an intermediate value that is recognized and sanctioned, the possibility of a real—if extraordinary—idea of space. To bring this idea into the domain of urban artifacts, we must return to the value of images, to the physical analysis of artifacts and their surroundings; and perhaps this will lead us to a pure and simple understanding of the value of the *locus*. For such an idea of place and time is seemingly capable of being expressed rationally, even if it embraces a series of values that

The *Locus*

63 One of the chapels of the Sacro Monte at Orta, Italy, circa 1600.

65

66

64 Chapels of the Sacro Monte at Orta, circa 1600.
65 View of the Sacro Monte at Varese, Italy, showing the chapels flanking the street to the Holy Sepulcher. Engraving by L. and P. Giarré.
66 Baveno, Italy, Renaissance portico built over Via Crucis.

are outside and beyond what we experience.

I realize the delicacy of this argument; but it is latent in every empirical study; it is part of experience. Henri Paul Eydoux,[2] in his studies on Gallic France, spoke specifically of places that have always been considered unique, and he suggested further analysis of such places, which seem to have been predestined by history. These places are real signs of space; and as such they have a relationship both to chance and to tradition.

I often think of the piazzas depicted by the Renaissance painters, where the place of architecture, the human construction, takes on a general value of place and of memory because it is so strongly fixed in a single moment. This moment becomes the primary and most profound idea that we have of the piazzas of Italy, and is therefore linked with our spatial idea of the Italian cities themselves. Ideas of this type are bound up with our historical culture, with our existence in built landscapes, with references that carry over from one context to another, and thus also with the rediscovery of singular points, which are virtually the closest approximation to a spatial idea that we have imagined. Henri Focillon speaks of psychological places, places without which the spirit of an environment would be opaque or elusive. Thus, to describe a particular artistic landscape, he offers the notion of "art as place." "The landscape of Gothic art, or rather, Gothic art as a landscape, created a France and a French humanity that no one could foresee: of outlines of the horizon, silhouettes of cities—a poetry, in short, that arose from Gothic art, and not from geology or from Capetian institutions. But is not the essential attribute of any environment that of producing, of shaping the past according to its own needs?"[3]

As is evident, the substitution of *Gothic art as place* for *Gothic landscape* is of enormous importance. In this sense, the building, the monument, and the city become human things par excellence; and as such, they are profoundly linked to an original occurrence, to a first sign, to composition, permanence, and evolution, and to both chance and tradition. As the first inhabitants fashioned an environment for themselves, they also formed a *place* and established its uniqueness.

The comments of the theoreticians on the framing of the landscape in painting, the sureness with which the Romans repeated certain elements in their building of new cities, acknowledging in the *locus* the potential for transformation— these and many other facts cause us to intuit the importance of certain artifacts; and when we consider information of this type, we realize why architecture was so important in the ancient world and in the Renaissance. It shaped a context. Its forms changed together with the larger changes of a site, participating in the constitution of a whole and serving an overall event, while at the same time constituting an event in itself. Only in this way can we understand the importance of an obelisk, a column, a tombstone. Who can distinguish anymore between an event and the sign that marks it?

I have asked many times in the course of this book, *where does the singularity of an urban artifact begin?* In its form, its function, its memory, or in something else again? We can now answer that it begins *in the event and in the sign that has marked the event.* This notion has traversed the history of architecture. Artists have always attempted to make something original, to make an artifact which precedes style. Burckhardt understood this process when he wrote, "There, in the sanctuary, they [the artists] took their first steps toward the sublime; they learned to eliminate the contingent from form. Types came into being; ultimately, the first ideals."[4] Thus, the close relationship that once was present between forms and elements proposes itself again as a necessary origin; and so while on the one hand architecture addresses its own circumscribed domain, its elements and its ideals, on the other it tends to become identified with an artifact, and the separation which occurred at its origin and which permitted it to develop autonomously no longer is recognizable. It is in this sense that we can interpret a comment by Adolf Loos: "If we find a mound six feet long and three feet wide in the forest, formed into a pyramid, shaped by a shovel, we become serious and something in us says, 'someone lies buried here.' That is architecture."[5] The mound six feet long and three feet wide is an extremely intense and pure architecture precisely because it is identifiable in the artifact. It is only in the history of architecture that a separation between the original element and its various forms occurred. From this separation, which the ancient world seemingly resolved forever, derives the universally acknowledged character of permanence of those first forms.

All of the great eras of architecture have reproposed the architecture of antiquity anew, as if it were a paradigm established forever; but each time it has been reproposed differently. Because this same idea of architecture has been manifested in different places, we can understand our own cities by measuring this standard against the actuality of the individual experience of each particular place. What I said at the beginning about the Palazzo della Ragione in Padua is perhaps subsumed in this idea, which goes beyond a building's functions and its history, but not beyond the particularity of the place in which it exists.

Perhaps we can better understand the concept of *locus*, which at times seems rather opaque, by approaching it from another perspective, by penetrating it in a more familiar, more visible—even if no longer rational—way. Otherwise, we continue to grasp at outlines which only evaporate and disappear. These outlines delineate the singularity of monuments, of the city, and of buildings, and thus the concept of singularity itself and its limits, where it begins and ends. They trace the relation of architecture to its location—the place of art—and thereby its connections to, and the precise articulation of, the *locus* itself as a singular artifact determined by its space and time, by its topographical dimensions and its form, by its being the seat of a succession of ancient and recent events, by its memory. All these problems are in large measure of a collective nature; they force us to pause for a moment on the relationship between place and man, and hence to look at the relationship between ecology and psychology.

"The greatest products of architecture are not so much individual as they are social works; rather the children of nations in labor than the inspired efforts of men of genius; the legacy of a race; the accumulated wealth of centuries, the residuum of the successive evaporations of human society—in a word, a species of formation."
Victor Hugo[6]

Architecture as Science

In his work of 1816 on the monuments of France, Alexandre de Laborde, like Quatremère de Quincy, praised the artists of the late eighteenth and early nineteenth century for going to Rome to study and master the immutable principles of knowledge, retraveling the great roads of antiquity. The architects of this new school presented themselves as scholars of the physical artifacts of their sci-

107

*67 Project for the stables of Count
Sangusko in southern France, Adolf
Loos, 1924.*

ence: architecture. Thus they were traversing a familiar route, since their masters too had devoted themselves to establishing a logic of architecture based on essential principles. "They are at once artists and scholars; they have mastered the habit of observation and of criticism . . . "[7]

But Laborde and his contemporaries failed to note the fundamental character of these studies: the fact that they provided an introduction to urban problems and to the human sciences, an introduction that tipped the balance in favor of the scholar rather than the architect. Only a history of architecture based on artifacts gives us a comprehensive picture of this delicate balance and allows us a well-articulated knowledge of the artifacts themselves.

We know that the basic subject of the theoreticians and their teachings was the elaboration of a general principle of architecture, of architecture as a science, of the formulation and applications of buildings. Ledoux[8] established his principles of architecture on the basis of the classical conception, but he was also concerned with places and events, situations and society. Thus, he studied the various buildings that society demanded with respect to their precise contexts.

For Viollet-le-Duc, too, the issue of architecture as science was unambiguous; for him there was only one solution to a problem. But, and here he expanded the thesis, since the problems addressed by architecture changed continually, therefore solutions had to be modified. According to the definition given by this French master, it was the principles of architecture together with the modifications of the real world that constituted the structure of the human creation. Thus in his *Dictionnaire* he set the great panorama of Gothic architecture in France before us with unparalleled power.

I know of few descriptions of architectural works which are as complete and persuasive as that of the Gaillard castle, Richard the Lionhearted's fortress.[9] In Viollet-le-Duc's prose, it acquires the force of a permanent image of how an architectural work is structured. Both the structure and the uniqueness of the castle are revealed by way of an analysis of the building relative to the geography of the Seine, a study of military art, and a topographical knowledge of antiquity, in the end investing the two rival *condottieri*, the Norman and the French, with the same psychology. Not only does the history of France lie behind this, but the castle becomes a place about which we acquire a personal knowledge and experience.

Likewise, the study of the house begins with geographical classifications and sociological considerations and by way of architecture goes on to the structure of the city and the country, the human creation. Viollet-le-Duc discovered that of all architecture the house offers the best characterization of the customs, usages, and tastes of a population; its structure, like its functional organization, changes only over long periods of time. From a study of the plans of houses, he reconstructed the formation of urban nuclei and was able to point the direction for a comparative study of the typology of the French house.

Using the same principle, he described the cities constructed *ex novo* by the French kings. Montpazier, for example, not only had a regular grid, but all the houses were of an equal size and had the same plan. The people who came to live in a special city like this found themselves on a plane of absolute equality. Thus, a study of the lots and the urban block allowed Viollet-le-Duc a glimpse of the history of social classes in France that was based on reality; in this respect he antici-

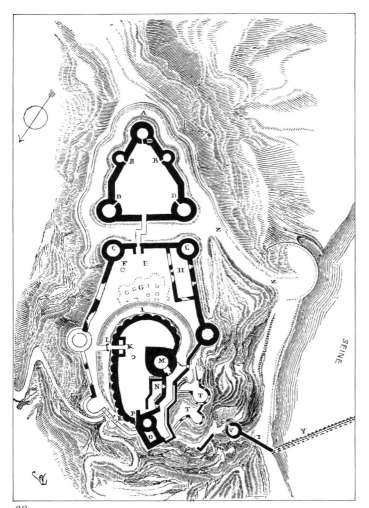

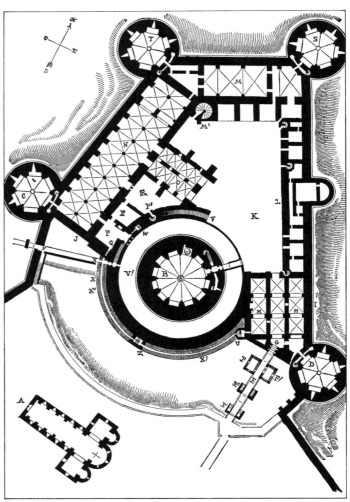

68

69

pates the social geographers and the conclusions of Tricart.

One must read the best texts of the French school of geography written in the first years of this century to find an equally scientific attitude, yet even the most superficial reading of Demangeon[10] on the rural house in France recalls the works of the great theoreticians of the past. Starting with a description of the man-made landscape of the countryside, Demangeon recognized in the house persistent elements that were modified only over long periods of time and whose evolution was longer and more complex than those of the rural economy to which they did not always or easily correspond; thus he proposed the existence of typological constants in housing and concerned himself with discovering the elemental types of housing.

Ultimately, the house, once extracted from its context, revealed that it derived not only from this local context, but manifested also external relationships, distant kinships, and general influences. Thus, by studying the geographical distribution of one type of house Demangeon avoided reducing many of his observations to the determinism of place, whether in terms of materials, economic structures, or functions; thereby he was able to delineate historical relations and cultural currents. Such an analysis necessarily falls short of a broad conception of the structure of the city and the region, something which the earlier theoreticians were able to recognize in overall form; but by comparison with Viollet-le-Duc's studies, it possesses in precision and methodological rigor what it lacks in general comprehensiveness.

It is as significant as it is surprising that it took an architect who was considered a revolutionary to take up and to synthesize themes which were seemingly remote from his analysis; thus, in his definition of the house as a machine and architecture as a tool (so scandalous at the time to the cultured academicians of art), Le Corbusier[11] did no less than combine all the practical teachings of this French school which, as we have said, were based on the study of reality. It was in the same years, in fact, that Demangeon spoke (in the work just referred to) of the rural house as a tool forged for the work of the farmer. The human creation and the forged tool seem, once again, to bracket this discourse and thrust it into a vision of architecture based on the real, a totalistic vision of which perhaps only artists are capable.

But such a conclusion only closes the discourse without having accomplished anything if it presumes the relationship between analysis and design to be a problem of the individual architect rather than of the progress of architecture as science. It denies the hope contained in Laborde's remark, that he saw in the new generation of men of art and culture those who had taken up the habit of criticism and observation—in other words, who saw the possibility of a more profound understanding of the structure of the city. I believe that this kind of study of the object of architecture as it is here understood, as a human creation, must precede analysis and design.

Such study must necessarily take in the full structure of the relationship between individual and communal work, the accumulated history of centuries, the evolution and the permanence of disparate cultures. Thus this section begins with a passage from Victor Hugo[12] which can serve as a program of study. In his often zealous passion for the great national architecture of the past, Hugo, like so many other artists and scientists, sought to understand the structure of this fixed scene of human events; and when he referred to architecture and the city in

68 Gaillard Castle, Normandy, France, plan by Viollet-le-Duc. A) Moat dug in the rock and main tower. B) Secondary towers. C) Principal towers. D)Secondary towers. E) First enclosure of the castle, surrounding the lower court. F) Well. G) Cellars leading to outside. H) Chapel. K) Castle entrance. L) Moat. M) Keep. N) Apartments of the commander. P) Emergency exit. R) Surveillance route. T) Towers and wall dug in the rock. V) Tower. X) Rampart. Y) River barricade. Z) Primary moat.

69 Castle of Coucy on the Ile de France, thirteenth to fourteenth century. Plan of ground floor by Viollet-le-Duc. A) Already existing chapels. B) Keep. C), D) Towers. E) Access bridge. K) Courtyard. L) Service buildings. M) Typical apartments. N) Storeroom on ground floor and large salon on upper floors. S), T) Towers.

their collective aspect as "a species of formation," he enriched our work with a reference as authoritative as it is suggestive.

Urban Ecology and Psychology

In the preceding section, I tried to emphasize the fact that through architecture, perhaps more than any other point of view, one can arrive at a comprehensive vision of the city and an understanding of its structure. In this sense, I underscored the studies of the house by Viollet-le-Duc and Demangeon, and suggested the usefulness of a comparative analysis of their findings. Moreover, I suggested that in Le Corbusier's work such a synthesis has already been accomplished.

I now wish to introduce into this discourse some observations on ecology and psychology, the latter in its application to urban science. Ecology as the knowledge of the relationships between a living being and his environment cannot be discussed here. This is a problem which has belonged to sociology and natural philosophy ever since Montesquieu, and despite its enormous interest, it would take us too far afield.

Let us consider only this question: how does the *locus urbis*, once it has been determined, influence the individual and the collective? This question interests me here in the ecological sense of Sorre: that is, *how does the environment influence the individual and the collective?* For Sorre, this question was far more interesting than the opposite one of how man influences his environment.[13] With the latter question, the idea of human ecology changes meaning abruptly and involves the whole history of civilization. We already responded to this question, or to the system that the two questions form, when at the beginning of this study we defined the city as a human thing par excellence.

But as we have said, even for ecology and the urban ecology to which we refer, this study has meaning only when the city is seen in the entirety of its parts, as a complex structure. The historically determined relationships and influences between man and the city cannot be studied by reducing them to a schematic model of the city as in the urban ecology models of the American school from Park to Hoyt. These theories can offer some answers, as far as I can see, relative to urban technics, but they have little to contribute to the development of an urban science founded on artifacts and not on models.

That the study of collective psychology has an essential part in the study of the city seems undeniable. Many of the authors to whom I feel closest in this work base their studies on collective psychology, which in turn is linked to sociology. This linkage has been amply documented. Collective psychology has bearing upon all the sciences where the city as an object of study is of primary importance.

Valuable information also may be obtained from the experiments conducted under the banner of Gestalt psychology, as undertaken by the Bauhaus in the domain of form and as proposed by the American school of Lynch.[14] In this book, I have particularly made use of some of Lynch's conclusions with respect to the residential district, as confirmation of the distinctive character of different districts within the city. There have been, however, some inappropriate extensions of the methods of experimental psychology; but before addressing these I should touch briefly on the relationship between the city and architecture as technics.*

*The dictionary defines "technics" (Italian *tecnica*) as "the study of principles of an art or of the arts in general, especially practical arts" (*Webster's New Twentieth Century Dictionary, Unabridged*, 2d ed.). This is the meaning intended here and in what follows.—*Ed.*

In speaking of the constitution of an artifact and of its memory, I am thinking of these problems largely in terms of their collective nature; they pertain to the city, and thus to its collective citizenry. I maintain that in an art or a science the principles and means of action are elaborated collectively or transmitted through a tradition in which all the sciences and arts are operating as collective phenomena. But at the same time they are not collective in all their essential parts; individuals carry them out. This relationship between a collective artifact, which is necessarily an urban artifact, and the individual who proposes and single-handedly realizes it can only be understood through a study of the technics by which the artifact is manifested. There are many different technics; one of them is architecture, and since this is the object of our study, we must here be concerned with it above all, and with economics and history only to the extent that they are manifested in the architecture of the city.

The relationship in architecture between the collective urban artifact and the individual is unique with respect to the other technics and arts. In fact, architecture presents itself as a vast cultural movement: it is discussed and criticized well beyond the narrow circle of its specialists; it needs to be realized, to become part of the city, to become "the city." In a certain sense, there is no such thing as buildings that are politically "opposed," since the ones that are realized are always those of the dominant class, or at least those which express a possibility of reconciling certain new needs with a specific urban condition. Thus there is a direct relationship between the formulation of certain proposals and the buildings that arise in the city.

But it is equally obvious that this relationship can also be considered in its separate terms. The world of architecture can be seen to unfold and be studied as a logical succession of principles and forms more or less autonomous from the reality of *locus* and history. Thus, architecture implies the city; but this city may be an ideal city, of perfect and harmonious relationships, where the architecture develops and constructs its own terms of reference. At the same time, the actual architecture of this city is unique; from the very first it has a characteristic—and ambiguous—relationship that no other art or science possesses. In these terms we can understand the constant polemical urge of architects to design systems in which the spatial order becomes the order of society and attempts to transform society.

Yet outside of design, even outside of architecture itself, exist urban artifacts, the city, monuments; monographs on single works in particular periods and environments demonstrate this. In his study of Florence in the Age of Humanism, André Chastel[15] demonstrates clearly all the links between civilization and art, history, and politics which informed the new vision of Florence (as also Athens, Rome, and New York) and the arts and processes that were shaping it.

If we consider Palladio and the historically determined cities of the Veneto in which we find his work, and how the study of these cities actually transcends Palladio the architect, we find that the concept of *locus* from which we began these arguments acquires its full meaning; it becomes the *urban context*, and is identifiable as a single artifact. Again we can ask, where does the singularity reside? It resides in the single artifact, in its material, the succession of events that unfolds around it, and the minds of its makers; but also in the place that determines it—both in a physical sense and above all in the sense of the choice of this place

113

and the indivisible unity that is established between it and the work.

The history of the city is also the history of architecture. But we must remember that the history of architecture is at most one point of view from which to look at the city. The failure to understand this has led to much time spent in studying the city and its architecture in terms of its images, or else an attempt to study the city from the standpoint of other sciences, for example psychology. But what can psychology tell us if not that a certain individual sees the city in one way and that other individuals see it in another? And how can this private and unculti- vated vision be related to the laws and principles from which the city first emerged and through which its images were formed? If we are concerned with the city architecturally from more than a stylistic point of view, it does not make sense to abandon architecture and occupy ourselves with something else. In- deed, no one would entertain the idea that when the theoreticians tell us that buildings must respond to criteria of firmness, commodity, and delight, they must explain the psychological motives behind this principle.

When Bernini speaks disdainfully of Paris because he finds its Gothic landscape barbarous,[16] we are hardly interested in Bernini's psychology; instead we are in- terested in the judgment of an architect who on the basis of the total and specific culture of one city judges the structure of another city. Similarly, that Mies van der Rohe had a certain vision of architecture is important not for ascertaining the "taste" or the "attitude" of the German middle class relative to the city, but for allowing us to appreciate the theoretical basis, the cultural patrimony of Schinkelesque classicism, and other ideas with which this is connected in the German city.

The critic who discusses why a poet has used a particular meter in a certain place in his poetry is considering what compositional problem has presented itself to the poet on a specific occasion. And thus in studying this relationship he is con- cerned with literature, and possesses all the means necessary for grappling with this problem.

How Urban Elements Become Defined

To take this analysis further, we must address ourselves to artifacts themselves, both typical and atypical, to try to understand how certain problems arise and become clarified in and through them. I often think, from this point of view, of the meaning of symbolism in architecture—and among the symbolists, of the "revolutionary architects" of the eighteenth century and of the Constructivists (who also were revolutionary architects). The present theory probably permits the most sensible explanation of symbolism, for to think of symbolism solely in terms of how a particular symbol actually served an event is simply a functionalist position. Rather, it is as if precisely at the decisive moments of his- tory architecture reproposed its own necessity to be "sign" and "event" in order to establish and shape a new era.[17]

Boullée writes, "A sphere, at all times, is equal only to itself; it is the perfect symbol of equality. No body possesses, as it does, this exceptional quality: that each of its facets is equal to all the others." The symbol of the sphere thus can sum up an architecture and its principles; at the same time, it can be the very condition for its being constructed, its motive. The sphere not only represents— or rather, does not represent, in itself is—the idea of equality; its presence as a sphere, and thus as a monument, is the *constituting* of equality.

114

One also thinks in this connection of the discussions (which were only superficially typological) of the central plan in the humanist period: "the function of the [central plan] building is double; it releases the soul as effectively as possible to its contemplative faculties and by this arrives at a sort of therapeutic spirituality that exalts and purifies the spectator; yet the very sublimity of the work constitutes an act of adoration that attains a religious tone through its absolute beauty."[18]

The disputes over the central plan, while they accompanied tendencies to reform or simplify religious practice within the church, led to the rediscovery of a type of plan that was one of the typical forms of early antiquity before it became the canonical church type of the Byzantine empire. It is as if a continuity of urban artifacts which had been lost had to be rediscovered amid new conditions, which then became new foundations. Chastel summarizes all of this when he states, "Three series of considerations come into play in the choice of the central plan: the symbolic value attributed to the circular form, the great number of geometric speculations prompted by studies of volumes in which the sphere and cube were combined, and the prestige of historical examples."[19]

The centrally planned church of San Lorenzo in Milan is a good example.[20] The scheme of San Lorenzo immediately reappears in the Renaissance; Leonardo continually, almost obsessively, analyzes it in his notebooks. The scheme becomes in Borromini's notebooks a unique artifact whose form is strongly influenced by two great Milanese monuments: not just San Lorenzo but also the Duomo. Borromini mediates between these two buildings in all of his architecture and, coupling the Gothic verticalism of the Duomo with the central plan of San Lorenzo, introduces into them strange, almost biographical characteristics.

In the San Lorenzo we see today, the various types of additions to it, from the medieval (the Chapel of St. Aquilinus) to the Renaissance (Martino Bassi's dome), are still apparent, while the entire structure occupies the place of the ancient Roman baths, in the very heart of Roman Milan. We are clearly in the presence of a monument; but is it possible to speak of it and its urban context purely in terms of form? It seems far more appropriate to look for its meaning, its reason, its style, its history. This is how it appeared to the artists of the Renaissance, and how it became an idea of architecture that could be reformulated in a new design. No one can speak of the architecture of the city without understanding such artifacts; they constantly demand further investigation for they constitute the principal foundations of an urban science. An interpretation of symbolic architecture in these terms can inform all architecture; it creates an association between the event and its sign.

Certain works which participate as original events in the formation of the city endure and become characteristic over time, transforming or denying their original function, and finally constituting a fragment of the city—so much so that we tend to consider them more from a purely urban viewpoint than from an architectural one. Other works signify the constitution of something new and are a sign of a new epoch in urban history; these are mostly bound up with revolutionary periods, with decisive events in the historical course of the city. Thus the need to establish a new standard of judgment arises more or less necessarily during certain periods of architecture.

115

I have tried to differentiate between an urban artifact and architecture in itself, but with respect to urban architecture, the most important and concretely verifiable facts occur through the coincidence of these two aspects, and through the influence that one exerts over the other. Although this book is about the architecture of the city, and considers the problems of architecture in itself and those of urban architecture taken as a whole to be intimately connected, there are certain problems of architecture which cannot be taken up here; I refer specifically to *compositional problems*. These decidedly have have their own autonomy. They concern architecture as a composition, and this means that they also concern style.

Architecture, along with composition, is both contingent upon and determinative of the constitution of urban artifacts, especially at those times when it is capable of synthesizing the whole civil and political scope of an epoch, when it is highly rational, comprehensive, and transmissible—in other words, when it can be seen as a *style*. It is at these times that the possibility of transmission is implicit, a transmission that is capable of rendering a style universal.

The identification of particular urban artifacts and cities with a style of architecture is so automatic in certain contexts of space and time that we can speak with discrete precision of the Gothic city, the baroque city, the neoclassical city. These stylistic definitions immediately become morphological definitions; they precisely define the nature of urban artifacts. In these terms it is possible to speak of civic design. For this to occur, it is necessary that a moment of decisive historical and political importance coincide with an architecture that is rational and definite in its forms. It is then possible for the community to resolve its problems of choice, to desire collectively one kind of city and to reject another. I will come back to this in the last chapter of this book in discussing the issue of choice in the context of the political problem of the city. For now it is enough to state that no choices can be made without this historical coincidence, that the constituting of an urban artifact is not possible otherwise.

The principles of architecture are unique and immutable; but the responses to different questions as they occur in actual situations, human situations, constantly vary. On the one hand, therefore, is the rationality of architecture; on the other, the life of the works themselves. When an architecture at a particular moment begins to constitute new urban artifacts which are *not* responsive to the actual situation of the city, it necessarily does so on the level of aesthetics; and its results inevitably tend to correspond historically to reformist or revolutionary movements.

The assumption that urban artifacts are the founding principle of the constitution of the city denies and refutes the notion of *urban design*. This latter notion is commonly understood with respect to context; it has to do with configurating and constructing a homogeneous, coordinated, continuous environment that presents itself with the coherence of a landscape. It seeks laws, reasons, and orders which arise not from a city's actual historical conditions, but from a plan, a general projection of how things should be. Such projections are acceptable and realistic only when they address one "piece of city" (in the sense we spoke of the city of parts in the first chapter), or when they refer to the totality of buildings; but they have nothing useful to contribute relative to the formation of the city. Urban artifacts often coexist like lacerations within a certain order; above all,

70

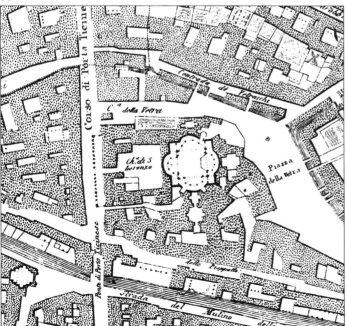

71

70 Basilica of San Lorenzo Maggiore,
Milan.
71 Plan of the Basilica of San Lorenzo
Maggiore and the surrounding area,
prepared by the Astronomers of
Brera, 1807.

they *constitute* forms rather than continue them. A conception which reduces the form of urban artifacts to an image and to the taste which receives this image is ultimately too limited for an understanding of the structure of urban artifacts. In contrast is the possibility to interpret urban artifacts in all of their fullness, to resolve a part of the city in a complete way by determining all the relationships that can be established as existing with respect to any artifact.

In a study on the formation of the modern city, Carlo Aymonino illustrated how the task of modern architecture is "to pinpoint a series of concepts and relationships which, if they have some fundamental laws in common from a technological and organizational standpoint, become verified in partial *models*, and are differentiated precisely through their resolution in a finished architectonic form which is specific and recognizable." He goes on to state that with "the end of the system of horizontal usage [zoning provisions], and with purely volumetric-quantitative building utilization [standards and regulations], the architectural section . . . becomes one of the governing images, the generating nucleus of the entire composition."[21]

It seems to me that to formulate a building *in the most concrete way possible*, especially at the design stage, is to give a new impulse to architecture itself, to reconstitute that total vision of analysis and design on which we have so urgently insisted. A conception of this type, in which the architectural dynamic prevails in the form powerfully and fundamentally, responds to the nature of urban artifacts as they really are. The constitution of new urban artifacts—in other words, the growth of the city—has always occurred through such a precise definition of elements. This extreme degree of definition has at times provoked non-spontaneous formulations, but even if their real modes of actualization could not be anticipated, these have served as a general framework. In this sense the developmental plan for a city can be significant.

This theory arises from an analysis of the urban reality; and this reality contradicts the notion that preordained functions by themselves govern artifacts and that the problem is simply to give form to certain functions. In actuality, forms in the very act of being constituted go beyond the functions which they must serve; they arise like the city itself. In this sense, too, the building is one with the urban reality, and the urban character of architectural artifacts takes on greater meaning with respect to the design project. To consider city and buildings separately, to interpret purely organizational functions in terms of representation, is to return the discourse to a narrow functionalist vision of the city. This is a negative vision because it conceives of buildings merely as scaffoldings for functional variations, abstract containers that embody whatever functions successively fill them.

The alternative to the functionalist conception is neither simple nor easy, and if on the one hand we reject naive functionalism, on the other we must still come to grips with the whole of functionalist theory. Thus we must mark out the limits within which this theory is continuously formulated and the ambiguities which it contains, even in the most recent proposals, which are sometimes self-contradictory. I believe that we will not transcend functionalist theory until we recognize the importance of both *form and the rational processes of architecture*, seeing in form itself the capacity to embrace many different values, meanings, and uses. Earlier I spoke of the theater in Arles, the Coliseum, and monuments in general as examples of this argument.

Once again, it is the sum of these values, including memory itself, which constitutes the structure of urban artifacts. These values have nothing to do with either organization or function taken by itself. I am inclined to believe that the way a particular function operates does not change, or changes only by necessity, and that the mediation between functional and organizational demands can occur only through form. Each time we find ourselves in the presence of real urban artifacts we realize their complexity, and this structural complexity overcomes any narrow interpretation based on function. Zoning and general organizational schemes can only be references, however useful, for an analysis of the city as a man-made object.

I now wish to return to the relationship between architecture and *locus*, first to propose some other aspects of this problem and then to consider the value of the monument in the city. We will take the Roman Forum as an example because it is a monument of fundamental importance for a comprehensive understanding of urban artifacts.[22]

The Roman Forum

The Roman Forum, center of the Roman Empire, reference point for the construction and transformation of so many cities of the classical world, and foundation of classical architecture and the science of the city practiced by the Romans, is actually anomalous with respect to the origins of Rome itself. The city's origins were at once geographical and historical. The site consisted of a low and marshy zone between steep hills. In its center, among willows and cane fields that were entirely flooded during the rains, was stagnant water; on the hills were woods and pastures. Aeneas described the sight in this way: ". . . and they saw herds of cattle lowing here and there in the Roman forum and in the elegant Carinae quarter."[23]

The Latins and Sabines settled on the Esquiline, the Viminale, and the Quirinale. These places were favorable for meetings of the peoples of Campania and Etruria as well as for settlement. Archaeologists have established that as early as the ninth century the Latins descended from the hills to dispose of their dead in the valley of the Forum, just one of the valleys of the Roman countryside, and thus the place entered into history. The necropolis discovered by Giacomo Boni in 1902–1905 at the foot of the Temple of Antoninus and Faustina constitutes the most ancient testament man has left there. First a necropolis, then the place of battles or more probably religious rites, the Forum increasingly came to be the site of a new form of life, the principle of a city being formed by tribes scattered throughout the hills who converged there and founded it.

Geographical formations indicated the way for paths, then for the roads that climbed up the valleys along the lines that were least steep (Via Sacra, Via Argiletus, Vicus Patricius), thereby charting the course of the extra-urban map. It was based not on a clear idea of urban design but instead on a structure indebted to the terrain. This link between the terrain and the conditions of the city's development subsequently persists throughout the whole history of the Forum; it is present in its very form, rendering it different from that of a city that is established by plan. The Forum's irregularity was criticized by Livy—"this is the reason that the ancient sewers, which formerly led through the public areas, now run here and there under private buildings, and the form of the city more resembles an occupied zone than one properly divided"[24]—who blamed it on the speed of reconstruction after the sack of the city by the Gauls and the impossibil-

119

ity of applying the *limitatio*; but in fact this kind of irregularity is characteristic of the type of growth Rome underwent and is quite similar to that of modern cities.

Around the fifth century the Forum ceased its activities as a marketplace (losing a function that had been fundamental to it) and became a true square, almost according to the dictum of Aristotle, who was writing at about this time, "The public square . . . will never be sullied by merchandise and artisans will be forbidden entrance . . . Far away and well separated from it will be the place destined as the market . . ."[25] Precisely during this period the Forum was being covered with statues, temples, monuments. Thus the valley that once had been full of local springs, sacred places, markets, and taverns now became rich with basilicas, temples, and arches, and furrowed by two great streets, the Via Sacra and the Via Nova, which were accessible from small alleys.

Even after Augustus's systematization and the enlargement of the central zone of Rome by the Forum of Augustus and the marketplace of Trajan, after Hadrian's works and until the fall of the Empire, the Forum did not lose its essential character as a meeting place, as the center of Rome; *Forum Romanum* or *Forum Magnum*, it became a specific artifact within the very heart of the city, a part that epitomized the whole. Thus Pietro Romanelli wrote, "On Via Sacra and the adjacent streets crowded with luxury stores, the people passed curiously without wanting anything in particular, without doing anything, only awaiting the arrival of the hour of the spectacles and the opening of the baths; we recall the episode of the "bore" who was so brilliantly described by Horace in his satire, *'ibam forte via Sacra . . . '* The episode was repeated thousands of times a day, every day of the year, except when some dramatic event up in the Imperial palaces on the Palatine or among the Praetorian Guards succeeded in stirring up the torpid soul of the Romans again. The Forum during the Empire was still on occasion the theater of bloody events, but they were events that almost always finished and exhausted themselves in the place where they unfolded, and one could say the same for the city itself: their consequences were stronger elsewhere than here."[26]

People passed by without having any specific purpose, without doing anything: it was like the modern city, where the man in the crowd, the idler, participates in the mechanism of the city without knowing it, sharing only in its image. The Roman Forum thus was an urban artifact of extraordinary modernity; in it was everything that is inexpressible in the modern city. It recalls a remark of Poète's about Paris, derived from his unique knowledge of the ancient and modern history of that French city: "A breath of modernity seems to waft to us from this distant world: we have the impression that we are not much out of our own environment in cities like Alexandria or Antioch, as in certain moments we feel closer to Imperial Rome than to some medieval city."[27]

What tied the idler to the Forum, why did he intimately participate in this world, why did he become identified in the city through the city itself? This is the mystery that urban artifacts arouse in us. The Roman Forum constitutes one of the most illustrative urban artifacts that we can know: bound up as it is with the origins of the city; extremely, almost unbelievably, transformed over time but always growing upon itself; parallel to the history of Rome as it is documented in every historical stone and legend, from the Lapis Niger to the Dioscuri; ultimately reaching us today through its strikingly clear and splendid signs.

120

72

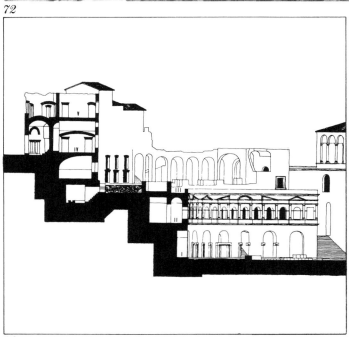

73

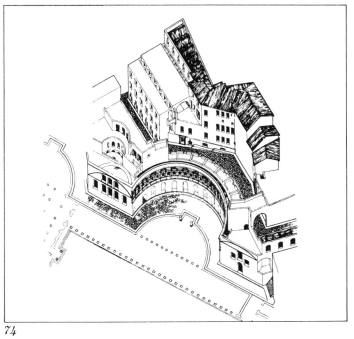

74

75 The Market of Trajan.
76 The Market of Trajan, plan of the covered street with shops on both sides.
77 A part of third-century Rome, including the Stadium of Domitian, Theater of Domitian, Baths of Agrippa, and Flaminian Circus.

75

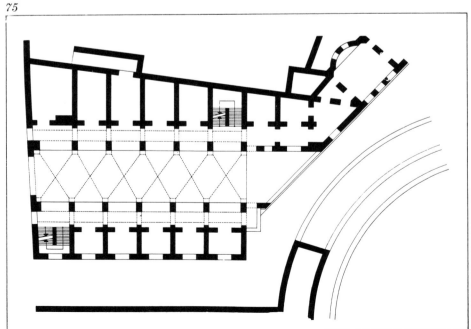

76

The Forum epitomizes Rome and is part of Rome and is the sum of its monuments; at the same time its uniqueness is stronger than its single monuments. It is the expression of a specific design or at least of a specific vision of the world of forms, the classical one; yet its design is also more ancient, as persistent and preexistent as the valley where the shepherds of the primitive hills gathered. I would not know how better than this to define an urban artifact. It is history and it is invention. It is also, then—and in this sense it particularly approaches the theory presented here—one of the foremost lessons of *architecture* that exists.

At this point it is appropriate to distinguish between *locus* and *context* as the latter is commonly understood in architectural and urban design discourse. The present analysis approaches the problem of the *locus* by attempting to set out an extremely rational definition of an artifact, approaching it as something which is by nature complex but which it is nonetheless necessary to attempt to clarify as the scientist does when he develops hypotheses in order to elucidate the imprecise world of matter and its laws. *Locus* in this sense is not unrelated to context; but context seems strangely bound up with illusion, with illusionism. As such it has nothing to do with the architecture of the city, but rather with the making of a scene, and as a scene it demands to be sustained directly in relation to its functions. That is, it depends on the necessary permanence of functions whose very presence serves to preserve forms as they are and to immobilize life, saddening us like would-be tourists of a vanished world.

It is hardly surprising that this concept of context is espoused and applied by those who pretend to preserve the historical cities by retaining their ancient facades or reconstructing them in such a way as to maintain their silhouettes and colors and other such things; but what do we find after these operations when they are actually realized? An empty, often repugnant stage. One of the ugliest things I have seen is the reconstruction of a small part of Frankfurt on the principle of maintaining Gothic volumes alongside pseudo-modern or pseudo-antique architecture. What became of the suggestiveness and illusion that seemed so much to inform the initial proposal I do not know.

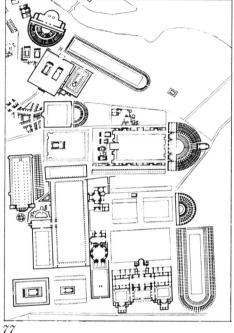

77

Of course, when we speak of "monuments" we might equally well mean a street, a zone, even a country; but if one of these is to be preserved everything must be preserved, as the Germans did in Quedlinburg. If life in Quedlinburg has taken on a kind of obsessive quality, it is justifiable because this little city is a valuable museum of Gothic history (and an extraordinary museum of much German history); otherwise there is no justification. A typical case which relates to this subject is that of Venice, but this city merits a special treatment, and I do not wish to linger now on it. It has been much debated elsewhere and requires the support of very specific examples. I will therefore return to the Roman Forum once more as a point of departure.

In July of 1811, Count De Tournon, prefect of Rome during Napoleon I's occupation of Italy, expounded his program for the Roman Forum to Count De Montalivet, Minister of the Interior:
"Restoration work on the ancient monuments. As soon as one addresses this issue, the first thing that comes to mind is the *Forum*, the celebrated place in which such monuments have been amassed and associated with the greatest memories. The restoration of these monuments consists above all in freeing them from the earth that covers their lower parts, connecting them to one

123

another, and finally, rendering access to them easy and pleasurable. . . .

"The second part of the project envisions the connection of the monuments to one another through an irregularly organized passageway. I have proposed a plan, drawn up under my direction, for one type of connection, to which I must refer you. . . . I will only add that the Palatine hill, an immense museum entirely covered with the magnificent remains of the palaces of the Caesars, must necessarily be comprised partly of a planted garden, a garden to enclose the monuments, for it is full of memories and will certainly be unique in the world."[28]

De Tournon's idea was not realized. It would probably have sacrificed most of the monuments to the design of the garden, depriving us of one of the purest of all architectural experiences; but as a consequence of his idea, and with the advent of scientific archaeology, the problem of the Forum became a major urban problem related to the very continuity of the modern city. It became necessary to conceive of the study of the Forum no longer as a study of its single monuments but as an integrated research into the entire complex, to consider the Forum not as the sum of its architecture but as a total urban artifact, as a permanence like that of Rome itself. It is significant that De Tournon's idea found support and was developed during the Roman Republic of 1849. Here too it was the event of a revolution that caused antiquity to be read in a modern way; in this sense, it is closely related to the experience of the revolutionary Parisian architects. However, the idea of the Forum proved to be even stronger than political events, and it persisted with various vicissitudes even under the Papal restoration.

When we consider this problem today from an architectural standpoint, many issues come to mind which demonstrate the value of the archaeological considerations of the last century relative to the reconstruction of the Forum and its reunification with the Forums of Augustus and of Trajan, and we can see the argument for actually reusing this enormous complex. But for present purposes it is sufficient to show how this great monument is still today a part of Rome which summarizes the ancient city, a moment in the life of the modern city, and a historically incomparable urban artifact. It makes us reflect that if the Piazza San Marco in Venice were standing with the Doge's Palace in a completely different city, as the Venice of the future might be, and if we found ourselves in the middle of this extraordinary urban artifact, we would not feel less emotion and would be no less participants in the history of Venice. I remember in the postwar years the sight of Cologne Cathedral in that destroyed city; nothing can conjure up the power that this work, standing intact among the ruins, had on the imagination. Certainly the pallid and brutal reconstruction of the surrounding city is unfortunate, but it cannot touch the monument, just as the vulgar arrangements in many modern museums can annoy but still do not deform or alter the value of what is exhibited.

This recollection of Cologne naturally must be understood only in an analogical sense. The analogy of the value of monuments in destroyed cities serves mainly to clarify two points: first, that it is not the context or some illusionistic quality that enables us to understand a monument; and second, that only by comprehending the monument as a singular urban artifact, or by contrasting it with other urban artifacts, can we attain a sense of the architecture of the city.

The significance of all this is epitomized, in my opinion, in Sixtus V's plan of Rome. Here the basilicas become the authentic places of the city; together they constitute a structure that derives its complexity from their value as primary artifacts, from the streets that join them, and from the residential spaces that are present within the system. Domenico Fontana begins his description of the principal characteristics of the plan in this way: "Our Lord now wishing to ease the way for those prompted by devotion or by vows who are accustomed to visit frequently the most holy places in the City of Rome, & in particular the seven Churches so celebrated for their great indulgences and relics, has opened a number of very spacious and straight streets in many places. Thus by foot, by horse, or in a carriage, one can start from any place in Rome one likes and continue virtually in a straight line to the most famous devotions."[29]

Sigfried Giedion, perhaps the first to understand the extreme importance of this plan, described it as follows: "His was no paper plan. Sixtus V had Rome, as it were, in his bones. He himself trudged the streets the pilgrims had to follow, and experienced the distances between points, and when, in March 1588, he opened the new road from the Coliseum to the Lateran, he walked with his cardinals all the way to the Lateran Palace then under construction. Sixtus spread out his streets organically, wherever they were demanded by the topographical structure of Rome. He was also wise enough to incorporate with great care whatever he could of the work of his predecessors."[30]

Giedion continues, "In front of his own buildings—the Lateran and the Quirinal—and wherever his streets came together, Sixtus V made provision for ample open space, sufficient for much later development. . . . By clearing around the Antonine Column and tracing the outline of the Piazza Colonna (1588), he created the present-day center of the city. Trajan's Column near the Coliseum with its enlarged surrounding square was a link between the old city and the new. . . . The instinct for civic design of the Pope and his architect is demonstrated again in their selection of a new site for the obelisk at just the right distance from the unfinished cathedral. . . .

"The last of the four obelisks that Sixtus V was able to set up was given perhaps the most subtle position of all. Placed at the northern entrance to the city, it marked the confluence of three main streets (as well as the often projected but never executed final extension of the Strada Felice). Two centuries later the Piazza del Popolo crystallized around this spot. The only other obelisk to occupy such a dominating position is that in the Place de la Concorde in Paris, set up in 1836."[31]

I believe that in this passage Giedion, whose personal contribution to the world of architecture has always been extraordinary, says many things about the city in general that go well beyond the plan under consideration. His comment that the first plan was not a paper plan but rather a plan derived from immediate, empirical experience is significant. Significant also are his remarks that the plan was, although fairly rigid, still attentive to the topographical structure of the city, and above all, that even in its revolutionary character, or by virtue of it, the plan incorporated and gave value to all of the preceding initiatives that had validity, that *were* in the city.

Added to this is his consideration on obelisks and their locations, those signs around which the city crystallized. The architecture of the city, even in the classical world, probably never again achieved such a unity of creation and comprehension. An entire urban system was conceived and realized along the lines of both practical and ideal forces, and it was thoroughly marked by points of union and future aggregation. The forms of its monuments and its topographical form remained stable within a changing system (recall the proposed transformation of the Coliseum into a wool factory), as if with the placement of the obelisks

125

in their particular places the city was being conceived in both the past and the future.

It might be objected that in presenting the example of Rome I am only concerned with an ancient city. Such a criticism can be answered with two different arguments: first, that a rigorously observed premise of this study is that no distinction can be made between the ancient city and the modern one, between a before and an after, because the city is considered as a man-made object; and second, that there exist few instances of cities which display exclusively modern urban artifacts—or at least such cities are by no means typical, since an inherent characteristic of the city is its permanence in time.

To conceive of a city as founded on primary elements is to my mind the only rational principle possible, the only law of logic that can be extracted from the city to explain its continuation. As such it was embraced during the Enlightenment, and as such it was rejected by the destructive progressivist theories of the city. One thinks of Fichte's critique of Western cities, where the defense of the communitarian (*Volk*) character of the Gothic city already contains the reactionary critique of subsequent years (Spengler) and the conception of the city as a matter of destiny. Although I have not dealt with these theories or visions of the city here, it is clear how they have been translated into an idea of city without formal references, and how they contrast, more or less consciously on the part of their modern imitators, with the Enlightenment emphasis on plan. From this point of view one can also make a critique of the Romantic Socialists, the Phalansterists, and others who proposed various concepts of self-sufficient community. These maintained that society could no longer express any transcendent values, or even any common representative ones, since the utilitarian and functional reduction of the city (to dwellings and services) had become the "modern" alternative to earlier formulations.

I believe instead that precisely because the city is preeminently a collective fact it is defined by and exists in those works that are of an essentially collective nature. Although such works arise as a means of constituting the city, they soon become an end, and this is their being and their beauty. The beauty resides both in the laws of architecture which they embody and in the collective's reasons for desiring them.

Monuments; Summary of the Critique of the Concept of Context

So far in this chapter we have principally considered the idea of *locus* in the sense of a singular place and event, the relationship of architecture to the constituting of the city, and the relationship between context and monument. As we have said, the concept of *locus* must be the object of specific research involving the whole history of architecture. The relationship between *locus* and design must also be analyzed in order to clarify the apparently unresolvable conflict between design as a rational element and an imposition, and the local and specific nature of place. This relationship takes in the concept of uniqueness.

As for the term *context*, we find that it is mostly an impediment to research. To context is opposed the idea of the monument. Beyond its historically determined existence, the monument has a reality that can be subjected to analysis; moreover, we can design a "monument." However, to do so requires an architecture, that is to say, a style. Only the existence of an architectural style permits fundamental choices, and from these choices the city develops.

126

I have also spoken of architecture as technics. The question of technics should not be underestimated by anyone addressing the problem of the city; clearly a discourse about images is fruitless if it is not concretized in the architecture that forms these images. Architecture becomes by extension the city. More than any other art, it has its basis in the shaping and subjection of material to a formal conception. The city presents itself as a great architectural, man-made object.

We have tried to show that a correspondence exists in the city between sign and event; but this is insufficient unless we extend our analysis to the problem of the genesis of architectural form. The architectural form of the city is exemplified in its various monuments, each of which has its own individuality. They are like dates: first one, then the other; without them we could not understand the passage of time. Although the present study is not concerned with architecture in itself but with architecture as a component of the urban artifact, we must note that it would be foolish to think that the problem of architecture can be resolved solely from the compositional viewpoint or newly revealed through a context or a purported extension of a context's parameters. These notions are senseless because context is specific precisely in that it is constructed through architecture. The singularity of any work grows together with its *locus* and its history, which themselves presuppose the existence of the architectural artifact.

I am therefore disposed to believe that the principal moment of an architectural artifact is in its technical and artistic formation, that is, in the autonomous principles according to which it is founded and transmitted. In more general terms, it is in the actual solution that each architect gives to his encounter with reality, a solution that is verifiable precisely because it relies on certain technics (which thus also necessarily constitute a limitation). Within technics, by which is meant the means and principles of architecture, is the capacity to be transmitted and to give pleasure: "We are far from thinking that architecture cannot please; we say on the contrary that it is impossible for it not to please, so long as it is treated according to its true principles . . . an art such as architecture, an art which immediately satisfies such a large number of our needs . . . how could it fail to please us?"[32]

From the initial constitution of any architectural artifact a series of other artifacts begins; and in this sense architecture is extended to the design of a new city like Palmanova or Brasilia. We cannot judge the designs of these cities strictly as architectural designs. Their formation is independent, autonomous: they are specific designs with their own history. But this history also belongs to architecture as a whole because they are conceived according to an architectural technic or style, according to principles and a general architectural idea.

Without such principles we have no way to judge these cities. Thus we can approach Palmanova and Brasilia as two notable and extraordinary urban artifacts, each with its own individuality and its own historical development. However, the architectural artifact not only embodies the structure of this individuality, but it is precisely this structure that affirms the autonomous logic of the compositional process and its importance. In architecture lies one of the fundamental principles of the city.

78 Plan of Brasilia, Lucio Costa, 1957.

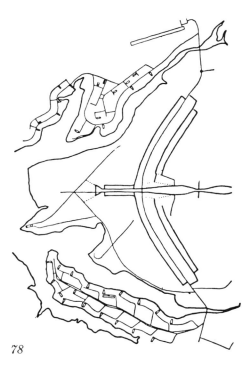

78

The study of history seems to offer the best verification of certain hypotheses about the city, for the city is in itself a repository of history. In this book we have

The City as History

127

made use of the historical method from two different points of view. In the first, the city was seen as a material artifact, a man-made object built over time and retaining the traces of time, even if in a discontinuous way. Studied from this point of view—archaeology, the history of architecture, and the histories of individual cities—the city yields very important information and documentation. Cities become historical texts; in fact, to study urban phenomena without the use of history is unimaginable, and perhaps this is the only practical method available for understanding specific urban artifacts whose historical aspect is predominant. We have illustrated this thesis, in part the foundation of this study, in the context of the theories of Poète and Lavedan as well as in relation to the concept of permanence.

The second point of view sees history as the study of the actual formation and structure of urban artifacts. It is complementary to the first and directly concerns not only the real structure of the city but also the idea that the city is a synthesis of a series of values. Thus it concerns the collective imagination. Clearly the first and second approaches are intimately linked, so much so that the facts they uncover may at times be confounded with each other. Athens, Rome, Constantinople, and Paris represent ideas of the city that extend beyond their physical form, beyond their permanence; thus we can also speak in this way of cities like Babylon which have all but physically disappeared.

I would now like to consider the second point of view further. The idea of history as the structure of urban artifacts is affirmed by the continuities that exist in the deepest layers of the urban structure, where certain fundamental characteristics that are common to the entire urban dynamic can be seen. It is significant that Carlo Cattaneo, with his positivist background, in his study of the civic evolution of cities which is considered the foundation of Italian urban histories, discovered a principle that could be articulated only in terms of the actual history of those cities.[33] He found in the cities the "unchanging terms of a geography prior to the Romans which remained attached to the walls of the cities (*municipi*)."[34]

In his description of the development of the city of Milan in the period after the Empire, he speaks of the city's predominance with respect to other Lombard centers, a predominance justified neither by its size, greater wealth or population, nor by other apparent facts. It was more something intrinsic to the nature of the city, almost a typological characteristic, of an undefinable order: "This predominance was innate to the city; it was the tradition of a greatness prior to the Ambrosian church, prior to the papacy, the Empire, the Roman conquest: *Mediolanum Gallorum Caput*."[35] But this quasi-mystical principle of order then became the principle of urban history, resolving itself into the permanence of civilization: "The permanence of the *municipio* is another fundamental fact and is common to almost all Italian histories."[36]

Even in the times of greatest decadence, as in the late Empire when the cities appeared as *semirutarum urbium cadavera* (the cadavers of half-ruined cities),[37] they were not in reality dead bodies, said Cattaneo, but only in a state of shock. The relationship between the city and its region was a characteristic sign of the *municipio* since "the city forms an indivisible body with its region."[38] In time of war and invasions, in the most trying moments for communal liberty, the unity between the region and the city was an extraordinary force; at times

128

the region regenerated the destroyed city. The history of the city is the history of civilization: "In the roughly four centuries of domination by the Longobards and the Goths, barbarism grew . . . cities were not valued except as fortresses. . . . The barbarians were extinguished along with the cities to which they had laid waste. . . ."[39]

Cities constitute a world in themselves; their significance, their permanence, is expressed by Cattaneo as an absolute principle: "Foreigners are astonished to see Italian cities persist in attacking one another, although they are not surprised to see this between one country and another; this is because they do not understand their own militant temperament and national character. The proof that the source of the enmity that encircled Milan was its power or, more correctly, its ambition, is that many of the other cities, when they saw it destroyed and in ruins, thought that they would no longer have to fear it and joined to raise it from the ruins."[40]

Cattaneo's principle can be associated with many of the themes developed here; it has always seemed to me that those very deep layers of urban life which he had in mind are largely to be found in monuments, which possess the individuality of all urban artifacts, as has been emphasized many times in the course of this study. That a relationship between a "principle" of urban artifacts and form exists in Cattaneo's thinking is apparent, even if one only examines his writings on the Lombard style and the beginning of his description of Lombardy, where the land, cultivated and made fertile over the course of centuries, immediately becomes for him the most important testimony of a civilization.

His comments on the polemics over the Piazza del Duomo in Milan bear witness, on the other hand, to the unresolved difficulties inherent in this complex problem. Thus his study of Lombard culture and Italian federalism finishes by refuting all the arguments, real and abstract, in the debate over Italian unification and over the old and new meanings that the cities of the Italian peninsula were coming to have in the national framework. His study of federalism not only allowed him to avoid all the errors endemic to the contemporary nationalist rhetoric, but also, in recognizing the obstacles to it, to see fully the new framework in which the cities had begun to find themselves.

To be sure the great Enlightenment and the positivist enthusiasm that had animated the cities had waned by the time of Italian unification; but this was not the only cause of the cities' decline. Cattaneo's proposals and the local style which Camillo Boito preached were able to give back to the cities a meaning that had been obscured. There was also a deeper crisis, which was characterized by the great debate in Italy which took place after unification over the choice of a capital. This debate turned on Rome. Antonio Gramsci's observation on this subject is most insightful: "To Theodor Mommsen, who asked what universal idea directed Italy to Rome, Quintino Sella responded, 'That of science. . .' Sella's response is interesting and appropriate; in that historical period science was the new universal idea, the basis of the new culture that was being elaborated. But Rome did not become the city of science; a great industrial program would have been necessary, and this did not happen."[41] Sella's response, that is, remained vague and ultimately rhetorical, even if fundamentally correct; to achieve such a goal it would have been necessary to implement an industrial program without fearing the creation of a modern and conscious Roman working class ready to participate in the development of a national politics.

The study of this debate over Rome as capital is of great interest for us even today; it engaged politicians and scholars of all persuasions, all of whom were concerned over which tradition the city should be the repository of, and toward which Italy it should direct its destiny as capital. Through this historical circumstance, the significance of certain interventions which tend to characterize Rome as a modern city and to establish a relationship between its past and the images of the other principal European capitals emerges more clearly. To see this debate over the capital merely as a manifestation of nationalist rhetoric—which was undoubtedly present—means to place this important process within limits too narrow to judge it; a similar process was typical for a number of other countries in various periods.

Instead, it is necessary to investigate how certain urban structures come to be identified with the model of a capital, and what relationships are possible between the physical reality of a city and this model. It is noteworthy that for Europe, but not only for Europe, this model was Paris. This is true to such a degree that it is not possible to understand the structure of many modern capitals—Berlin, Barcelona, Madrid, along with Rome and others—without recognizing this fact. With Paris the entire historical-political process in the architecture of the city takes a specific turn; but the meaning of this relationship can only be discerned by elaborating the specific ways in which it came about.

As always, a relationship is established between the urban artifacts structuring the city and the imposition of an ideal project or general scheme, and the pattern of this relationship is very complex. Certainly there are cities that realize their own inclinations and others that do not.

The Collective Memory

With these considerations we approach the deepest structure of urban artifacts and thus their form—the architecture of the city. "The soul of the city" becomes the city's history, the sign on the walls of the municipium, the city's distinctive and definitive character, its memory. As Halbwachs writes in *La Mémoire Collective*, "When a group is introduced into a part of space, it transforms it to its image, but at the same time, it yields and adapts itself to certain material things which resist it. It encloses itself in the framework that it has constructed. The image of the exterior environment and the stable relationships that it maintains with it pass into the realm of the idea that it has of itself."[42]

One can say that the city itself is the collective memory of its people, and like memory it is associated with objects and places. The city is the *locus* of the collective memory. This relationship between the *locus* and the citizenry then becomes the city's predominant image, both of architecture and of landscape, and as certain artifacts become part of its memory, new ones emerge. In this entirely positive sense great ideas flow through the history of the city and give shape to it.

Thus we consider *locus* the characteristic principle of urban artifacts; the concepts of *locus*, architecture, permanences, and history together help us to understand the complexity of urban artifacts. The collective memory participates in the actual transformation of space in the works of the collective, a transformation that is always conditioned by whatever material realities oppose it. Understood in this sense, memory becomes the guiding thread of the entire complex urban structure and in this respect the architecture of urban artifacts is distin-

130

guished from art, inasmuch as the latter is an element that exists for itself alone, while the greatest monuments of architecture are of necessity linked intimately to the city. ". . . The question arises: in what way does history speak through art? It does so primarily through architectural monuments, which are the willed expression of power, whether in the name of the State or of religion. A people can be satisfied with a Stonehenge only until they feel the need to express themselves in form. . . . Thus the character of whole nations, cultures, and epochs speaks through the totality of architecture, which is the outward shell of their being."[43]

Ultimately, the proof that the city has primarily itself as an end emerges in the artifacts themselves, in the slow unfolding of a certain idea of the city, intentionally. Within this idea exist the actions of individuals, and in this sense not everything in urban artifacts is collective; yet the collective and the individual nature of urban artifacts in the end constitutes the same urban structure. Memory, within this structure, is the consciousness of the city; it is a rational operation whose development demonstrates with maximum clarity, economy, and harmony that which has already come to be accepted.

With respect to the workings of memory, it is primarily the two modes of actualization and interpretation that interest us; we know that these depend on time, culture, and circumstances, and since these factors together determine the modes themselves, it is within them that we can discover the maximum of reality. There are many places, both large and small, whose different urban artifacts cannot otherwise be explained; their shapes and aspirations respond to an almost predestined individuality. I think, for example, of the cities of Tuscany, Andalusia, and elsewhere; how can common general factors account for the very distinct differences of these places?

The value of history seen as collective memory, as the relationship of the collective to its place, is that it helps us to grasp the significance of the urban structure, its individuality, and its architecture which is the form of this individuality. This individuality ultimately is connected to an original artifact—in the sense of Cattaneo's principle; *it is an event and a form.* Thus the union between the past and the future exists in the very idea of the city that it flows through in the same way that memory flows through the life of a person; and always, in order to be realized, this idea must not only shape but be shaped by reality. This shaping is a permanent aspect of a city's unique artifacts, monuments, and the idea we have of it. It also explains why in antiquity the founding of a city became part of the city's mythology.

The Attic historians, who tried to give their country a list of kings, made out that in Erichthonios, the second primaeval Athenian with the curious birth-legend, which we know from the stories concerning Athene, a Kekrops reappeared. . . . Allegedly also, he built the shrine of Athena Polias, already mentioned, set up the wooden image of the goddess in it, and was buried on the spot. . . . It seems rather that his significant name, which emphatically signifies a "chthonian," a being from the underworld, originally meant not a ruler, not a king of this our world above, but the mysterious child who was worshipped in mysteries and mentioned in seldom-told tales. . . . The Athenians called themselves Kekropidai after a primaeval being, but Erechtheidai after this their king and hero.[44]   **Athens**

131

79

79 Propylaea, Athens.
80 Temple of Apollo Patroos, Athens.
81 The Parthenon, Athens.
82 Athens. Approximate plan of the
city at the time of Pericles, middle of
the fifth century B.C., with residential
districts, dotted, surrounding
the public buildings, in black.
83 Plan of the Acropolis, Athens.
Among the principal buildings:
1) Beulé gate. 3)Temple of Athena
Nike. 4) Propylaea. 11) Parthenon.
12) Archaic Temple of Athena.
14) Erechtheum. 16) Temple of Rome
and Augustus. 26) Theater of
Dionysus. 32) Stoa of Eumenes.
33) Odeum of Herodos Atticus.
34) Aqueduct.

81

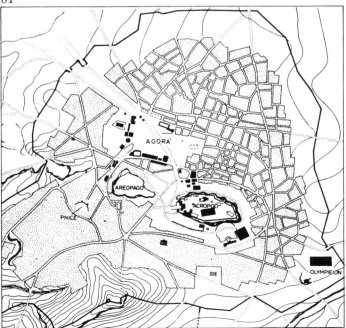

82

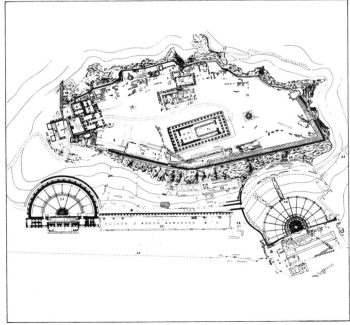

83

It may seem strange that this chapter, which is dedicated to history, commences with the recalling of a myth, a myth which precedes the history of a city we can no longer refrain from speaking about: Athens. Athens represents the first clear example for the science of urban artifacts; it embodies the passage from nature to culture, and this passage, at the very heart of urban artifacts, is conveyed to us by myth. When myth becomes a material fact in the building of the temple, the logical principle of the city has already emerged from its relationship with nature and becomes the experience which is transmitted.

Thus the memory of the city ultimately makes its way back to Greece; there urban artifacts coincide with the development of thought, and imagination becomes history and experience. Any Western city that we analyze has its origins in Greece; if Rome is responsible for supplying the general principles of urbanism and thus for the cities that were constructed according to rational schemes throughout the Roman world, it is Greece where the fundamentals of the constitution of the city lie, as well as of a type of urban beauty, of an architecture of the city; and this origin has become a constant of our experience of the city. The Roman, Arab, Gothic, and even the modern city have consciously emulated this constant, but only at times have they penetrated the surface of its beauty. Everything that exists in the city is both collective and individual; thus the very aesthetic intentionality of the city is rooted in the Greek city, in a set of conditions that can never recur.

This reality of Greek art and Greek cities presupposes a mythology and a mythological relationship with nature. This must be more extensively studied through a detailed examination of the city-states of the Hellenic world. At the basis of any such study must stand the extraordinary intuition of Karl Marx, who in a passage of the *Critique of Political Economy* speaks of Greek art as the childhood of humanity; what makes Marx's intuition astonishing is his reference to Greece as the "normal childhood," contrasting it to other ancient civilizations whose "childhoods" deviated from the destiny of mankind. This intuition crops up again in the work of other scholars, applied precisely to the life and the origins of the urban artifact:

"The difficulty, however, does not lie in understanding that Greek art and the Epic are associated with certain social developments. The difficulty is that they still give us aesthetic pleasure and are in a certain respect regarded as unattainable models. A man cannot become a child again, or he becomes childish. But does he not enjoy the naïveté of the child, and does he not himself have to strive on a higher level to reproduce the child's veracity? In every epoch, does not its essential character in its natural veracity live in the nature of the child? Why should not the historical childhood of humanity, where it unfolded most beautifully, exert an eternal charm, even though it is a stage that will never return? There are ill-bred children and precocious children. Many of the ancient peoples belong in this category. The Greeks were normal children. The charm their art has for us does not conflict with the undeveloped stage of the society in which it grew. On the contrary [its charm] is inseparably linked with the immature social conditions which gave rise to it, and which alone it could give rise to, and which can never recur."[45]

I do not know whether Poète knew this passage from Marx; in any case, in describing the Greek city and its formation he felt the need to differentiate it from the cities of Egypt and the Euphrates, which were examples of that obscure, undeveloped infancy, different from the normal infancy, of which Marx spoke. His statements recall irresistibly the contrasting myths of Athens and Babylon

134

84

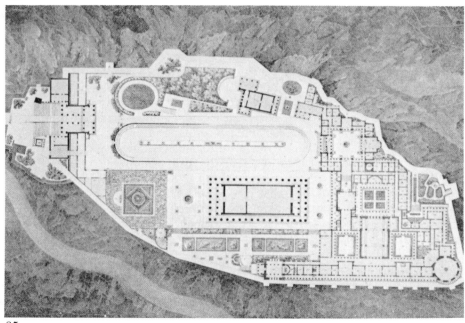

85

84 Project for a royal palace on the
Acropolis, Karl Friedrich Schinkel,
1834.
85 Plan of a project for a royal palace
on the Acropolis, Karl Friedrich
Schinkel, 1834.

that run through the history of mankind:

"Athens definitively offers us the lesson of a city different from those we have seen in Egypt or in the valleys of the Euphrates and the Tigris, in which the only formative element was the temple of the divinity or the palace of the sovereign. Here instead, beyond the temples—though they too differ from those of the preceding civilizations—we find as generating elements of the city the sites of the organs of a free political life (boule, ecclesia, areopagus) and the buildings connected with typically social needs (gymnasium, theater, stadium, odeum). A city like Athens represents a higher level of communal human life."[46]

In the structure of Athens, those elements which we have called primary urban artifacts here are effectively defined as the generating elements of the city: namely the temple and the organs of political and social life, variously located and in continuous evolution within the residential areas. The house too participates actively in the formation of the Greek city and constitutes a basic design through which we can account for the city's principal artifacts.

To understand more clearly the value ascribed to the Greek city and its modernity as an urban artifact that persists throughout subsequent history, it is useful to recall the original structure of the Greek city, especially in comparison to other cities, including Roman ones. Beyond its complex political composition, in the sense spoken of by Poète, the Greek city was characterized by a development from the interior toward the exterior; its constituting elements were its temple and its housing. Only after the archaic period, for purely defensive reasons, were the Greek cities encircled by walls, and in no case were these the original elements of the polis. In contrast, the cities of the Orient made walls and gates their *res sacra*, the constituting and primary elements of the city; the palaces and temples within the city walls were in turn encircled by other walls, like a series of successive enclosures and fortifications. This same principle of boundaries was transmitted to the Etruscan and Roman civilizations. But the Greek city did not have any sacred limits; it was a place and a nation, the abode of its citizens and thus of their activities. At its origin was not the will of a sovereign but a relationship with nature which took the form of a myth.

But this characteristic of the Greek city—and I repeat that it is an unparalleled model—cannot be completely understood without taking into account another decisive factor. The polis was a city-state; its inhabitants belonged to the city but in large part were dispersed throughout the countryside. The city's ties with the region were extremely strong. It is useful to cite another of Cattaneo's statements, since his observations on the nature of the city shed much light on the constitution of the Greek city in particular. To Cattaneo, as also to Poète, the different destiny of the polis of the Oriental cities, which were nothing but "great walled encampments" and barbarian installations and which "lived off their neighbors" (*per vicos habitant*), seemed very clear.[47]

Cattaneo correctly intuited that the walled encampments of the East were completely detached from the region around them, while in Italy "the city formed an inseparable body with its region."[48] ". . . This adhesion of the country to the city, where the most authoritative, wealthy, and industrious dwelt, established a political personage, an elementary, permanent, and indissoluble state."[49] We do not know how far Cattaneo took this analogy between the free communal city and the Greek city since he does not linger on this point. But this consonance between a historian's intuition and the actual structure of the city casts a positive light on the science of urban artifacts. Is not this link between the city and the re-

136

gion perhaps precisely what characterizes Athens as the democratic Greek city and city-state par excellence?

Athens was a city formed by citizens, a city-state whose inhabitants lived scattered over a reasonably large region that was still closely tied to the city. Even if many centers of Attica had local administrations they did not compete with the city-state. "The term *polis* that designated the city also designated the State; initially it was applied to the Acropolis, the primitive site of refuge, worship, and government, and as such the point of origin of the Athenian agglomeration. The Acropolis and the whole city in the sense of State—this is the double significance of the term *polis*."[50] Originally, then, polis meant the Acropolis; the word *astu* was used more generally to indicate the inhabited area.

The historical vicissitudes of Athens confirm the fundamental fact that the link uniting the Athenian citizen to his city was essentially political and administrative and not residential. The problems of the city did not interest the Athenian except from a general political and urban point of view. Roland Martin's observation on this subject is to the point; he noted that precisely because of this conception of the city as state, as the place of the Athenians, the first reflections on urban organization were of a purely theoretical type. That is, they were speculations concerning the best form of the city and the political organization most favorable to the moral development of the citizen.[51] In this ancient organization it seems that the physical aspect of the city was secondary, almost as if the city were a purely mental place. Perhaps the architecture of Greek cities owes its extraordinary beauty to this intellectual character.

It is at this point, however, that it seems detached from us, from our living experience. Whereas Rome in the course of its Republican and Imperial history reveals all of the contrasts and contradictions of the modern city, perhaps with a dramatic character that few modern cities know, Athens remains the purest experience of humanity, the embodiment of conditions that can never recur.

PHARMACIE · G. PLANCHE · ✶ NOUVEAUTÉS ✶ · DARUS

86a

The city, like all urban artifacts, can only be defined by precise reference to space and time. Although the Rome of today and the Rome of the classical period are two different artifacts, we can see the importance of permanent phenomena linking one to the other; nonetheless, if we wish to account for the transformations of these artifacts, we must always be concerned with highly specific facts. Common experience confirms what the most thorough studies have indicated: that a city changes completely every fifty years. One who lives in the city for some time gradually becomes accustomed to this process of transformation, but this does not make it any less true. The literature of all periods is rich with descriptions and records and often nostalgic laments about the transformation of the city's visage.

Of course, there are certain epochs or periods of time in which a city is transformed especially quickly—Paris under Napoleon III, Rome when it became the capital of Italy—and when the changes are impulsive and apparently unexpected. Mutations, transformations, small alterations—all of these take different lengths of time. Certain catastrophic phenomena such as wars or expropriations can overturn seemingly stable urban situations very rapidly, while other changes tend to occur over longer periods and by means of successive modifications of single parts and elements. In all cases many forces come into play and are applied to the city, and these forces may be of an economic, political, or some other nature. Thus, a city may change through its own economic well-being, which tends to impose strong transformations on styles of life, or, in another instance, may be destroyed by war. Yet whether one considers the transformation of Paris and Rome during the eras just mentioned, the destruction of Berlin and ancient Rome, the reconstruction of London and Hamburg after huge fires had devastated them, or the bombardments of the last war, in each case the forces which governed the changes can be isolated.

An analysis of the city also allows us to see how these forces are applied; for example, by studying the history of property through deed registries we can bring to light the sequence of landholdings and trace certain economic tendencies like the acquisition of land by large financial groups which, whenever it takes place, causes the end of lot subdivision and the formation of large areas destined for totally different programs. What still must be clarified are the precise ways in which these forces are manifested and, above all, the relationship that exists between their potential effect and that which they actually produce.

If we study the nature of speculation, for example, purely as a manifestation of certain economic laws, we will probably be able to establish several laws that are inherent to it; but these will only be of a general nature. Moreover, if we seek to discover why the application of these forces of speculation has such varying effects on the structure of the city, using the same approach, we will be even less likely to come up with an explanation. Far more useful for understanding the forces operating on the city are these two orders of facts: first, the nature of the city, and second, the specific way in which these forces produce transformations. In other words, the principal problem from our point of view is not so much to recognize the forces per se, but to know, first, how they are applied, and second, how their application causes different changes; to realize that changes depend, on the one hand, on the nature of the forces, and on the other, on the local situation and the type of city in which they arise. We must therefore establish a relationship between the city and the forces acting on it in order to recognize the modes of its transformation.

The City as Field of Application for Various Forces; Economics

86a Facade of a typical Paris bourgeois apartment house constructed during the Second Empire, from an English magazine of 1858.

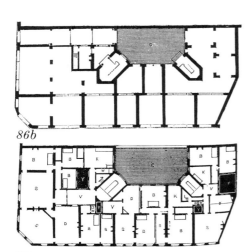

86b

86c

86b Typical ground-floor plan of a Paris bourgeois apartment house constructed during the Second Empire. This floor was used for commercial purposes.
86c Typical first-floor plan of a Paris bourgeois apartment house constructed during the Second Empire containing three apartments. B) Bedroom. C) Courtyard. D) Drawing room. K) Kitchen. S) Large Hall. V) Anteroom. W) Bathroom. Y) Passageway with skylight.

In the modern period a significant number of these transformations can be explained on the basis of planning, inasmuch as this constituted the physical form in which the forces controlling the transformation of the city were manifested. By planning we mean those operations undertaken by the municipality, either autonomously or in response to the proposals of private groups, which provide for, coordinate, and act on the spatial aspects of the city. We have spoken of planning especially as a modern phenomenon, but in fact cities, ever since they were founded, typically have possessed and partially grown through planning; the collective nature of urban artifacts in itself implies that a plan of some sort has existed, either at the beginning or over the course of development.

We have also seen how such plans impose themselves from a structural point of view with the same force as other urban artifacts; in this sense they too constitute a beginning. Economic forces tend to exert the major influence over planning, and it is interesting to study their application, especially in view of the fact that we have ample material on this subject. In the capitalist city the application of economic forces is manifested in speculation, which constitutes part of the mechanism by which the city grows. Here we are interested in exploring the relationship between speculation and the type of growth a city undergoes and how the city's form depends on this relationship—in other words, whether, or to what extent, the configurations of urban artifacts are dependent on the economic relationship. We know that forces like planning initiatives, expropriations, and speculation act on the city, but their relationship to real urban artifacts is highly complex.

In this chapter I wish to deal especially with two different theses that have been proposed relative to the city, taking them as fundamental references. The first of these was developed by Maurice Halbwachs and analyzes the nature of expropriations. Halbwachs maintains that economic factors by nature predominate in the evolution of the city up to the point when they give way to more general rules; however, he asserts, often the mistake is made from an economic point of view of ascribing primary importance to the particular way that a general condition arises. Economic conditions arise of necessity, in his view, and they do not change in meaning because they arise in one particular form, place, or moment as opposed to another.

For this reason, the sum total of economic factors fails to explain fully the structure of urban artifacts. But then what is the explanation for their uniqueness? Halbwachs attempts to respond to this question by examining the development of social groups in the city, and he attributes the relationship between the city's construction and its behavior to the complexly structured system of the collective memory. In his study of the nature of expropriations in Paris, *Les expropriations et le prix de terrains à Paris (1860–1900)*, which dates from 1925, the same year as his *Les cadres sociaux de la mémoire*, Halbwachs takes his scientific training as a point of departure for analyzing statistical information in masterly fashion, as he was also to do in his *L'évolution des besoins dans les classes ouvrières*.[1] Few works on the city based on these premises have been conceived with such rigor.

The second thesis to which I will refer is that of Hans Bernoulli. Bernoulli maintains that private land ownership and its parceling are the principal evils of the modern city since the relationship between the city and the land it occupies should be of a fundamental and indissoluble character. He therefore argues that the land should be returned to collective ownership. From here, his discourse on the urban structure extends to a number of considerations that are principally architectural in nature. He sees housing, the residential district, and public facilities all as strongly dependent on the use of the land. This thesis, presented and supported with great clarity, obviously addresses one of the major categories of urban issues.[2]

Several theorists have asserted that state ownership of property—that is, the abolition of private property—constitutes the qualitative difference between the capitalist city and the socialist one. This position is undeniable, but does it relate to urban artifacts? I am inclined to believe that it does, since the use and availability of urban land are fundamental issues; however it still seems only a condition—a necessary condition, to be sure, but not a determining one.

Of the many theses based on economics, I have chosen to emphasize those of Halbwachs and Bernoulli because of their clarity and correspondence to the reality of the city; I believe that they can provide valuable insights into the nature of urban artifacts. Ultimately, however, behind and beyond economic forces and conditions lies the problem of choices; and these choices, which are political in nature, can only be understood in light of the total structure of urban artifacts.

At the beginning of his study,[3] Halbwachs undertakes to consider the phenomena of expropriation in a large city from an economic standpoint. He starts out with a hypothesis which allows him to analyze expropriations in a scientific manner, viewing them as detached from their context; that is, he assumes that they possess their own character and constitute a homogeneous group. Thus, he can compare different cases without worrying about their differences; whether the cause of expropriation is accidental (for example, fire) or normal (obsolescence) or artificial (speculation), it does not alter for him the nature of the effect, which remains a case of either tearing down or building up, pure and simple.

The Thesis of Maurice Halbwachs

Expropriation does not occur in a homogeneous way in all parts of the city, however; it changes certain urban districts completely while respecting others more. It would seem to be necessary, then, in order to acquire a complete picture, to examine the variations from district to district; only from an overview of several districts at different periods can we measure the major variations in space and time.

There are at least two characteristics of these variations which are noteworthy. The first has to do with the role of the individual, that is, the effect exerted by a certain personality as such; the second simply with the order of succession of a given series of artifacts. " A street," writes Halbwachs, "is called 'Rambuteau,' an avenue 'Péreire,' or a boulevard 'Haussmann,' not, one would think, to render homage to these great speculators or administrators who served the public interest . . . these names are signs of origin."[4]

When municipal initiatives relate to needs that have been asserted and to proposals that have been discussed by the populace, there are many influences and factors at work, including accidental ones. But on the other hand, when the municipal government does not represent the popular will (as in Paris from 1831 to 1871), then we must attribute primary importance to ideas of aesthetics, hygiene, urban strategy, or to the practices of one or a few individuals in power. From this point of view, the actual configuration of a large city can be seen as a confrontation of the initiatives of different parties, personalities, and governments. In this way various different plans are superimposed, synthesized, and forgotten, so that the Paris of today is like a composite photograph, one that might be obtained by reproducing the Paris of Louis XIV, Louis XV, Napoleon I, and Baron Haussmann in a single image. Surely the unfinished streets and the solitude and neglect of certain districts are testimony to the diversity and relative independence of many projects.

The second characteristic we mentioned concerns the sequence in which a series of artifacts appears. Throughout history, there are constant forces that promote the building, acquiring, and selling of land, but these forces develop according to the specific directions that are offered to them, and in accordance with certain plans which they must address. These directions may change abruptly, often in unexpected ways; but when normal economic forces cannot by nature be easily modified, the intensity of their response to change may be much augmented or much diminished for reasons that are not strictly economic.

Haussmann suggested that there were certain tactical reasons, among others, for the transformation of Paris, for example the destruction of districts that were not favorable for assembling troops. That such a consideration should arise at the time of an authoritarian and non-popular government is not surprising, nor are others: for example, the attractions of working-class employment and rich prospects for speculators, both equally advantageous to a regime which sought to compensate for the minimum of political rights it offered by affording a maximum of material prosperity. Thus the large-scale expropriations in Paris under this regime are explicable on the basis of politics: the apparently decisive triumph of the party of order over that of revolution, the bourgeoisie over the working class.

Another characteristic example of the role played by specific historical circumstances during the revolutionary period in Paris is the planning of the great boulevards following the nationalization of emigrant and clerical property. The Commission of Artists simply marked out these large streets on the map, making use of the lands made available by the acquisition of the enormous new national property. The study of the transformations of Paris is thus bound up with the study of French history; the form of the city's transformations depends on both its historical past and the deeds of certain individuals whose wills acted as historical forces.

Acts of expropriation seem to differ by their very nature from all other acts which occur at the beginning of property changes. Related to this hypothesis is the fact that they generally do not occur in isolation; they are not so much focused on this street or that group of houses as connected to an entire system of which they are only one part. They are involved in the *tendencies* of the city's development.

In all cases where historical reasons are given as explanations for the transformations of Paris, there are also different possible explanations which relate the economic factors of expropriation to other economic factors. We have mentioned the nationalization of clerical property; of course, not all of the streets projected by the Commission of Artists were realized, but the expropriation of convent

142

property in itself was an economic issue. These properties constituted impediments, even in terms of their physical form, to the development of the city, and thus even under different circumstances, it is probable that they would have been expropriated by the king or sold by the clergy in a similar way to that which occurred later with the railroads.

As was pointed out by Halbwachs, it is not so much the precise way that a general condition arises which is significant; a condition arises out of necessity, and its meaning does not change because it arises in one particular form, place, and moment as opposed to another. This can be said of Haussmann's plan and all the military, political, and aesthetic arguments we have cited for it. The assembling of troops was not in itself responsible for modifying the street, not in its topographical form nor in its economic character, and thus it is no more necessary to account for it than it is for the chemist to account for the form and size of the test tube he uses for his experiments. Even if motives of order, hygiene, or aesthetics intervened, as they did not result in any important modification which can be explained on the basis of economics, the economist need not be concerned with them. Either these factors had a certain effect and therefore they cannot be ignored, or, after thorough research in which all the economic causes have been eliminated, their existence can be said to have had a "residual effect."

This hypothesis of the purely economic character of expropriations is predicated on their independence with respect to individual artifacts and political history. Moreover, since expropriations have a rapid and comprehensive effect, their different components being realized simultaneously and not successively, it is the total act that reveals the direction and influence of the forces present in a preceding period. The specific way in which expropriations occur, then, is unimportant, even from a legal point of view.

Whenever a consciousness of a collective need takes shape and becomes clear, total action can originate. Obviously the collective consciousness can be mistaken; the city can be induced to urbanize lands where there is no tendency to expand or to build streets where none are really needed, and such hastily created streets can remain deserted. (The causes of mistakes are many; for example, the creation of a street for emergency reasons could lead to the construction of others by analogy.) Thus expropriations themselves undergo a normal process of evolution.

Accordingly, Halbwachs does not consider expropriations as abnormal or extraordinary phenomena, but instead chooses to study them as the most typical phenomena of urban evolution. Since it is through expropriations and their immediate consequences that the economic tendencies by which the evolution of urban land can be analyzed are manifested in a reasonably condensed and synthetic form, the study of expropriations provides one of the clearest and surest points of view for examining a highly complex totality of phenomena.

Because of the importance I attribute to this thesis of Halbwachs, I would like to summarize the three elements that I consider fundamental:
1. the relationship between, and also the independence of, economic factors and the design of the city;
2. the contribution of the individual personality to urban changes, its nature and its limits; thus also the relationship between the precise, historically determined means by which a condition arises and its general causes;
3. urban evolution as a complex fact of social order which tends to occur accord-

143

ing to highly precise laws and orientations of growth.

To these three points I should add the importance of expropriations as a decisive moment in the dynamic of urban evolution, a valuable concept which Halbwachs established as a fundamental field of study.

Further Considerations on the Nature of Expropriations

One could study many different cities on the basis of Halbwachs's thesis. I attempted something along these lines in a study of one Milanese district,[5] stressing the importance of certain apparently accidental occurrences in the successive evolution of the city, such as the destructive effects of war and bombarding. I believe it can be shown, and I have attempted to do so in this study, that occurrences of this type only accelerate *certain tendencies that already exist*, modifying them in part, but permitting a more rapid realization of intentions which are previously present in economic form and which would otherwise still have produced physical effects—destructions and reconstructions—on the body of the city through a process which in effect would be hardly different from that of war. It is nonetheless evident that the study of these occurrences, because of the rapid and brutal form in which they arise, permits one to see far more vivid and immediate effects than those which appear as the outcome of a long series of historically sequential facts of land ownership and the evolution of the city's real-estate patrimony.

A modern study of this type derives considerable support from the study of urban plans—plans for expansion, for development, and so on. In substance these plans are closely linked to expropriations, without which they would not be possible and through which they are manifested. What Halbwachs stresses relative to the two important plans for Paris—that of the Commission of Artists and that of Haussmann (and in both cases the form of these plans does not differ substantially from that of many plans conceived under an absolute monarchy)—is true for most if not all cities. I have elsewhere attempted to relate the evolution of the urban form of Milan, for example, to the reforms promulgated by first Maria Theresa and then Joseph II of Austria and finalized under Napoleon. The relationship between these economically motivated initiatives and the design of the city is clearly apparent; above all it demonstrates the primary importance of the economic facts of expropriation in relation to the architectural artifacts of form. It also sheds light on how by nature expropriations—disregarding for the moment their political aspect, that is, how they can be used to the advantage of one class or another—are a necessary condition in the overall evolution of the city and are deeply rooted in urban social movements.

It can be shown how the Napoleonic Plan for Milan,[6] which was one of the most modern plans created in Europe despite its derivation from that of the Parisian Commission of Artists, explains, in its very physical form, the long series of expropriations and dispossessions of ecclesiastical holdings by the Austrian government. This plan thus is simply the precise architectural form of a particular instance of expropriation and can be studied as such; within these limits, if they can be so described, our study would benefit from an understanding of neoclassical culture, of the different personalities of architects like Luigi Cagnola and Giovanni Antolini, and of a whole series of spatial proprosals which, independent of economic considerations, preceded this plan and were resolved in it.

The relative autonomy of these spatial proposals can be measured on the basis of how strongly they survive in subsequent plans or link up with preceding ones

144

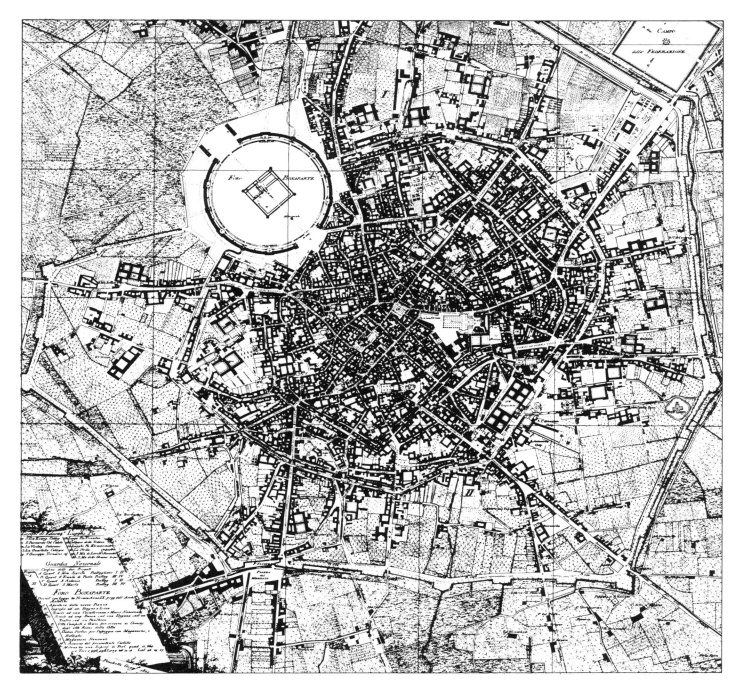

*87 Plan of Milan of 1801 with the
Bonaparte Forum of Giovanni
Antolini in upper left.*

but do not promote economic transformations. Thus, the success of strada Napoleone, at that time via Dante, is entirely comprehensible within the dynamics of urban life. The same dynamics that allowed the Beruto Plan to succeed in the northern section of the city insured its failure in the southern one, where its hypotheses were either too advanced or too remote from economic realities.

The economic dynamic erupted decisively following the acts taken by Joseph II of Austria during the twenty-year period from 1765 to 1785 to suppress religious orders. It was a matter of both politics and economics; the suppression of the Jesuits, of the Inquisition, and of the innumerable bizarre religious congregations which were flourishing in Milan as in few other cities, even in Spain, not only meant a step toward civic and modern progress but also signaled concretely the possibility for the city to take charge of vast urbanized areas, to systematize streets and rectify irregular situations, and to construct schools, academies, and gardens. The public gardens were set up directly next to the gardens of two convents and the Senate.

The Bonaparte Forum was certainly not an architectural necessity, but it was born of the city's need to give itself a modern face by establishing a business center for the new bourgeoisie that was in power. This need was independent of its form and the specific topographical, architectural, and historical conditions by which its location was chosen.

Antolini's idea remained a purely formal one, but as such, in a totally different political context, it was revived in the Beruto Plan with notable prominence, except that for reasons which once again were economic, the business center was no longer the Bonaparte Forum, and therefore, because of the complex nature of urban artifacts, the plan had a different impact on the urban equilibrium. This economic impact, I wish to emphasize, was independent of its design.

The way that Halbwachs develops his theory helps us to perceive, conversely, the confusion that generally arises in the theories of those who make presuppositions that are not at all scientific and ignore the nature of urban artifacts, blaming ruthless demolitions, grandiose plans, and so forth. In this regard, the way Haussmann's work is normally analyzed is typical. To avail ourselves of Halbwachs's point of view, one may or may not approve of Haussmann's plan for Paris when judged solely on the basis of its design—although naturally the design is very important, and it is certainly one of the things I want to consider here—but it is equally important to be able to see that the nature of Haussmann's plan is linked up with the urban evolution of Paris in those years; and from this standpoint the plan is one of the greatest successes ever, not only because of a series of coincidences but above all because of its precise reflection of the urban evolution at that moment in history.

The streets Haussmann opened followed the real direction of the development of the city and clearly acknowledged the role of Paris in the national and international setting. It has been said that Paris is too big for France and at the same time too small for Europe; this observation illustrates the fact that one cannot always estimate the size of a city or the workings of a plan, whatever the actual success of this plan, from a study of the urban condition that this plan encompasses. Thus, on the one hand, Bari, Ferrara, Richelieu; on the other,

88

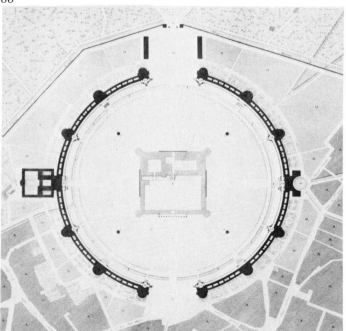

88 Sectional rendering of Bonaparte
Forum, Milan, Giovanni Antolini,
1801.
89 Plan of Bonaparte Forum, Milan,
Giovanni Antolini, 1801.

89

90

91a

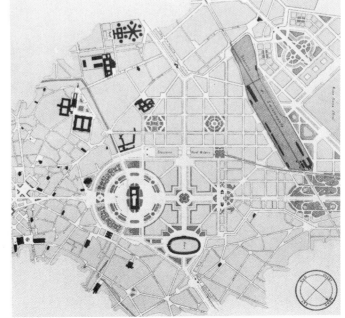

91b

90 *Porta Ticinese, Milan,*
Luigi Cagnola.
91a, 91b *Two of the variants proposed*
by the engineer Cesare Beruto,
designer of the first master plan of
Milan, for the organization of the
zone of the Castle, 1884.
92 *Corso Vittorio Emanuele, Milan,*
beginning of the twentieth century.

Barcelona, Rome, Vienna: in the former, the plan has undergone the effects of time or has even become only an emblem, an initiative not translated into reality except in an occasional building or street; in the latter, the plan has channeled, guided, and often accelerated the propulsive forces that act on, or are about to act on, the city. In still other instances, the plan tends to be projected toward the future in a particular way; for example, a plan which has been judged unfeasible at the time of its conception and whose initial manifestations have been opposed may then be recuperated in subsequent periods, demonstrating its foresight.

Certainly in many cases the relationship between economic forces and the development and design of the plan is not easy to define; one very important, and insufficiently known, example is that of the Plan Cerdá for Barcelona of 1859.[7] This plan, extremely advanced technically and entirely responsive to the economic transformations that were pressing upon the Catalan capital, was extensive and appropriate even if it offered too grandiose a forecast of the city's demographic and economic development. Not realized as it should have been, or in a strict sense not at all, the plan still determined the subsequent development of Barcelona. In fact, the Plan Cerdá was not realized precisely where its technological visions were too advanced for the times and where the solutions it offered demanded a level of urban evolution far superior to the existing one. Certainly more advanced than Haussmann's plan, it would have been difficult to realize not only for the Catalan bourgeoisie but for any other European city.

To describe briefly the plan's main characteristics, its viability was based on a general grid that allowed for a synthesis of the urban whole, as in the case of Haussmann's plan, and within this, an autonomous system of districts and residential nuclei. The plan thus presupposed not just more advanced technical but also certain political conditions, and fell short precisely on these points, as in the autonomous residential complexes it projected which demanded greater administrative attention and which were partially revived by the GATEPAC group in the 1930s.

At the same time, as Oriol Bohigas has rightly noted, the plan was untenable where it presupposed a very low density, a hypothesis entirely counter to the way of life and the very structure of Mediterranean cities. However, where it transformed the *illes*, or city blocks,[8] into massive constructed complexes and accepted the general principle of the rectangular fabric, it ended up lending itself magnificently to the aims of speculation, and as such only came to be realized in a degraded form. One can see in this case how complex the relationship between the design and the economic situation was—which does not contradict Halbwachs's thesis; quite the contrary.

Subsequently, the urban growth of Barcelona occurred as it could, and the Plan Cerdá was used to respond to that growth; it did not have the power to transform the city's political-economic objectives and was little more than a pretext or an image to which to conform. Its importance, however, independent from and unrelated to the economic forces operating in Barcelona, was that it represented a moment in the city's history and was taken as such.

As we have said, since the city is a complex entity, naturally it can coincide (and sometimes does so perfectly) or not coincide with a plan that issues from it. When it does not, it is either because of deficiencies in the plan or because of the

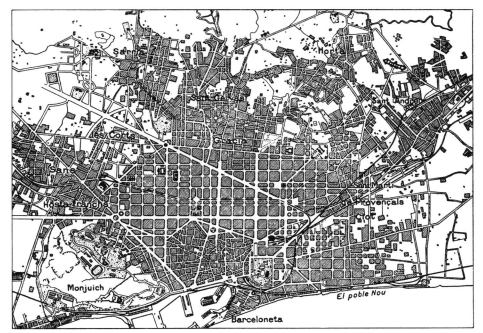

93

93 Plan of Barcelona.
94 Blocks in the zone of Barcelona
that was to be enlarged under the
plan of Idelfonso Cerdá, 1859. Above:
The progressive increase in density of
a typical block. Middle: Several
blocks as shown in a 1969 registry
map. Below, left: Plan of a corner
building, Calle Lauria no. 80, Juli
M. Fossas i Martinez, 1907; right:
Casa Lamadrid, Calle Gerona no.
113, Lluís Domènech i Montaner,
1902.

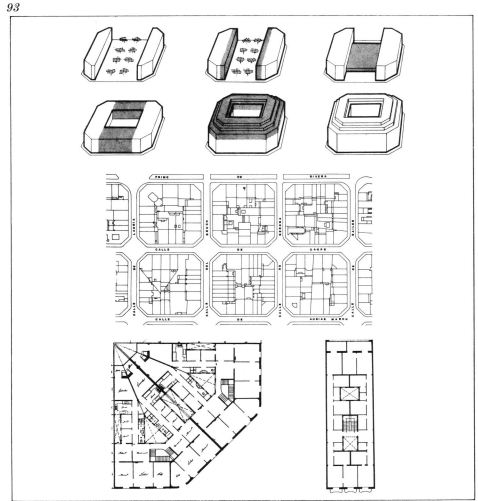

94

particular historical situation in which the city finds itself. In each case the relationship can be judged only outside of the actual development. Thus the Duke of Este's plan for Ferrara must be judged apart from its failure to be realized and its lack of provisions for development; otherwise we would have to say that it was worthless because of these shortcomings.

Another obvious example is the Muratti plan for Bari;[9] this is a typical example of expropriation as defined by Halbwachs, and it is characterized here as elsewhere by a series of precise political and historical circumstances. What is interesting in this case is that the plan projected under the Bourbons and approved in 1790 saw a subsequent development which, although subjected to various transformations, lasted up until 1918. Here too, and still today, the plan was altered in various ways precisely where it worked against speculation and in favor of isolated blocks, but it survives not as a mere impression recognizable to the historian but as the concrete form of the city, constituting the typical pattern of Bari and characterized by the separation between the old city and the modern Muratti *borgo*, a pattern also immediately recognizable elsewhere in Pugliese cities.

At the same time, it has rightly been observed that we should study not only how cities evolve but also *how they decline;* from this perspective we could undertake a study along the same lines as that of Halbwachs, but in the opposite direction. For example, to say that the city of Richelieu,[10] which was associated with the great cardinal-minister, declined rapidly with the disappearance of this personage from the political scene means nothing; he may have been the one who prompted the establishment and actually founded this urban center, but the city then should have been able to continue to grow on its own accord. The centuries of decline of certain large cities as well as certain small ones have modified these urban structures in different ways without damaging their original quality; otherwise we would have to say that there never was an urban life in cities like Richelieu and Pienza simply because they started out as artificial cities.

The same can be said of Washington, D. C., or of St. Petersburg. I do not think that the difference of scale, often extreme, between such cities matters here; actually it confirms the fact that we must ignore size in studying urban artifacts if we wish to arrive at a scientific framework for the problem. St. Petersburg can be considered at its beginning an arbitrary act of the czar; and the continuous bipolarity in Russia between Moscow and what is now Leningrad suggests that the growth of the latter to the rank of a capital and then to a great world metropolis was hardly uneventful. The real facts of this growth are probably as complex as those of the decline of Nizhniï Novgorod in Moscow or, to take another example, the rise of Milan to predominance over Pavia and other Lombard cities after a certain time.

Land Ownership

In *Die stadt und ihr Boden,*[11] Bernoulli illuminated one of the most important, perhaps the fundamental, problem of the city, one which constitutes a strong constraint on urban development. In this modest study, which is clearer and more basic than most of the articles and research undertaken subsequently on the problem, Bernoulli focuses on two principal issues. The first concerns not only the negative character of private property ownership but also the harmful consequence of its extreme division; the second, closely linked to this, sheds light on the historical reasons for this situation and its consequences after a certain point for the form of the city.

Land ownership, observes Bernoulli, whether of rural land or urban land, tends to be based on subdivision; the eccentric forms of fields are the equivalent of the complex and often irrational organization of urban property:
". . . To every innovation there is immediately opposed a tangle of property borders, defined since antiquity, and of a substantially different character from those rural borders along which the plow and harrow run, but no less rooted and immovable. These lots are not just encircled with stone, they are occupied by constructions of stone. As much as one knows that the new streets and new constructions that ought to be built would be better than the narrow, mean, and serpentine streets and the exhausted hovels, nothing can be done until the inevitable conflicts over property are resolved. These are long conflicts that demand patience and money, and very often the original intention is deformed along the way."[12]

In large measure the historical fact that initiated this process of dismembering the urban land was the French Revolution. When in 1789 land became free, the large estates of the aristocracy and the clergy were sold to the middle class and to farmers. But just as all of the landed rights of the nobility were largely dissolved, so also were those of the communes, and thus the great state-owned areas were broken up. The monopoly on land was transformed into private ownership; land became a marketable entity like anything else:
". . . The land casually slipped away from the community and fell into hands of prudent farmers and shrewd citizens, where it quickly became an object of true and real speculation. . . . The city found itself once again at that turn in the road where the right of private ownership of land was manifested in full in new building establishments. The new times, unexpectedly awakening to another industrial activity, gave proprietors an almost unbounded possibility to increase the value of their own lands."[13]

This analysis very rationally and clearly describes the situation at a precise moment of the city's history, but it must be countered with the following arguments. Bernoulli considers the evil of land subdivision to be among the specific consequences of the French Revolution, or at least a result of the fact that the revolutionaries of the time were unaware of the enormous communal capital they were alienating—the communal lands that should have been maintained as collective property and the great property holdings of the nobility and clergy that should have been confiscated and held by the communities rather than subdivided among private owners—thereby jeopardizing the rational development of cities (and countryside). On the other hand, where this did not occur, as in most of Germany including Berlin, the phenomenon occurred with similar consequences. When, in execution of Adam Smith's proposal, Berlin's financial law of 1808 permitted government lands to be used to liquidate government debts and to be transferred into private ownership "as freely and irrevocably as possible,"[14] here too the land, now a marketable good, became the object of economic monopoly. In his history of the modern development of Berlin, Hegemann[15] has portrayed in bold relief the fearful consequences that this had for the city and for the German workers, up to the time of the notorious master plan of 1853 of the President of the Police, which marked the beginning of the famous "Berlin courtyards."

Bernoulli's explanation and all the other theses of this type, though highly illuminating in many respects, must also be criticized on two other bases. The first

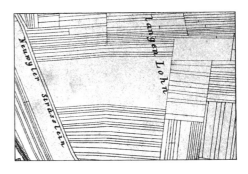

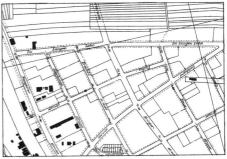

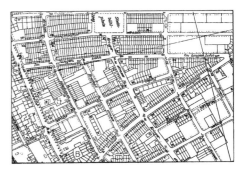

95 Organization and subdivision of land, as seen in the evolution of a suburban area of Basel, Switzerland: comparison of property boundaries in 1850, above; 1920, center; 1940, below. Initially land was used for agriculture, then reorganized for building purposes, and finally extensively subdivided into building plots. After Hans Bernoulli.

153

has to do with the validity of this analysis over time. That is, it explains certain striking features but not the definitive ones of the capitalist-bourgeois city. Furthermore, these features were subject to general economic laws that would have emerged anyway and thus, in my view, were actually a positive moment in the development of the city. In short, the breaking up of the land on the one hand led to the degeneration of the city, but on the other, it actually promoted its development.

We can return to Halbwachs's conclusion again, which says that we need not attribute primary importance to the precise way a general condition arises; it must arise of necessity, but it does not alter in meaning for having arisen in one form, place, and moment as opposed to another. We have just seen how the great expropriations and also the increased subdivision of urban land become central issues with the French Revolution and the Napoleonic occupation; however these phenomena already had clear precedents in the reforms of the Hapsburgs and even the Bourbons, and eventually they were even manifested in a country as profoundly reactionary as Prussia.

These phenomena had to do, in sum, with the working out of a general law to which all bourgeois states were subject, and as such it was positive. The division of the great estates, expropriations, and the formation of a new land registry system were all necessary economic phases in the evolution of Western cities. What varies from city to city is the political context in which this process came about; and only here, in terms of political choices, are significant differences to be found.

In fact, on this point the quite romantic aspect of socialists like Bernoulli and Hegemann cannot be ignored. In a historical and economic key, these writers echo the romanticism of William Morris and all the origins of the Modern Movement in architecture. It is in itself significant how Hegemann attacks the *Mietkasernen*—that is, without questioning whether in the end these large tenement houses were not equally as valid from a hygienic, technical, and aesthetic point of view as small houses. The same charge was to be made against the *Siedlungen* of Vienna and Berlin, where the critique took the form of a revival of certain local features. It is revealing that these authors always appeal to the Gothic city or to the state socialism of the Hohenzollerns—conditions that from an urban standpoint clearly had to be superseded, even at the price of possibly making the situation worse.

This reference to romantic socialism leads me to my second criticism of Bernoulli's thesis, which has to do with its connection to a vision in which the problem of modern urbanism is seen as determined by the city's historical relationship with the Industrial Revolution. In this vision, the emergence of the problem of the large city is taken to be coincident with the moment of the Industrial Revolution; before this time the urban problem is seen as qualitatively different. From this premise it is argued that the philanthropic and utopistic initiatives of romantic socialism were in themselves positive, and even constituted the basis for modern urbanism, so much so that when they disappeared, the urban culture, isolated from political debate, became increasingly shaped purely by technical processes in the service of the dominating power. I will concern myself here only with the first part of this assertion, since this entire book not only considers but denies the assumption of the second in the terms in which it is postulated. I maintain that the problem of the large city precedes the industrial period and is bound up with the city itself.

As Bahrdt has noted, the polemic against the industrial city issues from before the latter was born; at the time the romantic polemic was initiated only London and Paris already existed as large cities. The continuity of urban problems within these cities clearly belies the romantics' attribution of the evils of urbanism, real or presumed, to the growth of industry.[16] Moreover, in the first decades of the nineteenth century, Duisburg, Essen, and Dortmund were small cities with fewer than ten thousand inhabitants, while in large industrial cities like Milan and Turin, the problem of industry did not yet exist. The same is true of Moscow and Leningrad.

What is mysterious at first glance is to see how most urban historians have been able to reconcile the theses of the romantic socialists with the analysis made by Friedrich Engels. What is Engels's thesis? Simply this: "that the large cities have made the malady of the social organism, which was chronic in the country, acute, and in so doing have illuminated the true essence [of the problem] and the way to cure it."[17] Engels does not say that the cities before the Industrial Revolution were a paradise; rather in his indictment of the living conditions of the British working class he emphasizes how the rise of big industry only worsened and made apparent what were already impossible living conditions.

The consequences of the rise of big industry thus are not something that concerns large cities specifically; rather they are a fact that has to do with bourgeois society. Thus, Engels denies that a conflict of this type may be resolved at all in spatial terms, and the proof of his critique is to be found in Haussmann's projects, the attempts at slum clearance in the English cities, and the projects of the romantic socialists. As this implies, Engels also rejects the notion that the phenomenon of industrialism is necessarily bound up with urbanism; in fact, he declares that to think that spatial initiatives can affect the industrial process is a pure abstraction, and practically speaking a reactionary point of view. I believe that it would be a mistake to try to add anything to this position.

The Housing Problem

Further evidence of Engels's position on the relationship between socio-economics and the city is provided by his discourse on the problem of housing. Here the position is unequivocal. To focus on the problem of housing in order to resolve the social problem is in his view an error; housing is a technical problem that may or may not be resolved on the basis of a particular site, but it is not a characteristic of the working class. In this way Engels confirms what we have suggested above, that the problem of the large city precedes the industrial period. He writes, ". . . [the] shortage of houses is not something peculiar to the present; it is not even one of the sufferings peculiar to the modern proletariat in contradistinction to all earlier oppressed classes. On the contrary, all the oppressed classes in all periods suffered more or less uniformly from it . . ."[18]

It is well known by now that the problem of housing in ancient Rome, as soon as the city attained the dimensions of a large metropolis with all the problems inherent to it, was no less serious than it is in today's cities. Living conditions were desperate, and the descriptions that have come down to us from the classical writers show how this problem was foremost and fundamental; it appeared as such in the urban politics from Julius Caesar to Augustus down to the late days of the empire. Problems of this type also persisted throughout the Middle Ages; the vision that the romantics give us of the medieval city completely contradicts the reality. From documents, descriptions, and what still remains of the Gothic

155

cities, it is evident that the living conditions of the oppressed classes in these cities were among the sorriest in the history of mankind.

In this sense the history of Paris together with the entire subject of the urban way of life of the metropolitan French proletariat is paradigmatic. This way of life was one of the characteristic and decisive elements of the Revolution, and it persisted up until the time of Haussmann's plan. In this sense, Haussmann's demolitions, however else one may judge them, represented progress; those who are disturbed by his tearing down of the nineteenth-century city always forget that it nonetheless represents an affirmation, even if demagogical and single-minded, of the spirit of the Enlightenment, and that the conditions of life within the Gothic districts of the old cities represented something that was objectively impossible and indisputably had to be changed.

But the moralistic tendency implicit or explicit in the positions of scholars like Bernoulli and Hegemann did not prevent them from arriving at a scientific vision of the city. No one who has been seriously occupied with urban science has failed to note how the most important conclusions have always emerged from the work of scholars who devoted themselves exclusively to one city: Paris, London, and Berlin are indissolubly linked for the scholar with the names of Poète, Rasmussen,[19] and Hegemann. In these studies, so different in many respects, the relationship between general laws and the specific elements of the city is delineated in exemplary fashion. It is worth remarking that if for every branch of scientific thought the monograph affords a larger vista on its specific object, in the case of urban science it indubitably presents advantages because somehow, related as the city is to the concept of a work of art, the monograph addresses the total element which is peculiar to the city and which otherwise risks becoming ossified or opaque or even lost entirely in a more general treatment.

In this sense, one of the virtues of Bernoulli's work is that he never loses sight of the relationship with urban artifacts. He refers every general statement back to a specific urban artifact, and despite this never entirely becomes a historian, as happens even in the most convincing parts of Lewis Mumford's work. Bernoulli saw the city as a constructed mass, in his own definition, where every element has its particularity and its differentiation within the overall plan.

The subject of the relationship between the land and its buildings almost surpasses the economic relationship in scope, and perhaps for this reason it has never been formulated completely. In the polemics of the theoreticians of the Modern Movement, the treatment of the residential district as a single unit recalls the theories of earlier historians on large building complexes; it is significant how in seeking a historical foundation for their urban polemic the modernists turned to the great theoreticians of the Renaissance, especially to Leonardo da Vinci and his plan for a city containing a system of subterranean roads and canals for transporting cargo and servicing basement levels, with a network of streets for pedestrian traffic at the level of the ground floor of the houses. Following Leonardo's project, in a canonical succession that would be worth studying for its genealogical clarity, comes the project of the Adam brothers for the Adelphi residential district in London.

The Adelphi district was located south of the Strand between the City of London and Westminster, and the Adam brothers obtained the right to build from the Duke of St. Alban, the owner of the land. The district was sufficiently large to contain a building complex in which a system of superimposed roadways could be

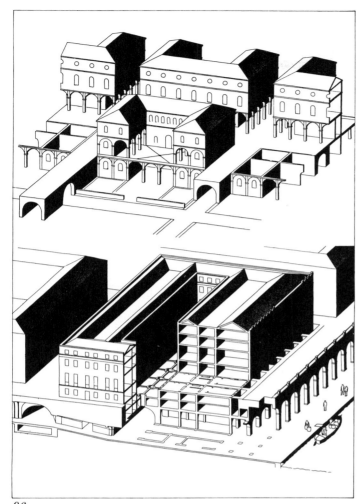

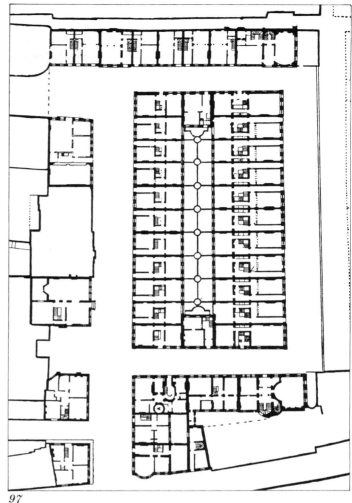

96

97

96 The Adelphi district, London,
James and Robert Adam. It was
constructed in 1768-72 and destroyed
in 1937; the design was based on a
sketch by Leonardo da Vinci.
Axonometric drawings showing
street systems at different levels: a
lower system, with open streets for
carts and underground streets for
services, connects the basements of
the complex with the loading docks on
the Thames. An upper street system
for pedestrians gives access to the
ground floor of the private apartments
and has terraces overlooking the
river. After Hans Bernoulli.
97 Adelphi district, London, James
and Robert Adam, 1768-72. Plan of
ground floor. After Steen Eiler
Rasmussen.

built whose lower streets would connect with the banks of the Thames. These are the terms in which the Adelphi project was presented. But is it only important in these terms? And can Leonardo's project be seen as something other than a unique proposal of a remarkable scale and a strongly rationalizing impulse?

In Bernoulli's view, Leonardo's project was not entirely in the realm of some of the other highly ambitious statements of the Renaissance—those which made the city into a supreme work of art at the limits of nature, engineering, painting, and politics. Leonardo's project was quite different from such ideal schemes because it was already *in* the city, a real city with its presumed relationships, as real as the piazzas of Bellini and the Venetian painters. It was connected to an actual experience of the city, and gave concrete form to the Milan of Lodovico il Moro, just as the great hospital there that translated the designs of Filarete was a concrete form, as the canals, the dams, and the new streets were concrete forms. No city was so much constructed in its totality as that of the Renaissance; I have already emphasized how this architecture was both sign and event, and was based on an order superior to that of function. This is precisely the case with the great Milan hospital, which is certainly not unrelated to Leonardo's meditations, and whose constitutive presence in the city has not changed in its importance even today.

Two and a half centuries later the Adam brothers found it possible to construct a whole part of the city, an actual urban artifact, despite all the real difficulties of this undertaking. But maybe such a work is not so exceptional; rather it indicates that a great primary element could originate, perhaps in an exceptional way, from a response to the problem of housing.

The Urban Scale

In the preceding section we pointed out several distortions which have characterized the study of the city: the overimportance attributed to the development of industry seen in a generic and conventional way with respect to the real dynamic of urban artifacts, the abstracting of problems out of the actual context of the city, and the confusion that certain moralistic attitudes have introduced, preventing the formation of a scientific habit of thought in urban studies. Although most of these distortions and prejudices do not issue from a single source and do not amount to a clearly systematic set of ideas, they are responsible for many ambiguities and it is worthwhile to consider certain aspects of them at greater length.

A number of the arguments that have been arbitrarily invented to explain the genesis of the modern city are to be found as the premises of various technical and regional studies.[20] These tend to turn on the problematical nature of the term *city* today; the problem arises, it is argued, essentially out of the city's physical and political homogenization following the rise of industrialism. Industry, the source of every evil and every good, becomes the true protagonist in the transformation of the city.

According to these arguments, the change wrought by industry is characterized historically by three phases. The first phase, and thus the origin of the transformation of the city, is marked by the destruction of the fundamental structure of the medieval city, which was based on an absolute identity between the place of work and the place of residence, both being within the same building. Thus began the end of the domestic economy as a unified entity of production and con-

158

sumption. This destruction of the basic form of life of the medieval city led to a chain of reactions whose ultimate ramifications would come to be measured fully in the city of the future. Contemporaneously, workers' housing, mass housing, and rental housing appeared; only at this point did the housing problem emerge as an urban and social problem. The distinctive sign of this phase in spatial terms, then, was the enlargement of the urban surface, with the house and the work place beginning to be slightly separated in the city.

The second phase, which was the decisive one, was characterized by a progressive expansion of industrialization. It engendered a definitive separation of house and work place and destroyed their former relationship to the neighborhood. The appearance of the first types of collective work was accompanied by a choice of housing that was not always in the immediate vicinity of the work place. Parallel to this evolution was the separation between work places that produced merchandise and those that did not. Production and administration were distinguished, and the division of labor in its most precise meaning began. From this division of work places the "downtown," in the English sense of the word, originated, creating specific interdependencies between offices that had increasing need for reciprocal contact. The central administration of an industrial complex, for example, sought to have banking, administration, and insurance as neighbors rather than production places. At first, when there was still sufficient room, this concentration came about in the center of the city.

The third phase of the city's transformation began with the development of means of individual transportation and the full efficiency of all means of public transportation to the work place. This development must have resulted not only from an increased technical efficiency but also from the economic participation of public administrations in transportation services. The choice of the place of residence became increasingly independent of the place of work. Meanwhile, as the service activities, which still tended to be located in the center, developed and acquired a primary importance, the search for housing outside the city in the adjacent countryside grew ever stronger. Work and its location came to play an increasingly subordinate role in the choice of housing. The citizen moved into any part of the territory he wished, giving rise to the phenomenon of the commuter. The relationship of residence and work now became fundamentally bound up with time; they became *Zeitfunktion*.

An explanation of this type contains a continuous mixture of true and false elements; it has its most evident limitations in its description of artifacts, lapsing into a sort of "naturalism" of the urban dynamic whereby the actions of men, the constitution of urban artifacts, and the political choices that the city makes are all assumed to be involuntary. It results in a consideration of certain legitimate, and technically important, urban proposals (for example, the real problems of decongestion and the work-residence relationship) as ends rather than means, virtually as principles and laws rather than instruments. Above all it makes a number of confused assumptions, based on a facile and schematic mixture of points of view, assertions, systems of interpretation, and disparate methods.

The major theses to take issue with in this explanation of the city are principally those relating to the housing problem and to scale. I have already dealt sufficiently with the first, given the scope of this work, particularly with reference to the thesis of Engels. The second issue, that of scale, requires a very extensive analysis; here I intend to consider only a few of its principal aspects as they relate directly to the arguments developed so far.

A correct treatment of the problem of scale ought to begin with the subject of the field or area of study and intervention. I have already discussed this in the first chapter of this book and again in my discussion of *locus* and quality in urban artifacts. Naturally this study of the field can also be applied in other senses, for example in the sense of operative scale. Here I intend to speak of scale only in the sense of what has been seen by some to be a "new urban scale."

It is logical that the extraordinary development of cities in recent years and the problems of the urbanization of the population, of concentration, and of the growth of the urban surface have taken on prime importance in the eyes of urbanists and all social scientists studying the city. This phenomenon of increased size is common to large cities and is noticeable to some degree everywhere; in some cases it has had extraordinary ramifications. Thus, in defining the region of the northeast coast of the United States between Boston and Washington and between the Atlantic and the Appalachians, Gottmann used the term *megalopolis*,[21] already coined and described by Mumford.[22] But if this is the most sensational case of increased urban scale, no less important instances of expansion exist in the large European cities.

These expansions constitute phenomena in themselves and must be studied as such; the various hypotheses of the megalopolis have brought to light interesting material which will undoubtedly be useful for further studies of the city. In these terms, the hypothesis of the city-region may truly become a working hypothesis, and it will become increasingly valuable the more it serves to illuminate situations that preceding hypotheses have been unable to explain completely.

What we want to contest, however, is that this "new scale" can change the substance of an urban artifact. It is conceivable that a change in scale modifies an urban artifact in some way; but it does not change its *quality*. Terms such as *urban nebula* may be useful in the technical language, but they explain nothing; however, even the inventor of the term stresses that he uses it "to explain the complexity and the lack of clarity of [the city's] structure," disputing in particular the thesis of a school of American ecologists for whom "the old notion of city as structured nucleus, defined in space and distinct from the neighboring area, is a dead concept" and who envision "the nucleus dissolving, forming a more or less colloidal fabric, the city being absorbed by the economic region or even the whole nation."[23]

The American geographer Ratcliff, coming from a different point of view from ours, has also disputed and rejected the popular thesis that metropolitan problems are problems of scale. To reduce metropolitan problems to problems of scale means to ignore completely the existence of a science of the city, in other words to ignore the actual structure of the city and its conditions of evolution. The reading of the city I have proposed here with reference to primary elements, historically constituted urban artifacts, and areas of influence permits a study of the growth of the city in which such changes of scale do not affect the laws of development.

It seems to me that the inappropriate interpretation of the "new scale" by architects can also be explained through certain suggestions of a more figurative nature. It is worth recalling how at the outset of the debate Giuseppe Samonà cautioned architects against the error of too easily being led by a perception of increased urban scale to gigantism in their projects. "It is absolutely out of the question in my opinion," he declared, "to nurture any idea of gigantic spatial parameters. In truth we find ourselves, as at all times, in a situation that, from a general point of view, presents man and his space in well-balanced proportion, and in a relationship analogous to that of the ancients, except that in today's relationship all the spatial measures are greater than were the more fixed ones of fifty years ago."[25]

Politics as Choice

So far in this chapter we have been concerned with raising some questions which are fundamentally related to the economic problems of the urban dynamic or at least derivable from them, and which did not emerge in the discussion in previous chapters (or only partially, apropos of Tricart's system of classification). I began by describing and commenting on two theses: that of Halbwachs, whose work has notably increased our knowledge of the city and the nature of urban artifacts, and that of Bernoulli, an agile and intelligent theoretician of one of the most widely debated problems of the modern city. These two authors introduced several elements of discussion which have been recurrent throughout this study and which continually demand to be reexamined. Bernoulli, developing his thesis on the relationship between land ownership and the architecture of the city, rapidly arrived at a scientific conception of the city; similarly, but starting from a design point of view, did architect-theoreticians like Le Corbusier and Ludwig Hilberseimer in the same climate of the Modern Movement.

In the preceding pages we also noted the romantic aspect of scholars like Bernoulli and Hegemann, and how their moralism, which so much gives value to their position as polemicists and innovators, ends up by vitiating their studies of reality. I am convinced that the moralistic component cannot so easily be eliminated from our valuation of the works of theoreticians of the city and that it would be an arbitrary act to do so.

Engels's position was no doubt an easier one to maintain; he addressed the problem from outside, so to speak, that is, from a political and economic point of view, telling us from this vantage point that the problem did not exist. This conclusion could appear paradoxical, but it is also the most clarifying aspect of his argument. When Mumford accused Engels of arguing that there were already enough houses in existence provided they were divided up, and of basing this assertion on his unverified presumption that what the rich possessed was good, Mumford was brutally deforming Engels's thought, although in substance reaffirming the worth of his thesis.[26] On the other hand, it is not surprising that Engels's thesis was not based on studies of the city; it could not have been developed in those terms because it was derived purely politically.

At this point it might be objected that while we have sought to comprehend the complexity of the urban problem in all of its terms and to refer every specific explanation back to the totality of the urban structure, we have failed to account for that which constitutes the first fact of the polis, *politics*, within our idea of the city's construction. In other words, if the architecture of urban artifacts is the *construction of the city*, how can politics, which constitutes the decisive moment, be absent from this construction?

Yet on the basis of all the arguments we have raised here, we not only affirm the
161

relevance of politics but even maintain that it is of primary importance and, indeed, decisive. *Politics constitutes the problem of choices.* Who ultimately chooses the image of a city if not the city itself—and always and only through its political institutions. To say that this choice is indifferent is a banal simplification of the problem. It is not indifferent: Athens, Rome, and Paris are the form of their politics, the signs of their collective will.

Certainly if we consider the city a man-made object, as the archaeologist does, then everything the city accumulates is a sign of its progress; but this does not diminish the fact that there may exist different valuations of this progress, as well as different valuations of its political choices. But here politics, which up to now may have seemed extraneous to or remote from this discourse on the city, makes its appearance in its own guise, presenting itself in the proper manner and at the essential moment.

Urban architecture—which, as we have repeated many times, is a human creation—is willed as such; thus the Italian piazzas of the Renaissance cannot be explained either in terms of their function or by chance. Although these piazzas are means in the formation of the city, such elements which originally start out as means tend to become ends; ultimately they *are* the city. Thus the city has as its end itself alone, and there is nothing else to explain beyond the fact of its own presence in its own artifacts. This mode of being implies a will to exist in a specific way and to continue in that way.

This "way" is what constitutes the beauty of the ancient city, which is always a paradigm for our own urban schemes. Certain functions, time, place, and culture modify our cities as they modify the forms of their architecture; but such modifications have value when and only when they are in action, as events and as testimony, rendering the city evident to itself. We have seen how periods of new events make this problem especially apparent, and how only a correct coincidence of factors yields an authentic urban artifact, one wherein the city realizes in itself its own idea of itself and registers it in stone. But this realization must always be evaluated in terms of the physical ways it occurs; there is as absolute and unambiguous a relationship between the element of chance and the element of tradition in urban architecture as there is between general laws and real elements:

In every city there are individual personalities; every city possesses a personal soul formed of old traditions and living feelings as well as unresolved aspirations. Yet still the city cannot be independent of the general laws of urban dynamics. Behind the particular cases there are general conditions, and the result is that no urban growth is spontaneous. Rather, it is through the natural tendencies of the many groups dispersed throughout the different parts of the city that we must explain the modifications of the city's structure.

Finally, a human being is not only an inhabitant of one country and one city, but of a highly precise and delimited place, and while no urban transformation does not also signify a transformation in the lives of its inhabitants, the reactions of people cannot be simply predicted or easily derived; to attempt to do so would be to attribute to the physical environment the same determinism that naive functionalism attributed to form. Reactions and relationships can be isolated for analysis only with difficulty; they must be understood within the overall structure of urban artifacts. This difficulty might even lead us to search for an irrational element in the growth of the city. The city is as irrational as any work of art, and its mystery is perhaps above all to be found in the secret and ceaseless will of its collective manifestations.

Thus the complex structure of the city emerges from a discourse whose terms of reference are still somewhat fragmentary. Perhaps the laws of the city are exactly like those that regulate the life and destiny of individual men. Every biography has its own interest, even though it is circumscribed by birth and death. Certainly the architecture of the city, the human thing par excellence, is the physical sign of this biography, beyond the meanings and the feelings with which we recognize it.

98

In the years between the first and second editions of this book, several of its themes have been debated and confirmed by material from other studies. The subject of the close tie between the study of the city and architecture has particularly dominated the debate in a large sector of the architectural culture. This confirmation of the direction initiated here has convinced me of the need to make an out-of-print text available again and the usefulness of reissuing this book. However, I think that it would be a mistake, at least for the central part of the book, to attempt to bring it up to date by modifying parts of some chapters or introducing them anew, because to do so would destroy the overall structure of the work and impose a complete face-lift upon it.

The success of this book is attested to by the numerous references made to it, the adoption of some of the terminology it introduced, and—uniquely—the way its title has been widely cited, both appropriately and inappropriately. *The Architecture of the City*, in fact, has a precise meaning worth recalling in as simple a way as possible: to consider the city as architecture means to recognize the importance of architecture as a discipline that has a self-determined autonomy (and thus is not autonomous in an abstract sense), constitutes the major urban artifact within the city, and, through all the processes analyzed in this book, links the past to the present. Architecture so seen is not diminished in terms of its own significance because of its urban architectural context or because a different scale introduces new meanings; on the contrary the meaning of the architecture of the city resides in a focus on the individual project and the way it is structured as an urban artifact.

This study of architecture not only considers and grows out of all of the past, but in it the architectural theories of the Modern Movement have a major place; it is, then, also an evaluation of the Modern Movement's legacy and its signficance. In the four years since the first edition of this book, there have been numerous publications, translations, and interpretations of the Modern Movement that testify to the difficulty of evaluating this legacy, but to accept it means to place the available material in a critical context. By now the view of the Modern Movement as a qualitative leap forward or as a moral-political movement has been abandoned by all but a few stubborn retrogrades whose work fails to enhance in any way the patrimony they defend. This book offers a preliminary evaluation of the modern legacy, seeking to find the terms within which it can usefully be accepted.

In rereading this book, there emerges from it as a fundamental problem the question of tendencies and of the relationship between urban analysis and design. These themes are related to each other. Few things better illustrate the poverty of some modern studies of architecture than the explicit assumption (or implicit in the worst cases) that scientific concepts are neutral. Neutrality is a stance that can be taken within a system of concepts or rules; but when the problem is to assign values to these same concepts, neutrality is meaningless. Architecture and architectural theories, like everything else, can only be described according to concepts which are neither absolute nor neutral, and these, depending on their importance, have the potential to modify man's way of seeing profoundly. In architecture problems of knowledge have always been connected to matters of tendency and of choice. An architecture that lacks a tendency has neither a field nor a manner in which to reveal itself. In constructing a theory of architecture, the relationship with history is also one of choice; my introduction and translation of Boullée's essay,[1] published after I wrote this book, exemplifies this.

Preface to the Second Italian Edition

98 "Capriccio," by Giovanni Antonio Canaletto, 1753–59, depicting Palladio's Basilica of Vicenza, his project for the Ponte di Rialto in Venice, and a partial view of the Palazzo Chiericati. National Gallery, Parma, Italy. "It is easily seen that the painting does not lack boats or gondolas, nor anything else to transport the viewer to Venice; and I know that many Venetians have asked what site in the city it was which they had not yet seen" (F. Algarotti, "Raccolta di lettere sopra la pittura e l'architettura" [Livorno, 1765], vol. LV).

The construction of a more complex rationalism than the schematic one offered by the historiography of modern architecture up to a few years ago entails a confrontation with modern architecture's own tradition, for only in coming to terms with this can a correct relationship with the present be discovered. The absence of a tendency illustrates the gratuitous and ad hoc nature of many studies. The relationship between urban analysis and design is thus an issue that can be resolved only within the framework of a tendency, within a certain system, and not through neutrality. In this respect the example of Hilberseimer's work is significant; his analyses of the city and of the structure of architecture are rigorously interdependent aspects of a general theory of rationalism in architecture. These two terms, analysis and design, seem to me to be coalescing into one fundamental area of study, in which the study of urban artifacts and of form becomes architecture. The rationality of architecture lies precisely in its capacity to be constructed out of a meditation on artifacts over time, with certain elements playing an integrating role in this construction. For the archaeologist and the artist alike, the ruins of a city constitute a starting point for invention, but only at the moment that they can be linked with a precise system, one based on lucid hypotheses which acquire and develop their own validity, do they construct something real. This construction of the real is an act mediated by architecture in its relationship with things and the city, with ideas and history.

After I wrote this book and from the concepts I postulated in it, I outlined the hypothesis of the *analogous city*, in which I attempted to deal with theoretical questions concerning design in architecture. In particular I elaborated a compositional procedure that is based on certain fundamental artifacts in the urban reality around which other artifacts are constituted within the framework of an analogous sytem. To illustrate this concept I gave the example of Canaletto's fantasy view of Venice, a *capriccio* in which Palladio's projects for the Ponte di Rialto, the Basilica of Vicenza, and the Palazzo Chiericati are set next to each other and described as if the painter were rendering an urban scene he had actually observed. These three Palladian monuments, none of which are actually in Venice (one is a project; the other two are in Vicenza), nevertheless constitute an *analogous* Venice formed of specific elements associated with the history of both architecture and the city. The geographical transposition of the monuments within the painting constitutes a city that we recognize, even though it is a place of purely architectural references. This example enabled me to demonstrate how a logical-formal operation could be translated into a design method and then into a hypothesis for a theory of architectural design in which the elements were preestablished and formally defined, but where the significance that sprung forth at the end of the operation was the authentic, unforeseen, and original meaning of the work.

Certain parts of this book touch on matters which remain to be developed further but which are quite important for a complete panorama of architectural studies. These include the theory of permanences and the meaning of monuments, the concept of *locus*, the evolution of urban artifacts, and the value that architecture as the physical structure of institutions gives to a place. Other questions treated here in a systematic way for the first time—such as building typology and urban morphology, or the issue of classification in architecture—have subsequently been amplified by important contributions which now must be taken into account.

The appeal in the introduction to this book for further analytical material on cities—and thus for more authentic knowledge of the greatest possible variety of urban situations, thereby providing some necessary background on the specific architectural construction of the city—still holds. The available material is still too fragmentary for us to proceed safely; on the basis of the elements that such analytical material could furnish, we might possibly have to revise our theory, little by little altering our hypotheses on the basis of new facts. Monographs of this type are necessary because it is above all through them that we can respond to the questions of urban analysis in a complete way. The urban configuration is a system where questions of topography and land ownership, of regulations, class struggles, and the idea of architecture tend slowly toward a single, precise construction, and every general theory must always be measured against this. In recent years some studies have been conducted in this domain, and I know that their publication has provided useful reference material.

Another issue raised in this book, one which also has been taken up recently in a different way and has produced interesting material for my own theses, is that of functionalism. The critique I make in this book is of a naive functionalism that oversimplifies reality and humiliates fantasy and liberty, especially when it is used either as a compositional tool—as is commonly the case in our schools—or as a standard zoning practice. Over the years I have pursued this critique, for example in my introduction to Boullée's essay, where I attempted to propose a vision of rationalism as an alternative to the functionalist position. The critique of functionalism must be considered a new theory of architectural composition and a basic principle for urban analysis. However, the rejection of naive functionalism does not mean the rejection of the concept of function in its most proper meaning. In other words, as I point out in this book, the concept of function must be used in an algebraic sense, by which I mean that values are knowable only as functions of one another, and that between functions and form there are more complex connections than the linear ones of cause and effect, which are belied by reality.

Finally, for the various welcomes this book has been given, I must thank all those who have reviewed, discussed, studied, and lingered over different aspects of it. The reviews by Carlo Aymonino, Giorgio Grassi, and Vittorio Gregotti[2] particularly interested me, especially because these authors, from different points of view, focused on the relationship this book establishes with architecture and in particular with the theoretical foundations of my own projects and teaching. As much for their authority as for the new elements they introduce, these essays could constitute part of the present work. I also thank Manfredo Tafuri, who, in his considerations on modern architectural theories, has placed the themes of this book into a larger framework of architectural phenomena, evaluating my writing and my designs as a total work of architecture.[3] Beyond the favorable judgments of these writers, the sense of their recognition has been most important to me, coming as it did during one of the most difficult and solitary periods of my architectural work. A particular thanks to Salvador Tarragó Cid for his translation of the book into Spanish and for the long introductory essay he wrote for the Spanish edition.[4]

December 1969

In writing this introductory essay, I intend not to modify or correct parts of this book, but rather to offer the scholar some amplification of certain of the themes I have dealt with, especially a tendency represented by this book, which in the six years since its first publication has engendered a number of related works.

I believe that the meaning of this book has been correctly grasped, even by those who have condemned it, as that of a *design for the architecture of the city*. Therefore, many of its assertions have not been greeted with the neutrality that is usually accorded to a critical work. I wish to emphasize, however, that it was the architectural treatise that served as a general model for this work; my intention was not to wage a battle of criticism or to discredit old idols like functionalism, but above all to advance a number of propositions on the nature of the design process and the study of form.

I purposely limited myself to citing architects rarely but scholars from other disciplines frequently, beginning with geographers and historians. I also purposely refrained from placing a precise boundary between ancient and modern architects. It might seem strange that someone concerned with defining the boundaries of the "corpus" of architectural studies should make use of theses from disciplines outside of architecture, but in fact I have never spoken of an absolute autonomy of architecture or of an architecture *an sich*, as some presume I have; I have primarily been concerned with establishing some of the characteristic propositions of architecture. The desire to do so in a theoretical rather than a design framework has aroused suspicions which I doubt that my architecture would otherwise provoke.

This observation, which may seem autobiographical, derives from a fundamental consideration without which it is difficult to understand the full range of the research I have undertaken, and which, for specific historical reasons, constitutes a major impasse for architecture above all. I refer to the *gap between theory and practice*. I have rarely seen it bridged even by those who have very clear ideas about their own activity. We can look at this argument in two different ways. The first, of a more general nature, has to do with the limiting of history to the historiographical act, to the amassing of a pure knowledge of the past without opening perspectives on the future, and to a substitution of a general faith in progress for a historical perspective. The latter connection seems quite clear to me, since the history of art and technology is inseparable from all the theories of art and technology. The second way of explaining this gap is on the basis of the insufficiency of current theoretical conceptions, as exemplified by the ideological fragility of contemporary architecture, which by now has entirely forgotten the positions of the Modern Movement and has put its trust in what is often a purely commercial taste.

In further investigating this gap, which still is posed as "theory or practice" and which ultimately becomes identified with the *institution* of architecture, I have sought out the statements of certain artists on the subject and read them carefully. Artists like Paul Klee, Henry van de Velde, Adolf Loos, and others clearly show us in a more or less systematic way the path of study, but their directions, which at first may have seemed compelling to follow, subsequently have often been forgotten. Thus artistic investigations have diminished while philological studies on this or that historical period, reconstructions of facts, and punctilious studies of events multiply. I do not deny the importance of the latter contributions, but they cannot be decisive for a theory of design. This becomes clear when one confronts the legacy of the Modern Movement, which is often either

99 Aerial view of Roman amphitheater transformed into a marketplace, Lucca, Italy.

taken as dogma (even though it is not well understood) or relegated to a historiographical event.

With my introduction and translation of Boullée's essay,[1] I specifically intended to elaborate a theory of architecture, taking as a point of departure a text which is a unique example of an architectural unity in that Boullée wrote it to formulate and comment on his own projects as well as to construct a theory of architecture. By *construction* I mean the establishment of a discourse on the corpus of architecture; it constitutes for architecture and art the same kind of frame of reference that exists for science.

For the artist, the problem of predecessors and models, of the particular situation in which he works—that is, of working within an already problematically structured context—places him in a position not unlike that of the scientist or philosopher. If he were not to operate within this context, art, like science and philosophy, would have no meaning. It is by now sufficiently clear that architecture does have such a context for the transmission of its models. Thus my studies on Lombard neoclassicism, on Loos,[2] and on Boullée are only incidentally historical, and in the end are nothing less than the cultural references from which I have constructed my theory of architecture; they have enabled me to establish with the greatest possible precision the context within which I can develop certain principles. Naturally the historical experience of the Enlightenment has also had a particular relevance for me.

Ultimately, *the history of architecture is the material of architecture*. In the process of constructing a large and unique project over time, working on certain elements which alter very slowly, one steadily arrives at an invention. Among those elements typological forms have a particular import. In *The Architecture of the City*, major though not primary importance is ascribed to typology. Subsequently, in my teaching, I have given typology the preeminent place, viewing it as the essential basis of design. I think it would be useful to describe the paths along which this development has occurred.

Aspects of classification and of architectural knowledge and the concept of typological form are the major themes developed in the typological discourse, and these themes are closely bound up with one another. Let us take the urban house as a reference. The urban house is an element of the city's construction defined by its double nature as an object of use and a work conforming to the institutional character of architecture. The material to study is thus within the field of architecture itself, and it involves the classification of existing typologies and their scope, and the investigation of the meaning they have had and continue to have outside of any preconceived scheme of development.

In this sense the relationship between the artifact and the category into which it is put becomes the object of analysis, an analysis which in turn becomes that of the process of architecture itself and the relation continuously established between a particular form and the life of the collective. But throughout its complex historical path, its constitution and definition as a discipline, architecture is identified with the city and cannot be defined without the city. A term such as *hôtel* or *Wohnhof* refers to a particular cultural artifact and corresponds to a specific area of culture; and even if such terms can also be distorted and adapted to various situations, they always correspond to clearly distinguishable artifacts. Only within the context of the logical succession of urban artifacts can one evaluate with some precision the *formal* character of specific proposals, as well as of that

170

particular group of proposals—whether more or less historically, practically, or partially realized—which are encompassed under the name *utopian*.

The present study derives its greatest support from studies of land ownership and topography. The block and the district, as permanent elements in the city, are seen as parts of a preconstituted urban structure in which topographical, sociological, linguistic, and other factors come together. These elements can be subjected to both an overall individuation and a typological characterization, thereby bringing to light local, regional, and national phenomena, which in turn become the elements of a norm.

Here the relationship between the general and the particular becomes increasingly precise; it becomes possible, for example, to establish characteristics of the Gothic lot which are closely related to the typology of the Gothic house, the so-called merchant's house. Typological relationships of this sort can be found in many different places—in Venice, Germany, Budapest, throughout Europe. Thus, while every place is characterized by its own particular aspect, by being precisely the architectural construction that it is, it can also be referred back to a more general design. We can define this general design as *typological form*.

The classification of various Gothic houses necessarily leads to our distinguishing the common characteristic that unites them and makes them unique; this is form. After arriving at its own specificity through its relationship with different realities, *a form becomes a way of confronting reality*, a way in which land is divided, for example, or the nature of the house established within a certain historical framework. In architecture such form has the value of a law, with its own autonomy and its own capacity to impose itself on reality. The Gothic lot, with its long and narrow form, the position of its stairs preestablished, and a constant relationship between solids and voids, constitutes a specific experience of unity. This experience coheres as a form even in different situations, even today; so that when an architect comprehends the beauty of a long and narrow cut in, say, an apartment design of Le Corbusier, he is referring to a specific experience which he knows through architecture.

Typological form refers, then, to a form which, either as a result of its being chosen during certain periods or the implications ascribed to it, has ended up by assuming the synthetic character of a process which exactly manifests the form itself. Architectural innovations always reveal particular tendencies, but they do not constitute typological inventions. We can understand that there is no possibility of typological invention if we realize that typology is shaped only through a long process of time and possesses highly complex links with the city and society.

A particularly interesting example is Palladio's use of classical typology. Palladio not only engaged in a heretical mixing of parochial and public elements, reducing religious buildings to buildings of state, but he also used indifferently, as forms in themselves, types that were associated with different uses, in particular the classical type of the centrally planned temple. In the former case, his architectural "inventions" (within certain limits) were precursors of the greatest discoveries of the "revolutionary architects"; in the latter his treatment of residential typology anticipated all of modern architecture beginning with Schinkel. Few examples better demonstrate how the immutable characteristics of typology are really those through which architectural design proceeds best.

Another thesis of this book which has provoked further studies is that of the *city*

171

100

101

102

100 Aqueduct, Segovia, Spain, from
the time of Trajan.
101 Aqueduct of Prata, called
Sértorio, between São Bento do Mato
and Evora, Portugal. Originally
attributed to the Romans, it was built
during the first half of the sixteenth
century.
102 Theater, Orange, France, from the
reign of Hadrian, c. 120 A.D. Later it
was used as a fortress, then as a
quarry.

of parts. Here the city is seen as a whole constituted of many pieces complete in themselves, and the distinctive characteristic of each city, and thus also of the urban aesthetic, is the dynamic that is created between its different areas and elements and among its parts. Moreover, such a city constituted of discrete parts permits greater freedom of choice.

This theory was developed by studying the physical reality of the city, and its truth emerges in each period of the city's history. I should also mention planning here, for it too represents a part of the city. The studies I made prior to this book on some of the larger European cities, in particular Vienna and Berlin,[3] together with some research I undertook on one part of the city of Milan,[4] convinced me that this principle was generalizable and constituted a fundamental hypothesis. A subsequent study of the cities of the Veneto, which by extension applied to all Mediterranean and mercantile cities, further verified this hypothesis. In some cities, there were enduring Roman features or Eastern influences that were stronger, while in others capitalism rapidly presented itself together with its specific attributes. One of the most interesting examples along these lines is the Venetian Ghetto and the structure of Venice generally.

I believe that all of these theses would benefit from further scientific investigation, from the point of view both of urban studies and of design, although I am also aware that they are susceptible to academic distortion. But in general, ever greater richness of information tends to lead to greater comprehension and potential for invention. I am thinking particularly of the theses of primary elements and of monuments, which were expounded for the first time in this book, and which subsequently have been validated by further documentation. There are several outstanding examples which also merit further investigation, including the amphitheater of Arles and the city of Vila Viçosa.

This discourse must be extended in a manner parallel to that on typology, that is, by demonstrating how the presence of *form*, of architecture, *predominates over questions of functional organization*, and by denying all theories that attempt to return questions of typology to the realm of the organization of buildings. Form is absolutely indifferent to organization precisely when it exists as typological form. I began this book by referring to the Palazzo della Ragione in Padua, and I still cannot think of a more illustrative example.

On an urban level, one example that I did not discuss is that of Split in Yugoslavia, which in my opinion constitutes, if not an outstanding example, then certainly a most revealing one. Here a large building, Diocletian's Palace, became a city, transforming its internal characteristics into urban ones and thereby demonstrating the infinite richness of analogical transformations in architecture when they operate on specific forms. Relative to examples like Vila Viçosa or Braganza, where a citadel became an urban nucleus and where ultimately the transformations were related to the more complex issue of the walls, the case of Split represents a true transformation of exterior spaces in a collective sense, that is, an urban sense. More than Arles, Nîmes, and Lucca (each with its different morphological implications), Split discovered in its own typological form an entire city, and thus the building came to refer *analogically* to the form of a city. This example is evidence that the single building can be designed by analogy to the city.

This concept is certainly not restricted to ancient and mythological examples; if we think of the *rue corridor* of Le Corbusier and the distorted meaning of

174

103
103 Sanctuary of Cape Espichel near
Lisbon.

"street" given to exterior gallery spaces by other modern architects, we realize that both were operating on a similar preestablished typology, that of an elongated element branching out into smaller rooms. An Italian archaeologist recently made this point succinctly in speaking of the way classical typology clearly stated how "the attribution of various functions to buildings based on a single typology" was standard.[5] This is valid for all architecture, and it tells us the meaning of the monument. It best applies to architecture that is most strongly identified with a typological form, for example, Palladio's use of the central plan. Modern architecture too has understood this relationship between architecture and the city in its development of the *unité d'habitation* and the large *Höfe*[6] of German architecture.

The development of these ideas led me to see more clearly the *connection between the study of typological form and architectural design*. In some cases, like that of Palladio's typology, the relationship is quite obvious; in others, like that of the Certosine and Benedictine convents which I analyzed in my lectures at the Polytechnic in Milan, the connections between typology, architecture, and city develop with increasing complexity and consequentiality.

The recognition of the existence of such complex but increasingly ordered relationships led me to postulate my theory of the *analogous city* in the introduction to my study of the cities of the Veneto as well as in other writings. This theory developed from many of the theses proposed in *The Architecture of the City*. I believe that many paths can lead to this concept of design, once the ideas presented in this book are established as a point of departure. One path sets out directly from urban studies. In analyzing the city of Milan, for example, I encountered en route all the difficulties which theoretical analysis calls into play, but unexpectedly these difficulties also led to the putting together of tables of elements that ultimately went into the ordering of a design. These tables, the fruit of work I undertook with Vanna Gavazzeni and Massimo Scolari, enabled us to accomplish a series of operations whose nature became increasingly compositional. The analogous city meant a system of relating the city to established elements from which other artifacts could be derived. At the same time, the suppression of precise boundaries in time and space allowed the design the same kind of tension that we find in memory.

In such an analogous system designs have as much existence as constructed architecture; they are a frame of reference for all that is real. When architects study the city of Milan, they have to take into consideration, as a real element, Antolini's unbuilt project for the Bonaparte Forum. This design is real in the sense that it was subsequently translated into a series of artifacts that cannot be explained without its existence and its form.

This path of research suggests a truly scientific direction for architecture. At the same time, I realize that the use of geographic texts, to refer to one discipline which receives particular attention in this book, has become a rigorous but closed form of research. I tried to use these texts as one uses materials of construction. The problem is to use them to establish an urban science and an architectural theory. Thus in writing on the cities of the Veneto I sought to give this material an interpretation and a form that could be assimilated into the theory of architecture.

It seems to me that urban science, understood in terms of all the foregoing arguments, is a web composed of many threads whose design appears increasingly

176

clear. If one looks at such subjects as the transformation of the walls of the ancient city, the existing body of archaeological material, the historical center as a part of the city, and finally, the city itself in terms of its parts, one can see all these as integral and inseparable elements of an overall formation.

Finally, I would like to express my heartfelt thanks to my students and friends José Charters Montiero and José da Nóbrega Sousa Martins who took on the task of translating this book into Portuguese and who, with their work on Portuguese cities and colonial cities, carry forward the work initiated here.

1971

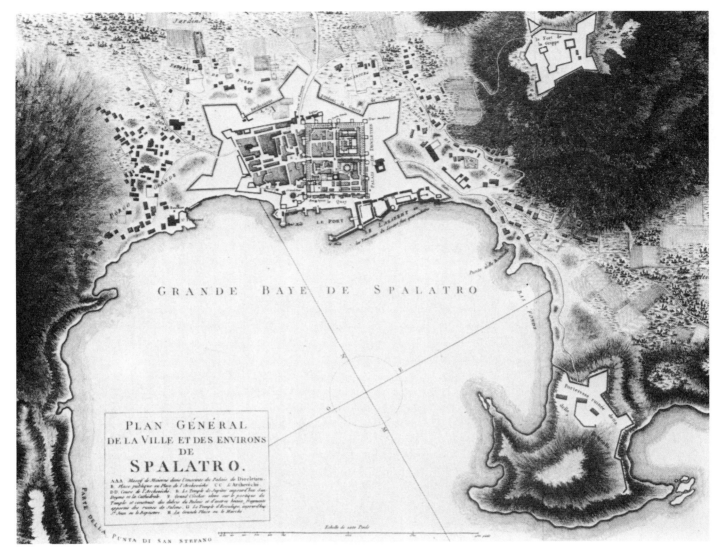

104 *General plan of Split, Yugoslavia, and surroundings at the end of the eighteenth century. Engraving by painter and architect L. F. Cassas, Paris, 1802.*

This book is an architectural project. Like any project it depends less on the material it draws on than on the relations it establishes between facts. An investigation of the meaning of the relationship between the singularity of form and the multiplicity of functions was the principal objective of this study. I still believe today that this relationship constitutes the meaning of architecture. Some of the elements analyzed in this book have subsequently become elements of a design theory: urban topography, the study of typology, the history of architecture as the material of architecture. In these elements time and space are continually intermixed. Topography, typology, and history come to be measures of the mutations of reality, together defining a system of architecture wherein gratuitous invention is impossible. Thus they are opposed theoretically to the disorder of contemporary architecture.

Like my architectural projects, this book has been interpreted in different ways, but those who have attempted to develop only one aspect, insisting either on a position of objectivity in urban research or on the autonomy of forms, have always taken the wrong road. These interpretations are erroneous because they obscure the complex nature of architecture. I have tried to show that to read topography as an architect means to recognize the formal values inherent in it, and above all to create a reference to design. The nature of a building is thus born from the nature of its city.

Fifty years ago Adolf Behne wrote about modern architecture, "By the concept of form I do not mean an accessory or an ornament . . . but rather something deriving from the particular character of the building . . . [the modern architect] desires the broadest adaptability to the greatest number of necessities."[1] In this book, the analysis of several great buildings of the past is conducted on precisely this rational basis. These buildings are seen as structures that have formed and still are forming the city, offering the maximum adaptability to new functions over time. The city of Split, which grew up within the walls of Diocletian's Palace and gave new uses and new meanings to unchangeable forms, is emblematic of the meaning of architecture and of the relationship between architecture and the city, where the broadest adaptability to a multiplicity of functions corresponds to an extreme precision of form.

August 1973

Comment on the German Edition

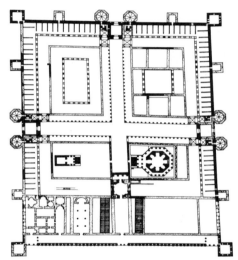

105 Plan of Diocletian's Palace, Split, Yugoslavia, according to the reconstruction by G. Niemann, 1910.

All quotations from foreign language sources have been put into English by the translators of this book unless otherwise noted.

**Introduction
to the First American Edition**
1. Javier Aguilera Rojas and Luis J. Moreno Rexach, *Urbanismo español en América* (Madrid: Editora Nacional, 1973).

**Introduction
Urban Artifacts and a
Theory of the City**
1. De Saussure, *Cours de linguistique générale*, ed. Charles Bally and Albert Sechehaye (Paris: Payot, 1922); trans. W. O. Henderson and W. H. Chaloner, *Course in General Linguistics* (New York: Philosophical Library, 1959).
2. Numa-Denis Fustel de Coulanges, *La Cité antique. Etudes sur le culte, le droit, les institutions de la Grèce et de Rome* (Paris: Durand, 1864; subsequent eds., Hachette); Mommsen, *Römische Geschichte*, 4 vols. (2d ed., Berlin: Weidmann, 1856-57); trans. William P. Dickson, *The History of Rome* (New York: Charles Scribner's Sons, 1891).
3. Freyre, *Casa-Grande & Senzala. Formãçao da Familia Brasileira sob o Regime de Economia Patriarcal* (Rio de Janeiro: José Olympio, 1958); Freyre, *Sobrados e mucambos. Decadência do patriarcado rural e desenvolvimento do urbano* (Rio de Janeiro: J. Olympio, 1951), vol. 2.
4. Vidal de la Blache, *Principes de géographie humaine* (1st ed., Paris: Armand Colin, 1922).
5. Milizia, *Principj di Architettura Civile* (Milan, 1832), ed. Giovanni Antolini; 2d ed. (Milan, 1847), ed. L. Masieri, S. Majocchi; reprinted with "Riproduzione anastatica conforme all'originale" (Milan: Gabrielle Mazzotta, 1972).

**Chapter 1
The Structure of Urban Artifacts**
1. Mumford discusses the idea of **the city as a work of art** in the introduction to his most beautiful book, synthesizing the most complex and stimulating material from studies on the city, especially from the Anglo-Saxon literature (not excluding Victorian eclecticism), and then developing it. "The city is a fact in nature, like a cave, a run of mackerel or an ant-heap. But it is also a conscious work of art, and it holds within its communal framework many simpler and more personal forms of art. Mind *takes form* in the city; and in turn, urban forms condition mind, for space, no less than time, is artfully reorganized in cities: in boundary lines and silhouettes, in the fixing of horizontal planes and vertical peaks, in utilizing or denying the natural site. . . . The city is both a physical utility for collective living and a symbol of those collective purposes and unanimities that arise under such favoring circumstances. With language itself, it remains man's greatest work of art" (Lewis Mumford, *The Culture of Cities* [New York: Harcourt, Brace & Co., 1938]), p. 5. The conception of the city as a work of art is often the characteristic content and experience in an artist's work; sometimes the name of an artist becomes associated with a city. One particularly important example of a study of the relationships between the city and the literary work, and of the city itself as a work of art, is Thomas Mann's lecture on Lübeck of June 5, 1926. Mann, "Lübeck als geistige Lebensform," in *Zwei Festreden* (Leipzig: Philipp Reclam, June 1928), pp. 7-47. A complex analysis of urban structure appears in modern form as early as Montaigne's travel journal, and is developed by scholars, travelers, and artists of the Enlightenment. Michel Eyquem de Montaigne, *Journal de voyage en Italie par la Suisse et l'Allemagne en 1580 et 1581*, with notes by M. De Querlon (Paris, 1774); ed. Maurice Rat (Paris: Garnier frères, 1955); trans. W. B. Waters, *The Journal of Montaigne's Travels in Italy by Way of Switzerland and Germany in 1850 and 1851*, 3 vols. (New York: E.P. Dutton & Co., 1903).
2. **The city and the nature of collective artifacts.** Lévi-Strauss, *Tristes Tropiques* (Paris: Plon, 1955); trans. John Russell (London: Hutchinson & Co., 1961). On p. 122 of the French text, the author speaks of "La ville . . . la chose humaine par excellence." On p. 121, he introduces some initial considerations on the quality of space and the mysterious character of the evolution of the city. In the behavior of individuals everything is rational, but this does not mean that an unconscious moment cannot be found in the city; for the city, in terms of the relationship between the individual and the collective, offers a strange opposition. "Cities have often been likened to symphonies and poems, and the comparison seems to me a perfectly natural one; they are, in fact, objects of the same kind. The city may even be rated higher since it stands at the point where nature and artifice meet" (p. 127). In his elaboration of this argument, Lévi-Strauss echoes the conclusions of ecological studies concerning the relationship between man and the environment and between man and the shaping of the environment. To under-

stand the city in a concrete way means to grasp the individuality of its inhabitants—an individuality that is the basis of the monuments themselves: "To understand a city, beyond its monuments, beyond the history of its stones, is to rediscover the specific way of being of its inhabitants."

3. Halbwachs, *La mémoire collective*, preface by Jean Duvignaud, introduction by J. Michel Alexandre (Paris: Presses Universitaires de France, 1950; rev. and enlarged ed., 1968).

4. **Cattaneo's conception.** Cattaneo, "Agricoltura e morale," first published in *Atti della Società d'incoraggiamento d'arti e mestieri. Terza solenne distribuzione dei premi alla presenza di S.A.I.R. il Serenissimo Arciduca Viceré nel giorno 15 maggio 1845* (Milan, 1845), pp. 3-11; later in the first volume of *Scritti completi editi ed inediti di Carlo Cattaneo*, ed. Arcangelo Ghisleri, 3 vols. (1st ed., Milan, 1925-26). It is now republished along with the other work attributed to Cattaneo, "Industria e morale," in the *opera omnia* published by F. Le Monnier: Carlo Cattaneo, *Scritti economici*, 3 vols., ed. Alberto Bertolini (Florence, 1956), vol. III, pp. 3-30. The passage cited is on pp. 4-5. On these pages the author gives the complete framework of his concept of *natural artifacts*, in an analysis in which linguistics, economics, history, geography, geology, sociology, and politics come together to characterize the structure of artifacts. Even more than his Enlightenment heritage, his positivism comes to light in his approach to individual problems. "The German language uses the same word for the art of building and the art of cultivating: the word 'agriculture' (*Ackerbau*) does not ring of cultivation, but of construction; the colonist is a builder (*Bauer*). When the ignorant German tribes saw in the shadow of the eagle how the Romans built bridges, streets, walls, and with little different effort transformed the shores of the Rhine and Mosel into vineyards, they embraced all of those works with only one name. Yes, a people must build its fields, just as it must build its cities" (p. 5). Bridges, streets, walls, are the beginning of a transformation; this transformation shapes man's surroundings and itself becomes history. The clarity of this formulation makes Cattaneo one of the first urban scholars in the modern sense when he applies it to the problem of the region; consider his intervention on the subject of the problems that arose with the new railroad routes. Thus Gabriele Rosa wrote in his biography of Cattaneo: "The problem was to open an artery between Milan and Venice. Mathematicians rigorously studied the geographical question,

not considering the population, history, and topical economics, elements which rebelled against mathematical ordering. The versatile and profound mind of Cattaneo was necessary to bring a clear light to bear on this new and serious question. . . . He sought a route that would permit the fullest private gain and public utility. He said that the work need not be sacrificed to the tyranny of the terrain; that the aim was not so much to pass through quickly, but to make speed profitable; that coming and going would be more frequent at short distances; that the greatest flow would be on the line uniting the persistent and most ancient centers; and that *in Italy whoever disregards individuals' love of their country will always sow on sandy ground*." Rosa, "Commemorazione di Carlo Cattaneo" (read at the meeting of the Lombard Institute of Science and Letters, November 11, 1869), in *Rendiconti del Reale Istituto Lombardo*, (Milan, 1869), pp. 1061-1082; republished as "Carlo Cattaneo nella vita e nelle opere," introduction to *Scritti completi editi ed inediti di Carlo Cattaneo*, vol. I, pp. XIII-XXXIX.

5. Lynch, *The Image of the City* (Cambridge, Mass.: Technology Press and Harvard Univ. Press, 1960).

6. Sorre, "Géographie urbaine et écologie," *Urbanisme et architecture. Etudes écrites et publiées en l'honneur de Pierre Lavedan* (Paris: Henri Laurens, 1954), pp. 341-44; Mauss, "Essai sur les variations saisonnières des sociétés eskimo. Étude de morphologie sociale," with M.H. Beuchat, in *L'année sociologique*, 1904-1905 (Paris: Félix Alcan, 1906), pp. 39-132. See also n. 1, chap. 3.

7. On **the city as a man-made object,** see Oscar Handlin and John Burchard, eds., *The Historian and the City* (Cambridge, Mass.: M.I.T. Press and Harvard Univ. Press, 1963). John Summerson speaks of "the city as artifact" in his essay "Urban Forms" in this anthology, pp. 165-76. Anthony N. B. Garvan, in "Proprietary Philadelphia as Artifact" (pp. 177-201), sheds light on the term from the standpoint of the archaeologist and the anthropologist and then argues that "if, therefore, the term can be applied to an urban complex at all, it should be applied in such a way as to seek all those aspects of the city and its life for which the material structure, buildings, streets, monuments were properly the tool or artifact" (p. 178). It is in this sense that Cattaneo speaks of the city as a physical thing, as a construction of human labor: "Labor builds houses, dikes, canals, streets" ("Industria e morale," *Scritti economici*, vol. III, p. 4).

8. Sitte, *Der Städtbau nach seinen*

künstlerichen Grundsätzen (Vienna: Carl Gräser Verlag, 1889); trans. George R. Collins and Christiane Grasemann Collins, *City Planning According to Artistic Principles* (London: Phaidon, and New York: Random House, 1965). The passage cited appears on p. 91 of the English edition. Sitte's biography is interesting. He was essentially a technician; he studied at the Vienna Polytechnic and founded the state professional school, the Staatsgewerbeschule, in 1875 in Salzburg, and later the one in Vienna.

9. Jean-Nicolas-Louis Durand, *Précis des leçons d'architecture données à l'Ecole Polytechnique*, 2 vols. (Paris, 1802-1805; 2d ed., 1809). The sentence quoted is from the 2d ed., vol. II, p. 21.

10. Francesco Milizia, *Principj di Architettura Civile*, cit. n. 4 of the Introduction to this book; the phrase quoted is from the beginning of the second part, "Della comodità," p. 221.

11. Antoine Chrysostôme Quatremère de Quincy, *Dictionnaire historique d'architecture comprenant dan son plan les notions historiques, descriptives, archaeologiques, biographiques, théoriques, didactiques et pratiques de cet art*, 2 vols. (Paris, 1832). The passage quoted is from vol. 2, the section on "Type." Quatremère's **definition of type** has recently been picked up by Giulio Carlo Argan in a particularly interesting way, in Argan, "Sul concetto di tipologia architettonica," in *Progetto e destino* (Milan: Casa editrice Il Saggiatore, 1965), pp. 75-81. See also Louis Hautecoeur, *Histoire de l'architecture classique en France*, 7 vols. (Paris: A. et J. Picard, 1943-57), in particular vol. V, *Révolution et Empire. 1792-1815* (1953), where Hautecoeur writes, "As Schneider noted, Quatremère affirmed that there is a 'correlation between scale, forms, and the impressions that our spirit receives from them'" (p. 122).

12. Among the new aspects of the research by architects on the **problems of typology**, the lectures given by Carlo Aymonino at the Istituto di Architettura di Venezia are particularly interesting. In one of them, "The Formation of a Concept of Building Typology," he states, "We can thus attempt to distinguish some 'characteristics' of building typologies which allow us to identify them better: a) singleness of theme, even if [the type is] subdivided into one or more activities in order to derive a reasonable elementary or simplicity from the organism; this also applies in more complex cases; b) indifference—in theoretical formulations—to context, that is, to a precise urban location (does a significant interchangeability derive from this?) and the

formation of a relationship concerned only with its own plan as the single relevant boundary (an incomplete relationship); c) the overcoming of building code regulations to the extent that the type is characterized precisely by its own architectural form. The type in fact is *also* conditioned by codes (of hygiene, security, etc.) but not *only* by them" (p. 9). Aymonino's lectures are found in two volumes published by the Istituto Universitario di Architettura di Venezia, *Aspetti e problemi della tipologia edilizia. Documenti del corso di caratteri distributivi degli edifici. Anno accademico 1963-1964* (Venice, 1964); and *La formazione del concetto di tipologia edilizia. Atti del corso di caratteri distributivo degli edifici. Anno accademico 1964-1965* (Venice, 1965). Some of these lectures are also republished with revisions in Carlo Aymonino, *Il significato della città* (Bari: Editori Laterza, 1975).

13. Malinowski, *A Scientific Theory of Culture and Other Essays* (Chapel Hill: Univ. of North Carolina Press, 1944). **Functionalism in geography.** The concept of organic function was introduced by Friedrich Ratzel in 1891, who, by analogy with physiology, compares the city to a bodily organ; the functions of the city are those which justify its own existence and development. More recent studies distinguish between functions associated with centrality and the relationship to the general region *(Allgemeine Funktionen)* and those which are associated with particular functions *(Besondere Funktionen)*. In the latter studies, function has a greater spatial reference. For the use of this term in relation to ecology, see n. 29 of this chapter. From its inception, geographical functionalism found itself in serious difficulty in trying to classify *commercial functions*, which had naturally acquired prominence. In *Anthropogeographie*, Ratzel defined the city as "a longstanding concentration of men and their houses, which covers a considerable amount of land and is found at the center of the major commercial arteries." Hermann Wagner too insists on the city as a point of concentration of commerce *(Handel und Verkehr)*. Ratzel, *Anthropogeographie*, 2 vols. (Stuttgart: J. Engelhorn, 1882 and 1891; 3d ed., 1909 and 1922). For a summary of the theses of the German geographers, see the dictionary *Allgemeine Geographie*, Gustav Fochler-Hauke, ed. (Frankfurt am Main: Fischer Bücherei, 1959), in particular the entry "Siedlungsgeographie," by Günter Glauert, pp. 286-311. See also Jacqueline Beaujeu-Garnier and Georges Chabot, *Traité de géographie urbaine* (Paris: Armand Colin, 1963), and John Harold George Lebon, *An*

Introduction to Human Geography (London: Hutchinson Univ. Library, 1952; 5th ed. rev., 1963).

14. Chabot, *Les villes. Aperçu de géographie humaine* (Paris: Armand Colin, 1948; 3d ed., 1958). Chabot classifies the principal functions of the city as military, commercial, industrial, therapeutic, intellectual and religious, and administrative. Ultimately he admits that in the city the various functions become mixed with one another, ending up acquiring the value of an original artifact; however, he is more concerned with elementary and original functions than with permanent artifacts. In Chabot's system, function, together with the plan, is seen as a moment of urban life. His conception is thus the richer and more articulated.

15. Weber, *Wirtschaft und Gesellschaft. Grundriss der Verstehenden Soziologie*, 4th ed., ed. and with an introduction by Johannes Winckelmann, 2 vols. (Tübingen: J.C.B. Mohr–Paul Siebeck, 1956).

16. Jean Tricart, *Cours de géographie humaine*, 2 vols: vol. I, *L'habitat rural;* vol. II, *L'habitat urbain* (Paris: Centre de Documentation Universitaire, 1963). Tricart observes, "Like every study of artifacts considered in themselves, urban morphology presupposes a convergence of givens customarily drawn from different disciplines: urbanism, sociology, history, political economy, law itself. It is sufficient that this convergence has as its aim the analysis and explanation of a concrete artifact, of a landscape, for us to be able to state that it has its place in the framework of geography" (vol. II, p. 4).

17. Richard Updegraff Ratcliff, "The Dynamics of Efficiency in the Locational Distribution of Urban Activities," in Harold Melvin Mayer and Clyde Frederick Kohn, eds., *Readings in Urban Geography* (Chicago: Univ. of Chicago Press, 1959), pp. 299-324; the passage cited is on p. 299.

18. Marcel Poète, *Introduction à l'Urbanisme. L'évolution des villes, la leçon de l'antiquité* (Paris: Boivin & Cie., 1929). Concerning the influence which Poète exercised on urban studies, see the journal *La vie urbaine*, published by the Institut d'Urbanisme de l'Université de Paris à la Sorbonne, under the direction of Lavedan. The journal, issued three times yearly from 1920 to 1940, published studies and research on the city, primarily historical in character and of a notably high level. Poète's monumental work, perhaps unequaled in the entire body of studies on the city, is *Une vie de cité. Paris de sa naissance à nos jours*, 4 vols. (Paris: Auguste Picard, 1924-1931): vol. I, *La jeunesse. Des origines aux temps modernes* (1924); vol.

II, *La cité de la Renaissance. Du milieu du XVᵉ siècle à la fin du XVIᵉ siècle* (1927); vol. III, *La spiritualité de la cité classique. Les origines de la cité moderne (XVIᵉ-XVIIᵉ siècles)* (1931); album, *Six cents illustrations d'après les documents, accompagnées de légends et d'un exposé historique* (1925). The studies on Paris are condensed in Marcel Poète, *Comment s'est formé Paris* (Paris: Hachette, 1925). Mumford described this book as a basic text rich with the learning of an entire lifetime.

19. *Introduction à l'Urbanisme . . .*, p. 60.

20. Lavedan's works include *Géographie des villes* (Paris: Gallimard, 1936; rev. ed., 1959) and *Histoire de l'urbanisme*, 3 vols. (Paris: Henri Laurens, 1926-1952): vol. I, *Antiquité. Moyen-Age* (1926; 2d ed. with the section on antiquity completely revised, with Jeanne Hugueney, 1966); vol. II, *Renaissance et temps modernes* (1941; rev. ed., 1959); vol. III, *Epoque contemporaine* (1952). Also by Lavedan, *Les villes françaises* (Paris: Vincent, Fréal & Cie., 1960).

21. **Enlightenment thought.** On the relationship between buildings and the city, Voltaire, for example, wrote: "Many citizens have constructed magnificent buildings, but more refined in *le grand goût* on the inside than the outside, and satisfying the taste for luxury of private individuals still more than they enhance the city." François Marie Arouet de Voltaire, *Le siècle de Louis XIV* (first definitive ed., 1768), in *Oeuvres complètes de Voltaire*, 4 vols. (Paris, 1827-29). The passage is from vol. III, p. 2993. See also, Jean Mariette, *L'Architecture françoise, ou Receuil des Plans, Elevations, Coupes et Profiles des Eglises, Palais, Hôtels, & Maisons particulières de Paris & des Chateaux et Maisons de Campagne ou de Plaisance des Environs, & des plusieurs autres Endroits de France, Bâtis nouvellement pas les plus habils Architectes et levés et mesurés exactement sur les lieux*, 3 vols. (Paris, 1727-1832). This great collection of reliefs of buildings, edited by publisher and print dealer Jean Mariette, was re-edited by Louis Hautecoeur, *L'architecture française* (Paris-Brussels: G. Van Oest, 1927). See also Anthony Blunt, *François Mansart and the Origins of French Classical Architecture* (London: Warburg Institute, 1941).

22. Francesco Milizia, *Principj di Architettura Civile*. Milizia's treatise is divided into three parts: "Parte prima. Della bellezza," "Parte seconda. Della comodità," "Parte terza. Della solidità delle fabbriche."

23. Ibid., p. 371, from "Parte seconda."

24. Ibid., p. 663, from "Conclusione della

terza parte e di tutta l'opera."

25. Ibid., p. 418, from "Parte seconda."

26. Ibid., p. 420, from "Parte seconda."

27. Ibid., p. 235, from "Parte seconda."

28. Ibid., p. 236, from "Parte seconda."

29. A treatment of this problem would have to take into account the great theme of **ecology** developed in the classic works of Humboldt, Grisebach, and Warming, and continuing up to the modern period. Alexandre de Humboldt [Alexander von Humboldt], *Essai sur la géographie des plantes, accompagnée d'un tableau physique des régions équinoxiales . . .* (Paris, 1805). August Grisebach, *Die Vegetation der Erde nach ihrer klimatischen Anordnung. Ein Abriss der Vergleichenden Geographie der Pflanzen*, 2 vols. (Leipzig: Wilhelm Engelmann, 1872). Eugenius Warming, *Oecology of Plants. An Introduction to the Study of Plant Communities* (Oxford: Clarendon Press, 1909); original edition in Danish (Copenhagen: P.G. Philipsen, 1895). Their points of departure are the recognition of the "growth forms" of species and their effort to bring to the fore the recognition of external factors (physical surroundings) without neglecting to consider the reciprocal actions among living beings, including man. For an extensive bibliography, see Jean Brunhes, *La géographie humaine. Essai de classification positive. Principes et exemples* (Paris: Félix Alcan, 1910; 4th ed. rev. in 3 vols., with expanded bibliography, 1934); trans. T. C. Le Compte, ed. Isaiah Bowman and Richard Elwood Dodge, *Human Geography; An Attempt at a Positive Classification; Principles and Examples* (Chicago: Rand McNally, 1920). The fascination with urban science in these studies is evident. The term *human ecology* goes back to Robert Park (1921). Amos H. Hawley, *Human Ecology. A Theory of Community Structure* (New York: Ronald Press, 1950). See also n. 13 of this chapter and n. 1, chap. 3.

30. The following essay is interesting, though not really based on a study of the city as a concrete artifact: Etienne Souriau, "Contribution à la physiologie des cités. Le végétal ville ou rhyme et raison," in *Urbanisme et architecture. Etudes écrites en l'honneur de Pierre Lavedan* (Paris: Henri Laurens, 1954), pp. 347-54.

31. Milizia, *Principj di Architettura Civile*, p. 235. ·

32. Charles Baudelaire, *Les Fleurs du Mal*, 2d ed. (Paris: Poulet-Malassis et de Braise, 1861). Among the critical editions of this work, see esp. J. Crépet, G. Blin, C. Pichois, eds. (Paris: J. Corti, 1968). The verses quoted are from "Tableaux parisiens," no. 89, "Le Cygne." Baudelaire is one of the literary figures whose critical intuitions about architecture and the city are among the most remarkable.

Chapter 2
Primary Elements and the Concept of Area

1. This type of conception of **the city and its parts** is the basis of the urban theory of Fritz Schumacher; it appears in the plan of 1921 for Cologne and in the more famous one of 1930 for Hamburg. For Schumacher's theory, the most important work is his *Vom Städtebau zur Landesplanung und Fragen städtebaulicher Gestaltung* (Tübingen: Ernst Wasmuth, 1951). See in particular the paragraph on p. 37 concerning "the different requirements (*Anforderungen*) of the parts of the city": the differentiation of the modern city is the principal feature of its individuality (*Eigenart*), as all of its zones tend to be divided with ever more clarity from one another. The way it is shaped and its objectives (*Gestaltungsaufgabe*) characterize its structure independently of any single law or formal principle. For the plan of Hamburg, see Fritz Schumacher, *Zum Wiederaufbau Hamburgs*, record of the discussion in Hamburg Town Hall on October 10, 1945 (Hamburg: Johann Trautmann, 1945); republished in Schumacher, *Strömungen in deutscher Baukunst seit 1800* (Leipzig: E. A. Seemann, 1935; 2d ed., Cologne, 1955). Also see Gemeinsamer Landesplanungsrat Hamburg/Schleswig-Holstein, *Leitgedanken und Empfehlungen* (Hamburg-Kiel, 1960). On the study area and some interpretations of the "natural area" in the sense of the original area, see my study, Aldo Rossi, *Contributo al problema dei rapporti tra tipologia edilizia e morfologia urbana. Esame di un'area di studio di Milano, con particolare attenzione alle tipologie edilizie prodotte da interventi privati* (Milan: Istituto Lombardo per gli Studi Economici e Sociali [I.L.S.E.S.], 1964).

2. On the subject of **American sociology and the Chicago School,** see the following: Ernest W. Burgess, "The Determination of Gradients in the Growth of the City," in *Proceedings of the American Sociological Society*, XXI, 1927, pp. 178-84; Burgess, "The Growth of the City," in *Proceedings of the American Sociological Society*, XVIII, 1923, pp. 85-97, republished in Robert E. Park, Ernest W. Burgess, Roderick D. McKenzie, *The City* (Chicago: Univ. of Chicago Press, 1925), and with an introduction by Morris Janowitz (Chicago and London: Univ. of Chicago Press, 1967).

3. Homer Hoyt, *The Structure and Growth of Residential Neighborhoods in Ameri-*

can Cities (Washington: Federal Housing Administration, 1939). For a discussion of some of the theses of the American urban sociologists, see Sorre, "Géographie urbaine et écologie" (cit. n. 6, chap.1).

4. The major work of Baumeister is *Stadt-erweiterungen in technischer, baupolizei-licher und wirtschaftlicher Beziehung* (Berlin: Ernst und Korn, 1876). This is the first German handbook which was widely read.

5. On the **Berlin codes,** see Werner Hegemann, *Das steinerne Berlin . . .*, cit. n. 12 of this chapter, and esp. the section on "The Typological Problem of Housing in Berlin" in chap. 2 of this book.

6. The urban vicissitudes of the city of **Vienna** are particularly interesting because of the historical importance of this city and the ample existing documentation. The *Weichbild* identified by Hassinger is not really the periphery; it is distinguished by its own image, and even today this zone constitutes as highly typical an aspect of Vienna as the Josefplatz. The general evolution of the city can best be understood by studying the constitution and disposition of the individual areas which constitute it, especially those areas whose use is intimately associated with housing. The nature of housing in Vienna is largely explained by the *Hofquartierspflicht*. This regulation had to do with the establishment of the Hapsburg court in the city; unable to satisfy the residential needs of the numerous court followers, the law was altered so that private landlords were obliged to provide quarters as needed during court sessions. This meant the destruction of three-story Gothic houses in the baroque period for the erection of six- and seven-story houses with two or three basement stories. The value of the land within the walls had already become so high in 1700 that the poorest classes of the population and the artisans were forced to migrate to the external districts, which were created after 1683. It is interesting to note how in this case a schematic interpretation of the phenomenon of urbanism does not explain the formation of the city up to the nineteenth century; when, after 1850, the growth process of the industrial period began, Vienna had already destroyed part of its old city. See Aldo Rossi, "Un piano per Vienna," *Casabella-continuità*, no. 277 (July 1963), pp. 2-21, republished in Aldo Rossi, *Scritti scelti sull'architettura e la città, 1956-1972*, ed. and with an introduction by Rosaldo Bonicalzi (Milan: Clup [Cooperativa Libreria Universitaria del Politecnico], 1975), pp. 193-208; Hugo Hassinger, *Kunsthistorischer Atlas der K. K. Reichshaupt- und Residenzstadt Wien und Verzeichnis der erhaltenswerten historischen, Kunst- und Naturdenkmale des Wiener Stadtbildes* (Vienna: Anton Schroll & Co., 1916); Roland Rainer, *Planungskonzept Wien* (Vienna: Verlag für Jugend und Volk, 1962). See also the journal *Der Aufbau:* in particular no. 4/5 of 1961, *Gemeinwirtschaft, Planen und Bauen;* no. 7/8 of 1961, *1946–1961, 15 Jahre,* with Georg Conditt's article, "Stadtplanung und Planungsgrundlagen"; no. 11/12 of 1962, *Aussenbezirke der Stadt Wien,* with articles by Sokratis Dimitriou, "Die Wiener Gürtelstrasse," and Karl Feltinek, "Kulturelle Mittelpunkte in den Wiener Aussenbezirke." Finally, see Robert E. Dickinson, *The West European City: A Geographical Interpretation* (London: Routledge & Kegan Paul, 1951; rev. ed., 1961); see esp. the section in chap. 10, "Vienna: Capital of Austria," pp. 184–94.

7. Lynch, *The Image of the City*, pp. 66-67.

8. Ibid., pp. 70-71.

9. Eugène-Emmanuel Viollet-le-Duc. *Dictionnaire raisonné de l'architecture française du XIᵉ au XVIᵉ siècle*, 10 vols. (Paris: Ancienne Maison Morel, 1854-69); the passage cited is from vol. VI, "Maison," p. 214.

10. For an explanation of the *Hofquartierspflicht* law, see n. 5 of this chapter.

11. Behrens, "Die Gemeinde Wien als Bauherr," *Bauwelt*, no. 41 (1928); published in Italian with my introduction, "Peter Behrens e il problema dell'abitazione moderna," *Casabella-continuità*, no. 240 (June 1960). In this article I argued that the fundamental thematics of this German master in the field of housing can be summarized in two principal points: 1) only a system of low houses with gardens, in combination with houses of several stories, in a carefully chosen and studied area, renders a quarter harmonious, publicly livable, and economical; 2) materials and individual constructional parts must be standardized. By 1910 Behrens had already clarified the formative process of a new urban space. Concerning the problem of **Modern Movement housing,** see Internationale Kongresse für Neues Bauen, Zurich, *Die Wohnung für das Existenzminimum* (Frankfurt am Main: Englert & Schlosser, 1930; 3d ed., Stuttgart: Julius Hoffmann, 1933). This book, which reports on the proceedings of the 2d C.I.A.M. (Congrès Internationaux d'Architecture Moderne), held in Frankfurt in 1929, contains the principal writings of the architects of the Modern Movement on the housing problem, among them: Ernst May, "Die Wohnung für das Existenzminimum"; Walter Gropius, "Die soziologischen Grundlagen der Minimalwohnung für die städtische Industriebevölkerung"; Le Cor-

busier and Pierre Jeanneret, "Analyse des éléments fondamentaux du problème de la 'Maison Minimum' "; Hans Schmidt, "Bauvorschriften und Minimalwohnung." The book has been translated into Italian, with a long introduction by Carlo Aymonino, together with the proceedings of the 3d C.I.A.M. held in Brussels in 1930, which focused on the question of "Metodi construttivi razionali. Case basse, medie e alte." On some of the methodological aspects of the Modern Movement, see Ernesto Rogers, "Problemi di metodo (La prefabbricazione)," 1944 and 1949; republished in Rogers, *Esperienza dell'architettura* (Turin: Giulio Einaudi, 1958), pp. 80-81. The problem of housing in the Modern Movement is analyzed in a masterly way by Giuseppe Samonà, who deals with the full range of these issues, focusing on the relationship between architecture and the city. It is worth quoting the following passage from Samonà's essay: "An organism was sought that was polemically opposed to the chaotic corpulence of the existing city, and therefore suited in all of its activities and services to the needs of an associative life, capable of being programmed in its behavior with the schematic exactness of a preconstituted *standard* for all activities, and able to be translated into well-determined dimensions. The almost institutional meaning of 'scale' as a measure of all activity prevented one from experiencing urban situations in the context of their own social applications, of penetrating their discontinuities and complexities, because the explosive impetus of their forces and contradictory interests would have been irreducible to a single scheme, even if it were technically perfect." Giuseppe Samonà, *L'urbanistica e l'avvenire della città negli stati europei* (Bari: Laterza, 1969; 2d ed. enlarged, 1971), pp. 99-100 of the 1st edition.

12. Jean Gottman, *Megalopolis. The Urbanized Northeastern Seaboard of the United States*, introduction by August Heckscher (New York: Twentieth Century Fund, 1961; 2d ed., Cambridge, Mass.: M.I.T. Press, 1964).

13. This study of housing in **Berlin** is developed in my article, Aldo Rossi, "Aspetti della tipologia residenziale a Berlino," *Casabella-continuità*, no. 288 (June 1964), pp. 10-20; republished in *Scritti scelti . . .*, pp. 237-52. Major publications on Berlin include Louis Herbert, *Die Geographische Gliederung von Gross-Berlin. Länderkündliche Forschungen* (Stuttgart, 1936); Werner Hegemann, *Das steinerne Berlin. Geschichte der grössten Mietkasernenstadt in der Welt* (Berlin: Kiepenhauer, 1930; republ., Berlin: Ullstein, 1963);

Robert E. Dickinson, *The West European City . . .* (cit. n. 5 to this chapter), esp. chap. 13, "Berlin," pp. 236-49; Fritz Schumacher, *Strömungen in deutscher Baukunst seit 1800* (cit. n. 1 to this chapter); Erich Haenel, Heinrich Tscharmann, *Das Kleinwohnhaus der Neuzeit* (Leipzig: J. J. Weber, 1913); Walter Müller-Wulckow, *Deutsche Baukunst der Gegenwart* (Königstein im Taunus-Leipzig: Karl Robert Langewiesche, 1909); Herman Ziller, *Schinkel* (Bielefeld-Leipzig: Velhagen & Klasing, 1897); W. Fred, *Die Wohnung und ihre Ausstattung* (Bielefeld-Leipzig: Velhagen & Klasing, 1903); Heinz Johannes, *Neues Bauen in Berlin. Ein Führer mit 168 Bildern* (Berlin: Deutscher Kunstverlag, 1931); Rolf Rave, Hans-Joachim Knöfel, *Bauen seit 1900 in Berlin* (Berlin: Kiepert, 1968); Adolf Behne, *Vom Anhalter bis zum Bauhaus* (1922; republ. in *Bauwelt*, no. 41-42, 1961); Peter Behrens, "Il futuro di Berlino," *Casabella-continuità*, no. 240 (June 1960), p. 33, translation of an article published in the newspaper *Berliner Morgenpost*, November 27, 1912. Also see the following journals: *Moderne Bauformen* (esp. the years between 1920 and 1930); *Bauwelt; Deutsche Architektur;* and the publications of the Deutsche Bauakademie, Berlin, and the Institut für Raumforschung, Bad Godesberg.

14. In the Italian literature *Siedlung* has been imprecisely and unfortunately translated as *quartiere*. The word actually has a more general meaning of "settlement" and "colony"; it is also widely used to indicate new residential developments on the periphery of German cities. Hassinger defines *Siedlung* in the following way: "*Siedlung*, in the broadest sense of the word, is any human settlement, even the itinerant hunter's shelter . . . as well as the encampment of nomadic shepherds remaining in one place for some time, or an established dwelling place, like the farm, the village, or the city." Fritz Klute, ed., *Allgemeine Geographie. Handbuch der Geographischer Wissenschaft*, (Potsdam: 2 vols., 1933), vol. II, p. 403. This is part of a vast work under the direction of Klute consisting of, in addition to the two volumes just cited (vol. I, *Physikalische Geographie;* vol. II, *Das Leben auf der Erde*), 11 vols. on regional geography published between 1930 and 1939. Hugo Hassinger is responsible for the part on "Die Geographie des Menschen (Anthropogeographie), vol. II, pp. 167-542, with a chapter on "Siedlungsgeographie," pp. 403-56.

15. Rasmussen, *Towns and Buildings Described in Drawings and Words* (1st American ed., Cambridge, Mass.: Harvard Univ. Press, 1951). On **Ville Radieuse,** see

Le Corbusier, *La Ville Radieuse. Eléments d'une doctrine d'urbanisme pour l'équipement de la civilisation machiniste* (Boulogne-sur-Seine: Editions de "L'Architecture d'Aujourd'hui," 1935; republ., Paris: Vincent, Fréal & Cie., 1964). For a modern evaluation of the **Garden City,** the most up-to-date opinion is still that of Rodwin, who gives a precise and practical evaluation of the New Towns and the entire English urban experience. Lloyd Rodwin, *The British New Town Policy* (Cambridge, Mass.: Harvard Univ. Press, 1956). Summarizing the various English proposals, Rodwin states, "The proposals also afford, particularly to the proponents, another illustration of the British propensity and ingenuity at compromise, in short, 'the English mind at its best: always in touch with the practicable, always in sight of the ideal.' Of all Howard's inventions, this one proved to be the most successful. How great an impact these ideas had on the thinking of some persons is brought out forcibly by Lewis Mumford's observation: 'At the beginning of the twentieth century, two great new inventions took form before our eyes: the airplane and the Garden City, both harbingers of a new age: the first gave man wings and the second promised him a better dwelling place when he came down to earth' " (p. 12). The passage cited by Rodwin is from Lewis Mumford, "The Garden City Idea and Modern Planning," introduction written in 1945 for Ebenezer Howard's *Garden Cities of Tomorrow* (London: Faber and Faber, 1945; first published as *Tomorrow: A Peaceful Path to Real Reform* in 1898; 2d ed. rev. titled *Garden Cities of Tomorrow*, 1902).

16. A suggestive if problematic evaluation of the English experience was made by Doglio in an article that I consider one of the most stimulating and intelligent in the Italian postwar literature on urbanism, "L'equivoco della città-giardino," *Urbanistica*, XXIII, no. 13 (1953), pp. 56-66; this article is excerpted from a larger essay published in parts in *Volontà*, VIII, nos. 1/2, 3, 4, 5, 6/7 (1953); republished with the same title in pamphlet form (Naples: Edizioni R. L., 1953; 2d ed., Florence: Crescita Politica Editrice, 1974). The Garden City, in all of its implications, constitutes a focal point of great importance for European architecture and demands very substantial study.

17. Doglio, op. cit., p. 56.

18. Willy Hellpach, *Mensch und Volk der Grosstadt* (Stuttgart: Ferdinand Enke, 1939; 2d ed. rev., 1952). The quotation, from the Preface of the book (p. 9), concluded a report on "The origin and formation of urban ethnic types," given by Hellpach in 1935 at the International Congress of Demographers in Berlin.

19. David Lewis, "Complesso residenziale Park Hill a Sheffield. Un'esperienza rivoluzionaria," *Casabella-continuità*, no. 263 (May 1962), pp. 5-9, passage cited p. 7.

20. Bahrdt, *Die moderne Grossstadt, Soziologische Uberlegungen zum Städtebau* (Hamburg: Rowohlt, 1961).

21. Milizia, *Principj di architettura civile*, p. 663.

22. Fontana, *Della Trasportatione dell' Obelisco Vaticano et delle Fabriche di Nostro Signore Papa Sisto V, fatto dal Cav. Carlo Fontana, Architetto di Sua Santità* (Rome, 1590; 2d ed., Naples, 1604), pt. II, fol. 18; cited in Sigfried Giedion, *Space, Time and Architecture* (Cambridge, Mass.: Harvard Univ. Press, 5th ed. rev., 1967), p. 106. Giedion discusses the transformation of the Coliseum in his chapter on "Sixtus V (1585-1590) and the Planning of Baroque Rome," pp. 75-106. The importance of this transformation was noted for the first time by Gideon, even if not with the same implications.

23. Françoise Lehoux, *Le Bourg Saint-Germain-des-Prés depuis ses origines jusqu'à la fin de la Guerre de Cent Ans* (Paris: the author, 1951); Pierre Lavedan, *Les villes françaises*. On the formation of **Paris,** in addition to Marcel Poète's books, there are some particularly important studies of historical topography. In the series Bibliothèque d'histoire de Paris, see Louis Halphen, *Paris sous les premiers Capétiens (987-1223). Etude de topographie historique* (Paris: Ernest Leroux, 1909). Several works have acquired an exceptional importance for the history of the urban structure, providing a series of dates and information that allow one to understand profoundly the mechanism of the urban dynamic in the formation of the modern city. See, in the same series, Georges Huisman, *La juridiction de la Municipalité parisienne, de Saint Louis à Charles VII*ᵉ (Paris: Ernest Leroux, 1912); see esp. chap. VII: "La juridiction du domaine de la ville," "La juridiction du domaine municipal public," "La juridiction du domaine privé."

24. Pirenne, *Les villes et les institutions urbaines*, 2 vols. (4th ed., Paris: Félix Alcan, and Brussels: Office de Publicité, 1939). Also, Henri Pirenne, *Les villes du Moyen-Age. Essai d'histoire économique et sociale* (Brussels: Maurice Lamertin, 1927); trans. I. E. Clegg, *Economic and Social History of Medieval Europe* (New York: Harcourt, Brace and World, 1937).

25. Pirenne, *Les villes et les institutions urbaines*, p. 345.

26. Ibid., p. 338.

27. Ibid., p. 48.

28. Vincenzo Rizzi, *I cosidetti Statuti Murattiani per la città di Bari. Regolamenti edilizi particolari* (Bari: Leonardo da Vinci, 1959).

29. Hall, *London 2000* (London: Faber and Faber, 1963). See pp. 26, 162-64.

30. Barral, *Diecinueve figuras de mi historica civil* (Barcelona: Jaime Salinas, 1961).

31. Eugène-Emmanuel Viollet-le-Duc, *Dictionnaire raisonné de l'architecture française . . .*, vol. VIII, "Style," p. 480. For Viollet-le-Duc architecture is the consequence of profound observation of the principles on which art can and must rest. The architect must seek these principles and deduce all of their consequences with rigorous logic.

32. Compare this passage from John Summerson's "Urban forms," in Handlin and Burchard, *The Historian and the City*, pp. 165-76: " . . . because I am disposed to condemn the kind of urban history which concentrates on architecture at the expense of total building output, such work may or may not be good architectural history but it is not the history of the city as an artefact. Our historian has to be on terms with the whole physical mass of marble, bricks and mortar, steel and concrete, tarmac and rubble, metal conduits and rails—the total artefact. He has to deal with all this and he has to deal with it within limits."

33. Berenson, *The Italian Painters of the Renaissance* (London: Phaidon, 1952), p. 10. The book consists of four essays published separately between 1894 and 1907.

34. Smailes, *The Geography of Towns* (London: Hutchinson Univ. Library, 1953; rev. ed., 1957), p. 103 of 1st edition.

35. Lavedan, *Géographie des villes* (cit. n. 20, chap. 1), pp. 91-92. The passage continues, "This generating element is not necessarily the same as the one that generates the city. We have seen, for example, that many cities owe their origin to a spring; these springs almost never had an influence on the routings of roads; rather, they often were found outside of the actual agglomeration. Thus is the case with Cahors, the antique 'Divona Cadurcorum'; the spring that attracted the first inhabitants is as far from Roman Cahors as it is from the medieval or modern city. If Cahors is originally a city by a spring, its plan is that of a city on a thoroughfare . . . the generating element of the plan corresponds to the element of growth, not to the element of the city's origin" (p. 92).

36. Georges Gusdorf, *L'Université en question* (Paris: Payot, 1964), p. 83.

37. Claude Lévi-Strauss, *Tristes Tropiques* (cit. n. 2, chap. 1), p. 126 of the English edition.

Chapter 3
The Individuality of Urban Artifacts; Architecture

1. Concerning the *locus* and **theories of the division of space,** see Maximilien Sorre, "Géographie urbaine et écologie" in *Urbanisme et architecture* (cit. n. 6, chap. 1); Sorre, *Rencontres de la géographie et de la sociologie* (Paris: Librairie Marcel Rivière & Cie., 1957); Claude Lévi-Strauss, *Tristes Tropiques* (cit. n. 2, chap. 1); Marcel Mauss, "Essai sur les variations saisonnières des sociétés eskimos" (cit. n. 6, chap. 1). In this last study, Mauss comments upon how group names are often also place names, and how *mut*, the last syllable of Eskimo names, signifies "inhabitant of." In this way, primitive peoples were defined according to their territory: this man is the one from this mountain, from that river, etc. The meaning of this origin becomes clear in terms of the connecting of two points; the route then acquires a subjective value. See also Maurice Halbwachs, *La topographie légendaire des Evangiles en Terre sainte. Etude de mémoire collective* (Paris: Presses Universitaires de France, 1941). The importance of this work was brought to light by Georges Friedmann in his preface to another work by Halbwachs; Friedmann emphasized how Halbwachs's study, although not conceived expressly with this in mind, comes on the heels of other great works, such as those of David Friedrich Strauss and Ernest Renan, dedicated to the problems of Christian origins. Friedmann's preface is in Halbwachs, *Esquisse d'une psychologie des classes sociales* (Paris: Librairie Marcel Rivière & Cie., 1955).

2. Eydoux, *Monuments et trésors de la Gaule. Les récentes découvertes archéologiques* (Paris: Plon, 1958; 2d ed., Union Générale d'Editions, 1962). See esp. chap. 2, "Dieux, héros et artistes à Entremont, capitale de la confédération gauloise des Salyens." Also, Henri Paul Eydoux, *Cités mortes et lieux maudits de France* (Paris: Plon, 1959). The study of archaeological sites in Provence is of particular interest for urban studies because of the living presence of the monuments in these places and the quantity of material. In this respect the archaeological maps of Roman Gaul constitute a body of material that is of primary importance. See Institut de France, Académie des Inscriptions et Belles Lettres, *Forma Orbis Romani. Carte archéologique de la Gaule Romaine* (Paris: Ernest Leroux). Nos. I, II, IV, V,

VI, and VII were published between 1931 and 1939; others were published after the war. Each map, at a scale of 1:200,000, includes several regions. For the study of urban development in Provence, see also Paul-Albert Février, *Le développement urbain en Provence de l'époque romaine à la fin du XIVe siècle (Archéologie et histoire urbaine)* (Paris: E. de Broccard, 1964).

3. Focillon, *Vie des formes* (Paris: Ernest Leroux, 1933); *Vie des formes. Editions nouvelle, suivie de l'éloge de la main* (Paris: Félix Alcan, 1939); trans., *The Life of Forms in Art* (2d ed., New York: Wittenborn, Schultz, 1948). The concept expressed in the quotation can be taken in very general terms as the basis of Focillon's scientific work. See also Focillon, *Art d'occident. Le Moyen Age roman et gothique* (Paris: Armand Colin, 1938). Focillon commented in the preface, "Our work is then not an initiation, nor an archaeological handbook, but a history, that is, a study of the relations, different according to time and place, that are established between facts, ideas, and forms, the latter of which cannot simply be considered to have ornamental value. They participate in historical activity; they represent the parabola which they have vigorously helped to delineate. Medieval art is not a natural concretion, nor the passive expression of a society; in large measure the Middle Ages themselves are its creation."

4. Jacob Burckhardt, *Weltgeschichtliche Betrachtungen* (Stuttgart: Alfred Kröner, 1963); trans., *Force and Freedom: Reflections on History* (New York: Pantheon, 1943), p. 318.

5. Loos, *Trotzdem. Gesammelte Aufsätze 1900-1930* (Innsbruck: Brenner, 1931). The quotation is from the 1910 "Architektur," one of the writings in the book. *Trotzdem* is one of the two books that Loos published during his lifetime and is a compilation of his articles, lectures, and other writings; the second is *Ins Leere gesprochen. Aufsätze in Wiener Zeitungen und Zeitschriften aus den Jahren 1897-1900* (Paris: Georges Crès, 1921; 2d ed. rev., Innsbruck: Brenner, 1932). Both books are republished in the first volume of the collected writings, *Adolf Loos, Sämtliche Schriften* (Vienna–Munich: Herold, 1962), ed. Franz Glück. For a bibliography and evaluation of Loos's work with respect to the theses of this book, see Aldo Rossi, "Adolf Loos. 1870-1933," *Casabella-continuità*, no. 233 (November 1959), pp. 5-12, 23, republished in Aldo Rossi, *Scritti scelti . . .*, pp. 78-106.

6. Hugo, *Notre-Dame de Paris*, in *Oeuvres complètes de Victor Hugo* (Paris: Albin Michel-Ollendorf, 1904; trans., Boston: Estes and Lauriat, n.d.). The quotation from the novel, first published in 1832, is from Bk. III, chap. 1, p. 170 of the English edition. See also n. 12 to this chapter.

7. Laborde, *Les Monuments de la France classés chronologiquement et considérés sous le rapport des faits historiques et de l'étude des arts*, 2 vols. (Paris, 1816-36). The passage quoted is from vol. I, p. 57.

8. Claude-Nicolas Ledoux, *L'Architecture considerée sous le Rapport de l'Art, des Moeurs et de la Législation* (Paris, 1804). See also the second and posthumous edition, *L'Architecture de Claude-Nicolas Ledoux* (Paris: Lenoir, 1847).

9. Eugène Emmanuel Viollet-le-Duc, *Dictionnaire raisonné . . .*, cit. n. 9, chap. 2. The description of the Gaillard Castle is in vol. III, pp. 82-102. The castle, near Andelys, was built by Richard the Lionhearted. The construction of this fortress, the gateway to Normandy, was directed against the offensives of the kings of France. The castle-fortress is a complete system of defense works on the Seine at a point where the river is able to protect Rouen from an army coming from Paris. Its strategic disposition proved to be extraordinary, especially during the struggles between England and the French kings. Viollet-le-Duc gave much consideration to this aspect, referring to the work of A. Deville, *Histoire du château Gaillard et du siège qu'il soutint contre Philippe-Auguste, en 1203 et 1204* (Rouen: E. Frère, 1929; 1st ed., 1849).

10. Albert Demangeon, *Problèmes de Géographie humaine* (Paris: Armand Colin, 1952). See in particular, "L'habitation rurale en France. Essai de classification des principaux types," pp. 261-87; first published in *Annales de Géographie*, XXIX, no. 161 (September 15, 1920), pp. 352-75. The book, published posthumously for the first time in 1942, is a collection of Demangeon's writings which for the most part had already appeared in *Annales de Géographie*.

11. Le Corbusier, *Manière de penser l'Urbanisme* (Paris: Editions de l'Architecture d'Aujourd'hui; rev. ed., Editions Gonthier, 1963); François de Pierrefeu and Le Corbusier, *La maison des hommes* (Paris: Plon, 1942).

12. On Hugo and architecture, a splendid study addressing all the relationships between nineteenth-century culture and architecture has recently appeared in France: Jean Mallion, *Victor Hugo et l'art architectural* (Paris: Presses Universitaires de France, 1962).

13. **The relationship between man and the environment.** See Maximilien Sorre,

"Géographie urbaine et écologie"; Sorre, *Rencontres de la géographie et de la sociologie;* Willy Hellpach, *Mensch und Volk der Grossstadt;* all cit. *supra.* Also see my review "L'uomo della metropoli," *Casabella-continuità,* no. 258 (December 1961), pp. 22-25. Here, repeating a famous comment by Bismarck which Hellpach also cites (pp. 23-24), I wrote that in the Wilhelmian city, the immigrant enjoyed a certain, fully calculated measure of liberty, or at least greater freedom than he had enjoyed in the countryside; this freedom also consisted in the fact that it was a form of city where certain structures or modes of growth were appropriate for the entire urban aggregate. Even if the preoccupation with the beautification and aggrandizement of the capitals often masked powerful forces of speculation, the resultant embellishment could at least in part be enjoyed by all the citizens. Moreover, this form of the bourgeois city had a meaning, and its citizens participated in its residential and administrative structures and its larger monumental projects; certainly the man of Hellpach's metropolis could improve and refine his perceptions there, and the farmer of whom Bismarck spoke was able to walk under the lime trees on the wide streets and find a place to sit and "listen to a bit of music" and "down some beer." In regard to the polemics on the large bourgeois city, see also my discussion of Engels and Hegemann in chapter 4 of this book.

14. Kevin Lynch, *The Image of the City,* cit. n. 5, chap. 1.

15. Chastel, *Art et Humanisme à Florence au temps de Laurent le Magnifique. Etudes sur la Renaissance et l'Humanisme platonicien* (Paris: Presses Universitaires de France, 1959).

16. Paul Fréart Sieur de Chantelou, "Journal du voyage du Cavalier Bernini en France," *Gazette des Beaux Arts* (Paris), published periodically 1883-85; republished as an extract (Paris, 1815); trans. into Italian by Stefano Bottari, *Bernini in Francia* (Rome: Edizioni della Bussola, 1946).

17. Concerning the **revolutionary architects,** see the work of Emil Kaufmann: *Von Ledoux bis Le Corbusier. Ursprung und Entwicklung der autonomen Architektur* (Leipzig-Vienna: Dr. Rolf Passer, 1933); *Three Revolutionary Architects. Boullée, Ledoux and Lequeu* (Philadelphia: The American Philosophical Society, 1952); *Architecture in the Age of Reason. Baroque and Post-Baroque in England, Italy, and France* (Cambridge, Mass.: Harvard Univ. Press, 1955). On the coinage of the term *revolutionary ar-*

chitects, and developing a contrary thesis, see the work of Hans Sedlmayr, *Die Revolution der modernen Kunst* (Hamburg: Rowohlt, 1955); *Verlust der Mitte, Die bildende Kunst des 19 und 20 Jahrhunderts als Symptom und Symbol der Zeit* (Salzburg: Otto Müller, 1948). For a broad evaluation of these theses, see my studies: Aldo Rossi, "Emil Kaufmann e l'architettura del'Illuminismo," *Casabella-continuità,* no. 222 (November 1958), pp. 42-47; "Una critica che respingiamo," *Casabella-continuità,* no. 219 (May 1958), pp. 32-35; both republished in *Scritti scelti . . .* An indispensable analysis of these works and general critical evaluation is that of Louis Hautecoeur, *Histoire de l'architecture classique,* cit. n. 11, chap. 1. For an evaluation of the relationship between the arts and the sciences in France during the Revolution, see Joseph Fayet, *La Révolution française et la science. 1789-1795* (Paris: Marcel Rivière & Cie., 1960).

18. André Chastel, *Art et Humanisme à Florence,* p. 148; Rudolf Wittkower, *Architectural Principles in the Age of Humanism* (London: Warburg Institute, 1949; 2d ed., Alec Tiranti, 1952).

19. Chastel, *Art et Humanisme à Florence,* p. 149.

20. It is well known that the **central plan** is one of the classic themes of the history of architecture. In the case of San Lorenzo in Milan, which is also an extraordinary urban artifact and an exceptional object of permanence in a city where the urban dynamic has been extremely strong, architecture and history together constitute the church's image. This image is linked with the collective idea that the city has of its monuments. Following are a series of essential works for an understanding and analytical study of this monument: Aristide Calderini, *La zona monumentale di San Lorenzo in Milano* (Milan: Ceschina, 1934); Julius Kohte, *Die Kirche San Lorenzo in Mailand* (Berlin: Ernst und Korn, 1890); Gino Chierici, "Un quesito sulla basilica di San Lorenzo," in *Palladio. Rivista di storia dell'architettura,* II, no. 1 (1938), pp. 1-4; Fernand de Dartein, *Etude sur l'Architecture lombarde et sur les origines de l'Architecture romano-byzantine,* 2 vols. (Paris: Dunod, 1865-82; reprinted Milan: Grafiche Mariani Ritti, 1963, under the direction of Novindustria di Mario Botti); Eberhard Hempel, *Francesco Borromini* (Vienna: Anton Schroll & Co., 1924); Henry de Geymüller, *Les projets primitifs pour la Basilique de Saint-Pierre de Rome par Bramante, Raphael Sanzio, Fra-Giocondo, les Sangallo, etc., publiés pour la première fois in fac-simile avec des restitutions nombreuses et un*

texte, 2 vols. (Paris: J. Baudry, and Vienna: Lehmann et Wentzel, 1875-80).

21. Aymonino, "Analisi delle relazioni tra i servizi e le attrezzature," pp. 33-45, cit. n. 12, chap. 1. The passage quoted is on p. 44. This essay was republished. in Aymonino, *Il significato delle città*, cit. n. 12, chap. 1.

22. On **Rome** and the **Roman Forum,** see the following works: Ferdinando Castagnoli, Carlo Cecchelli, Gustavo Giovannoni, and Mario Zocca, *Topografia e urbanistica di Roma* (Bologna: Licinio Cappelli, 1958); Jérôme Carcopino, *La vie quotidienne à Rome à l'apogée de l'empire* (Paris: Hachette, 1939); Leon Homo, *Rome impériale et l'urbanisme dans l'antiquité* (Paris: Albin Michel, 1951); Giuseppe Lugli, *Roma antica. Il centro monumentale* (Rome: Giovanni Bardi, 1946); Ludovico Quaroni, "Una città eterna—quattro lezioni da ventisette secoli," in *Urbanistica, Roma città e piani* (Turin, n.d.), pp. 5-72; enlarged and republished in Quaroni, *Immagine di Roma* (Bari: Laterza, 1969; 2d ed., 1976); Pietro Romanelli, *Il foro romano* (Bologna: Licinio Cappelli, 1959). Of exceptional interest for information about Roman artifacts seen as part of a continuum, and concerning the emergence of urban artifacts, see Quaroni's work, for example this passage on p. 15: "What interests us most, however, is that the *pomoerium* was the boundary of the city in terms of building, the boundary, we would say, of the developmental plan and of the building code; these had no value outside of it since the city was considered to terminate beyond this point. For economy of defense, distance, and administration, it was understood as a zone of continuous building, as restricted as possible. Naturally, nothing stopped the poorest segment of the population, those who did not enjoy all the rights of citizenship, among other things, from building their illegal *barrache* outside the *pomoerium;* the *continentia* accounted for vast villages, just as do the *bidonvilles* and illegal and semi-rural suburbs that proliferate today around Rome, where the low price of land and the presence of easy means of communication favor settlement." From an analytical standpoint such as this, Rome, and especially Imperial Rome, with its defects, abuses, and contradictions, ends up as an image strangely akin to that of the large modern city. Further on Quaroni insists upon the relationship between the Roman principle of administration and of construction and the concrete conditions of life in Rome, a relationship that characterized the persistence of original characteristics and their mixture with more heterogeneous imported elements. A major and systematic study of the urban vicissitudes of Rome by way of the enormous analytical material that is available would certainly be of fundamental value to the urban sciences.

23. Virgil, *Aeneid*, Bk. VIII, 11. 359-60. The *Carinae* were located on the Esquiline hill, where one of the richest and most monumental quarters of Augustan Rome rose; Rosa Calzecchi Onesti notes that they were located "on the small elevation where S. Pietro in Vincoli sits today and in the valley below." See Calzecchi's translation and introduction of *Eneide* (Turin: Giulio Einaudi, 1967).

24. Titus Livius, *Ab urbe condita*, Bk. V, chap. LV.

25. Aristotle, *Politics* (Cambridge, Mass.: Harvard Univ. Press, 1962), Bk. VII, p. 593.

26. Pietro Romanelli, *Il foro romano*, p. 26.

27. Marcel Poète, *Introduction à l'urbanisme*, p. 368.

28. Ferdinando Castagnoli, Carlo Cecchelli, et al., *Topografia e urbanistica di Roma*. De Tournon's comment is quoted in the Appendix to "Parte Terza. Roma dal Rinascimento al 1870," by Gustavo Giovannoni, pp. 537-38. See also, Paolo Marconi, *Giuseppe Valadier* (Rome: Officina Edizioni, 1964), esp. chap. IX, "L'occupazione francese," pp. 168-87.

29. Domenico Fontana, *Della trasportatione dell'Obelisco Vaticano . . . ,* Bk. I, p. 101; cited by Sigfried Giedion, *Space, Time and Architecture* (cit. n. 22, chap. 2), p. 93.

30. Giedion, op. cit., p. 93.

31. Ibid., pp. 96-98.

32. Jean-Nicolas-Louis Durand, *Précis des leçons d'architecture . . . ,* vol. I, p. 17 (cit. n. 9, chap. 1). See also, Durand, *Partie graphique des cours d'architecture faits à l'Ecole Royale Polytechnique depuis sa réorganisation, précédée d'un sommaire des leçons relatives à ce nouveau travail* (Paris, 1821), as well as Aymonino's references to Durand in the texts cited n. 12, chap. 1.

33. Carlo Cattaneo, *La città considerata come principio ideale delle istorie italiane* (Milan, 1858); ed. G. A. Belloni (Florence: Vallecchi, 1931); republished as *La Città*, ed. G. Titta Rosa (Milan-Rome: Valentino Bompiani, 1949); and included in the complete works, *Carlo Cattaneo. Scritti storici e geografici*, 4 vols., ed. Gaetano Salvemini and Ernesto Sestan (Florence: Felice Le Monnier, 1957), vol. II, pp. 384-487. Salvemini, in his introduction to *La più belle pagine di Carlo Cattaneo scelte da G. Salvemini* (Milan, 1922), calls Cattaneo's *Notizie naturali e civili su la Lom-*

bardia . . . (of 1844) the "model of regional anthropogeography, even today unsurpassed in Italy" (pp. I-XXXI, republished in Salvemini, *Opere*, vol. II: *Scritti sul Risorgimento* [Milan: Giangiacomo Feltrinelli, 1961], pp. 371-92). See also Croce's judgment; he saw it as a rift in Italian history ("Cattaneo did not write a history of Italy, but offered a 'rift' in *Notizie naturali e civili della Lombardia* . . . [sic], which for their admirable objectivity hardly seem to have been written just a few years before 1848"). Benedetto Croce, *Storia della storiografia italiani nel secolo decimonono*, 2 vols. (4th ed., Bari: Laterza, 1964), vol. I, p. 211.

34. Cattaneo, *La città considerata* . . . , in *Scritti storici e geografici*, vol. II, p. 391.

35. Ibid., p. 416.

36. Ibid., p. 387.

37. Ibid., p. 396.

38. Ibid., p. 386.

39. Ibid., p. 406.

40. Ibid., p. 421.

41. Gramsci, *Quaderni del carcere, 3: Il Risorgimento* (Turin: Giulio Einaudi, 1964). The quotation is from the paragraph on Quintino Sella, pp. 160-61. Concerning the debate on **Rome as capital,** see Alberto Caracciolo's beautiful book, *Roma capitale. Dal Risorgimento alla crisi dello stato liberale* (Rome: Edizioni Rinascita, 1976); and Italo Insolera, *Roma moderna. Un secolo di storia urbanistica* (2d ed., Turin: Giulio Einaudi, 1962). Caracciolo reports parts of Cavour's speech of March 25, 1861, where the Piedmontese maintained that Rome was "the only Italian city that did not have exclusively municipal [local] memories" (p. 20). See also the passage on pp. 10-11 of Caracciolo's book: "In the national movement, Rome was above all a unifying force of extraordinary moral power. If there was a common tradition to be found in the entire peninsula, it was called Rome. No study of the origins of Italian national consciousness can fail to take into account the magnetic attraction of this name over the centuries. Every time an attempt has been made to recover a unity in the history of Italy, one has had to return, by one route or another, to this point. The power of ancient Rome and the authority of Papal Rome are the characteristic elements that determine and almost fill up by themselves the history of Italy over two millenia. Every active force in the peninsula must reckon with the religious, political, and moral power summarized in the name of this city. . . . Again at the dawn of the Risorgimento, the name of Rome appears frequently, as much with the neo-Guelphs as with liberal and democratic laymen, because the problem of the Church is always there, and it is such as to condition the success of every instance of unification and renewal. One can attempt to destroy it, or put it in the background, or neutralize it, but in no case can this decisive entity in Italy be ignored."

42. P. 132 (cit. n. 3, chap. 1).

43. Jacob Burckhardt, *Force and Freedom* (cit. n. 4, chap. 3), p. 163.

44. Károly Kerényi, *Die Mythologie der Griechen, Die Götter- und Menschheitgeschichten* (Zurich: Rhein-Verlag, 1951); *Die Heroen der Griechen* (Zurich: Rhein-Verlag, 1958); trans. H. J. Rose, *The Heroes of the Greeks* (London: Thames and Hudson, 1959). The passage cited is from the English edition, p. 213. See also, Carl Gustav Jung and Karl Kerényi, *Einführung in das Wesen der Mythologie* (Zurich: Rascher, 1941); trans. R. F. C. Hull, *Essays on a Science of Mythology* (London: Routledge and Kegan Paul, 1951). I would have liked to explore some of the ramifications of Kerényi's work on the concept of *locus* and on the significance of the origin of urban artifacts. However, in addition to its being beyond the scope of this study, a research effort of this type would demand years of work and the availability of a vast quantity of analytical material. In his *Science of Mythology* Kerényi investigates the founding of cities, as this subject continually touches on his work on the gods and heroes of Greece; he sheds light on both the multiplicity and the originality which constitute cities and also on the significance of the founder of the city as well as of its original design. "It is not only the psychologist who finds tri- and quadripartite [systems existing] together. Ancient traditions know the importance of the number three in city plans, in Etruria as in Rome itself: they tell of three towers, three streets, three quarters, three temples or tripartite temples. We cannot but observe a multiplicity even when we seek the singular and the shared: this is the nature of the original. And this already implies at least an answer to the question of whether it is worthwhile to inquire into the particular origin of different local and chronological formations."

45. Karl Marx, *Zur Kritik der politischen Oekonomie*, in *Marx-Engels Werke* (Berlin: Dietz, 1961), vol. 13. The passage is from the introduction which Marx wrote between August and September of 1857. English version in Karl Marx, *On History and People*, vol. 7 of The Karl Marx Library, ed. Saul K. Padover (New York: McGraw-Hill, 1977), pp. 79-80.

46. Marcel Poète, *Introduction à l'Urbanisme* (cit. n. 18, chap. 1), p. 232.

47. Carlo Cattaneo, *La città con-*

siderata . . ., in *Scritti storici e geografici*, vol. II, pp. 384-85.

48. Ibid., p. 386.

49. Ibid., pp. 386-87.

50. Poète, *Introduction à l'Urbanisme*, p. 215.

51. Roland Martin, *L'urbanisme dans la Grèce antique* (Paris: A. & J. Picard, 1956; 2d ed. enlarged, 1974).

Chapter 4
The Evolution of Urban Artifacts

1. Maurice Halbwachs, *Les expropriations et le prix des terrains à Paris (1860-1900)* (Paris: E. Cornély, 1909); *Les cadres sociaux de la mémoire* (Paris: Presses Universitaires de France, 1925); *La population et les tracés de voies à Paris depuis un siècle*, 2d ed. enlarged of the first part of *Les expropriations . . .* (Paris: Presses Universitaires de France, 1928); *L'évolution des besoins dans les classes ouvrières* (Paris: Presses Universitaires de France, 1933).

2. Hans Bernoulli, *Die Stadt und ihr Boden* (Erlenbach-Zurich: Verlag für Architektur, 1946; 2d ed. rev., 1949).

3. Halbwachs, *La population et les tracés de voies . . .* For an application of the method and the results of my study, see also, Aldo Rossi, *Contributo al problema dei rapporti tra tipologia edilizia e morfologia urbana . . .* (cit. n. 1, chap. 2).

4. Halbwachs, *La population et les tracés de voies . . .* , p. 4.

5. Aldo Rossi, *Contributo al problema dei rapporti tra tipologia edilizia e morfologia urbana . . .* The zone in Milan treated in this study consists of the triangular area between the former Spanish bastions, two axes of corso Italia and corso di Porta Romana (converging in piazza Missori), and part of the former Commune of Vigentino to the south.

6. Aldo Rossi, "Il concetto de tradizione nell'architettura neoclassica milanese," in *Società*, XII, no. 3 (June 1956), pp. 474-93; republished in Rossi, *Scritti scelti . . .* (cit. n. 6, chap. 2), pp. 1-24. In this work, which began with an analysis of Milanese urban history, I already foresaw the possibility of a larger urban theory which could account for the unity of development of urban artifacts notwithstanding their multiplicity of aspects. Thus the architecture of the eighteenth century became emblematic for me of the contrast between a rational, enlightened conception of the city and the importance of specific situations. The principal facts relating to the formation of the **Napoleonic plan for Milan** are as follows. With the Viceroy's decree of January 9, 1807, the municipalities of Milan and Venice were accorded a *Commissione di Or-*

nato which had vast powers and a large sphere of action. The task of the Commission was specifically to "plot out a general type of internal city street for subsequent systematization; to undertake, at the request of the Municipality, the requisite projects for the symmetrical improvement of buildings fronting on the streets and for the enlargement and straightening of the same and for the execution of the same projects worked out in detail . . . ; to be vigilant concerning the public security with regard to buildings, etc. . . . ." This Commission, appointed by the government, was composed of the most illustrious personalities in the field then in Milan, among them Luigi Cagnola and Luigi Canonica. Naturally the first task the Commission undertook was that of the master plan, the project for which was completed that year, but it also did not fail to take an active role in guiding, making provisions for, and continuously and directly intervening in the development of the city in the years 1807-1814. To sketch the general outlines of the plan: the construction of a large new center, the Bonaparte Forum, was projected by Antolini to stand in front of the Sforza Castle; the broad strada Napoleone (roughly where via Dante is today) was to take off from here, opening up around the Cordusio in an interesting triangular plaza and then continuing along in a straight line with the Ospedale Maggiore and San Nazaro as a backdrop. Almost parallel to this, another street starting out at the bottom of via San Giovanni sul Muro was to lead to the temple of San Sebastiano del Tibaldi, isolated and circumscribed within a large rectangular plaza, whose expansion around its central plan emphasized its volume. The corso della Riconoscenza (formerly corso di Porta Orientale and today corso di Porta Venezia) flowed between the Residence of the Archbishop and the Palace of Justice. The Piazza del Duomo was enlarged without disrupting the ancient Roman grid. As I wrote at the end of my study, "Ultimately they took into consideration and respected the artistic buildings and historical memories of the city; the monuments were seen as the seat and testimony of municipal history, and placed as backdrops to the straight streets and the centers of piazzas, almost as constitutive elements of that larger plan of construction and of ordering which history forms over time and in which cities come to be mirrored." *Scritti scelti . . .* , p. 21. A vast amount of analytical material and useful critical evaluation exists concerning the urban history of Milan.

7. Oriol Bohigas, *Barcelona, entre el Plan Cerdá i el barraquisme* (Barcelona: Edi-

cions 62, 1963). Ildefonso Cerdá, *Teoría General de la Urbanización y aplicación de sus principios y doctrinas a la Reforma y Ensanche de Barcelona*, 2 vols. (Madrid: Imprenta Español, 1867); facsimile reproduction with bibliography and other principal published writings of Cerdá, ed. Fabián Estapé (Barcelona: Instituto de Estudios Fiscales–Editorial Ariel–Editorial Vicens Vives, 1968). Bohigas studied and perhaps was first to draw attention to **Cerdá's plan** and his teaching; he notes how the 1867 work preceded by twenty-three years Joseph Stübben's treatise *Der Städtebau* (Darmstadt: Bergsträsser, 1890), pt. IV, vol. IX, of Stübben's *Handbuch der Architektur* (1883-90), which was considered the first treatise on urbanism. It is interesting to quote a few passages from Cerdá's work, as cited by Bohigas, including the Catalan scholar's evaluation of Cerdá's work and the plan for Barcelona: "The large city . . . is not much more than a kind of station or inn. . . . It will always have one or more streets which come from the highway grid that furrows the surface of our globe. From these principal streets then depart others which distribute movement . . . for the entire city. From these, the properly urban streets, others detach which communicate with the individual residences. . . . The areas formed by the urban streets crossing reciprocal intersections should be much smaller than those formed by the principal streets. These relatively small areas are those which . . . are called *barrios*. . . . [They are] refuges which man has reserved for his own short visit or for a permanent one, whenever he wants to separate himself from the great movement that agitates humanity." Bohigas brings out very acutely how, even if many of Cerdá's themes have their roots in Romantic literature, he nonetheless stands completely apart for the importance he gives to urban classification and to the analysis of actual situations.

8. *Illa*, plural *illes*, is Catalan for "block."

9. See, Vincenzo Rizzi, *I cosidetti Statuti Murattiani per la città di Bari* . . . (cit. n. 2, chap. 2).

10. Pierre Lavedan, *Les villes françaises* (cit. n. 20, chap. 1), pp. 102-103. The city of Richelieu was created by the great cardinal-minister of Louis XIII between 1635 and 1640. Around 1638, the walls of the city, the church, and a certain number of buildings were begun. In 1641 the whole plan appeared finished. The plan is highly regular, with a large central axis dividing the city into two symmetrical parts. This axis, coming from a gate, is lined on both sides by a uniform row of houses and culminates in a square plaza with closed corners, where the principal buildings are located. At Richelieu, order was imposed not only on a plaza or a street, but on an entire city; it is a magnificent monumental unity which has been preserved up to our own time. On the other hand, the castle has disappeared; from the beginning it was never connected with the city. A larger composition of which the castle could have been a developmental element was never attempted in the design of the city. The other great French city which was developed as a royal residence—Versailles—has a far more complex topological evolution.

11. Cit. n. 2, chap. 4.

12. Ibid.

13. Ibid.

14. Ibid.

15. Werner Hegemann, *Das steinerne Berlin* . . . (cit. n. 13, chap. 2). Hegemann's volume constitutes one of the most important contributions on the urban history of Berlin. It is an outstanding book whose political commitment to a democratic renewal of civic institutions is based on an extraordinary knowledge of the development of the city. For Hegemann, Berlin, a city which had a very large number of "rental barracks" owing to its unfortunate police code, was also a city which had within itself great possibilities for renewal. See esp. the passages excerpted in *Casabella-continuità*, no. 288 (June 1964), pp. 21-22.

16. Hans Paul Bahrdt, *Die moderne Grossstadt* . . . (cit. n. 19, chap. 2). See esp. the first part of the book, "Kritik der Grossstadtkritik," pp. 12-34.

17. Engels, "Zur Wohnungsfrage," three articles published in the magazine *Volksstaat* in 1872 (2d ed. rev., Leipzig, 1887); trans. C. C. Dutt, *The Housing Question* (London: Lawrence and Wishart, 1936).

18. Engels, *The Housing Question*, pt. I, p. 21.

19. Steen Eiler Rasmussen, *London, The Unique City* (1st English ed., rev. from the Danish ed. of 1934, London: Jonathan Cape, 1937; repub. Cambridge, Mass.: M.I.T. Press, 1967). For Poète's work, see n. 18, chap. 1; for Hegemann, see n. 13, chap. 2.

20. For example, see *Städte verändern ihr Gesicht* (Stuttgart: Stadtplanungs und Vermessungsamt Hannover, 1962), which has a mostly socio-economic bibliography interesting for this type of formulation of the problem. It is necessary to keep in mind, however, that the assumption that the first Industrial Revolution was a qualitative urban leap accompanies (and paralyzes) all of the historiography of the Modern Movement.

21. Gottmann, *Megalopolis. The Urbanized Northeastern Seaboard* . . . (cit. n. 12,

chap. 2).

22. Lewis Mumford, *The Culture of Cities* (cit. n. 1, chap. 1).

23. Jean Gottmann, "De la ville d'aujourd'hui à la ville de demain. La transition vers la ville nouvelle," *Prospective*, no. 11 (June 1964), pp. 171-80. See also Pierre Massé's introduction (pp. 5-16) to this issue dedicated to urbanization.

24. Richard Updegraff Ratcliff, "The Dynamics of Efficiency . . . " (cit. n. 17, chap. 1).

25. Samonà, contribution to the "Tavola rotonda sulle componenti urbanistiche e gli strumenti di intervento," in *La città territorio. Un esperimento didattico sul centro direzionale di Centocelle in Roma* (Bari: Leonardo da Vinci, 1964), pp. 90-102; the passage cited is on p. 91.

26. Mumford, *The Culture of Cities*, p. 168; the judgment on Engels is to be found in the annotated bibliography, p. 519.

Preface to the Second Italian Edition

1. Aldo Rossi, "Introduzione a Boullée" in Etienne-Louis Boullée, *Architettura. Saggio sull'arte*, trans. into Italian by Aldo Rossi (Padua: Marsilio, 1967), pp. 7-24.

2. Aymonino, "Per la formazione di una scienza urbana," in *Rinascita*, no. 27 (July 2, 1966); Grassi, "La costruzione logica della città," in *Architettura libri. Rivista di informazione bibliografica a cura del servizio di documentazione della CLUVA*, no. 2/3 (Venice, July 1966), pp. 95-106; Gregotti, "L'architettura della città," in *Il Verri*, no. 23 (March 1967), pp. 172-73.

3. Tafuri, *Teorie e storia dell'architettura* (Bari: Laterza, 1968), pp. 90-92, 114, 160, 190, 192-93, 201-202.

4. Tarragó Cid, "Prólogo a la edición castellana," in Aldo Rossi, *La arquitectura de la ciudad*, trans. Josep Maria Ferrer-Ferrer and Salvador Tarragó Cid (Barcelona: Gustavo Gili, 1971, 1976), pp. 9-42.

Introduction
to the Portuguese Edition

1. Aldo Rossi, "Introduzione a Boullée," in Etienne-Louis Boullée, *Architettura. Saggio sull'arte* (cit. n. 1 to the Preface to the Second Italian Edition), pp. 7-24.

2. Aldo Rossi, "Il concetto di tradizione nell'architettura neoclassica milanese" (cit. n. 6, chap. 4); Rossi, "Adolf Loos, 1870-1933" (cit. n. 5, chap. 3).

3. Aldo Rossi, "Un piano per Vienna" (cit. n. 6, chap. 2); Rossi, "Aspetti della tipologia residenziale a Berlino" (cit. n. 13, chap. 2).

4. Aldo Rossi, *Contributo al problema dei rapporti tra tipologia edilizia e morfologia urbana* . . . (cit. n. 1, chap. 2).

5. Guido Mansuelli, *Architettura e città.*

Problemi del mondo classico (Bologna: Alfa, 1970).

6. *Hof* (pl. *Höfe*), courtyard, court.

Comment on the German Edition

1. Adolf Behne, *Der moderne Zweckbau* (Munich: Drei Masken, 1923); republished with an introduction by Ulrich Conrads (Frankfurt am Main and Berlin: Ullstein GmbH, 1964).

Figure Credits

1b From Hermann Kern, *Labirinti* (Milan: Giangiacomo Feltrinelli Editore, 1981).

2-3 Courtesy Peter H. Dreyer.

4 From Ludwig Münz and Gustav Kunstler, *Adolf Loos: Pioneer of Modern Architecture* (New York and Washington: Frederick A. Praeger, 1966).

5 Courtesy Douglas Harnsberger.

6 Courtesy Ed Roseberry.

7 Courtesy Lindsay Stamm Shapiro.

8-9 From Edgard de Cerquairo Falcão, *Relíquias de Bahia* (São Paulo, Brazil: Romiti & Lanzara, 1940).

10 Collection Cranbrook Academy of Art Museum, Bloomfield Hills, Michigan.

11 Courtesy Hellmuth, Obata & Kassabaum, St. Louis, Missouri.

12 From *Souvenir de la Suisse*, a collection of nineteenth-century engravings by R. Dikenmann.

13 From Javier Aquilera Rojas and Luis J. Moreno Rexach, *Urbanismo español en América* (Madrid: Editora Nacional, 1973).

15-17 Courtesy Giulio Dubbini.

18 *above*, 71, 87, 91a, 91b Raccolta Bertarelli, Milan.

18 *below* Collection Museo Civico, Padua.

19-21 From Francesco Milizia, *Principj di Architettura Civile*, 2d ed. rev. (Bassano, 1804).

22 From Francesco Milizia, *Principj di Architettura Civile*, 1st Milanese ed. (Milan, 1832).

1a, 23, 25, 26, 66, 70, 90 Courtesy Roberto Freno.

14, 24, 37, 40-42, 44-45, 50, 54, 57a, 57b, 67, 72, 78, 81, 84-85, 88-89, 92-93, 99-102, 105 Courtesy the author.

27-28, 30-31 From G. Calza, "Contributo alla storia dell'edilizia imperiale romana," in *Palladio. Rivista di storia dell'architettura* V, no. 1 (1941).

29 From G. Calza, G. Becatti, I. Gismondi, G. De Angelis D'Ossat, and H. Bloch, eds., *Scavi di Ostia. Topographia generale* (Rome: Libreria dello Stato, 1953).

32-34 Courtesy *Lotus International*.

35-36, 38 From *Antichità arabe in Spagna*, an album published around 1830, Raccolta Bertarelli.

39 From a plan published by the Commercial Club of Chicago, 1909.

43 From Eugène Emmanuel Viollet-le-Duc, *Dictionnaire raisonné de l'architecture française de XIe au XVIe siècle*, vol. VI (Paris, 1854-59).

48-49 From *Casabella-Continuità* 288 (June 1964).

46 From Rud Eberstadt, *Handbuch des Wohnungswesens und der Wohnungsfrage*, 4th ed. (Jena: Verlag von Gustav Fischer, 1920).

47,53 From Werner Hegemann, *Das steinerne Berlin* (Berlin: Kiepenhaur, 1930).

51-52 From Hans-Joachim Knöfel and Rolf Rave, *Bauen seit 1900 in Berlin* (West Berlin: Verlag Kiepert, 1968).

55 From Henri Paul Eydoux, *La France antique* (Paris: Librairie Plon, 1962).

56 From a collection of engravings published by Alberts (The Hague, 1724; the drawing first appears in Domenico Fontana, *Libro Secondo in cui si ragiona di alcune fabriche fatte in Roma et in Napoli dal Cavaliere Domenico Fontana* [Naples, 1603]), Raccolta Bertarelli.

58 From Achille Ardigo, Franco Borsi, and Giovanni Michelucci, *Il quartiere di S. Croce nel futuro di Firenze* (Rome: Officina edizioni, 1968).

59 From Carlo Fontana, *L'anfiteatro Flavio descritto e delineato dal Cavaliere Carlo Fontana* (The Hague, 1725).

60 From a collection of engravings published by Alberts (The Hague, 1724; original ed., Amsterdam, 1704), Raccolta Bertarelli.

61 From Leonardo Benevolo, *Corso di disegno per i licei scientifici*, vol. V (Bari: Editori Laterza, 1974-75).

62 From Luigi Dodi, *Dell'antica urbanistica romana nel Medio Oriente* (Milan: Politecnico di Milano. Istituto di Urbanistica della Facoltà di Architettura, 1962).

63-64 Courtesy Max Bosshard.

65 From an engraving by L. and P. Giarré, 1845, Raccolta Bertarelli.

68-69 From Eugène-Emmanuel Viollet-le-Duc, *Dictionnaire raisonné de l'architecture française de XIe au XVIe siècle*, vol. III (Paris, 1854-59).

73-74, 76 From W. L. MacDonald, *The Architecture of the Roman Empire* (New Haven: Yale University Press, 1965).

75 From Heinz Kähler, *Roma e l'arte imperiale* (Milan: Il Saggiatore, 1963).

77 From a plan drawn by Alois K. Strobl, in Edmund Bacon, *Design of Cities* (New York:

Viking Press, 1967).

79-80 Courtesy Gianni Braghieri.

82-83 From Leonardo Benevolo, *Corso di disegno per i licei scientifici*, vol. II (Bari: Editori Laterza, 1974-75).

86a, 86b, 86c From the British magazine *The Builder: An Illustrated Weekly Magazine for Architect, Engineer, Archeologist* . . . XVI, no. 159 (6 March 1858).

94 *above* From *2C. Construcción de la Ciudad* 1, 1972; *center* from Gruppo Architettura, *Per una ricerca di progettazione 6. Ruolo dell'abitazione nell sviluppo e nella trasformazione della città contemporanea*, Istituto Universitario di Architettura di Venezia, 1973; *below* from J. Emili Hernández-Cros, Gabriel More, and Xavier Populana, *Arquitectura de Barcelona, Guía*, 2d ed. (Barcelona: Editorial La Gaya Ciencia, 1973).

95-96 From Hans Bernoulli, *Die Stadt und ihr Boden*, 2d ed. rev.(Erlenbach-Zurich: Verlag für Architektur, 1949).

97 From Steen Eiler Rasmussen, *London: The Unique City*, rev. ed. (Cambridge, Mass.: The M.I.T. Press, 1967).

98 Courtesy Casa editrice Electa.

103 Courtesy José da Nóbrega Sousa Martins.

104 From L. F. Cassas, *Voyage pittoresque et historique de l'Istrie et de la Dalmatie* (Paris, 1802).

Publishing History of *The Architecture of the City*

Italian Edition

L'architettura della città (Padua: Marsilio Editori, 1966), in Biblioteca di Architettura e Urbanistica, no. 8, Paola Ceccarelli, general ed.; 2d ed. (1970), with a preface by the author; 3d ed. (1973); 4th ed. (Milan: Clup [Cooperativa Libreria Universitaria del Politecnico], 1978), ed. Daniele Vitale, with revised notes, and introductions and presentations from previous Italian and Portuguese editions.

Spanish Edition

La arquitectura de la ciudad (Barcelona: Editorial Gustavo Gili, 1971), trans. Josep Maria Ferrer-Ferrer and Salvador Tarragó Cid, with a prologue by Salvador Tarragó Cid, and bibliographic revision by Joaquim Romaguera i Ramió, in Coleccion Arquitectura y Critica, Ignacio de Solá-Morales Rubió, general ed.; 2d, 3d, 4th, 5th eds. (1976, 1977, 1979, 1981) in Colección Punto y Linea.

German Edition

Die Architektur der Stadt, Skizze zu einer grundlegenden Theorie des Urbanen (Düsseldorf: Verlagsgruppe Bertelsmann GmbH/Bertelsmann Fachverlag, 1973), trans. Adrianna Giachi, with a preface by the author, in Bauwelt Fundamente, no. 41, Ulrich Conrads, general ed.

Portuguese Edition

A Arquitectura da cidade (Lisbon: Edições Cosmos, 1977), ed. and trans. José Charters Montiero and José da Nóbrega Sousa Martins, with an introduction by the author.

French Edition

Forthcoming.

Biographical Note

Born in Milan on May 3, 1931, Aldo Rossi studied architecture at the Milan Politecnico and received his degree there in 1959. While a student and then after, he worked on the architectural magazine *Casabella-Continuità* at a time when it played a leading role in Italian culture. Rossi participated in the magazine in several capacities during the period that Ernesto Rogers was its director: first as a collaborator (1955-1958, nos. 208-219), then as a member of the study center (1958-1960, nos. 221-248), and finally as an editor (1961-1964, nos. 249-294).

Rossi began his teaching activity as an assistant in Ludovico Quaroni's urbanism course in Arezzo in 1963, and as an assistant for Carlo Aymonino's course "Organizational Characteristics of Buildings" at the Istituto Universitario di Architettura in Venice in 1963-1965. In 1965 he joined the faculty of the School of Architecture in Milan and became involved in the important cultural activities promoted by the Italian student movement. In 1972, 1973, and 1974 he taught at the Eidgenössische Technische Hochschule in Zurich. Since 1975 he has been Professor of Design at the Istituto Universitario di Architettura in Venice. In September-October 1976, he directed the First International Seminar of Architecture in Santiago de Compostela, Spain, on the theme "Design and Historic City" (1st S.I.A.C., Seminario Internacional de Arquitectura en Compostela; proceedings published in Salvador Tarragó Cid and Justo Beramendi, eds., *Proyecto y ciudad historica* [Santiago de Compostela, 1977]), as well as the second of these seminars in 1978. He was Visiting Professor at the Cooper Union School of Architecture in New York City in 1977 and at the Yale School of Architecture in 1980. He has participated in numerous conferences throughout Europe, Latin America, and the United States.

Rossi's major written work, *The Architecture of the City*, was published in 1966 and has since been translated into several languages (see the "Publishing History of *The Architecture of the City*" that appears in this volume). Some of Rossi's other writings appear in *L'analisi urbana e la progettazione architettonica* (Milan, 1970), including the results of the study group he directed at the Milan School of Architecture; in the volume *Scritti Scelti sull'architettura e la città 1956-1972* (Milan, 1st ed., 1975; 2d ed., 1978); and in numerous journals published in Italy and elsewhere. From 1965 to 1972 he directed the series Polis-Quaderni di architettura e urbanistica for Editori Marsilio in Padua. In 1973 he directed the international section on architecture of the XV Triennale of Milan, at which time the collective volume *Architettura Razionale* was published with his introduction (Milan, 1973). Rossi's *Scientific Autobiography* was published in 1981 in the OPPOSITIONS BOOKS series.

Following Vittorio Savi's essay *L'architettura di Aldo Rossi* (Milan: Franco Angeli, 1976), numerous articles and several monographs on Rossi's work have been published, including *Aldo Rossi in America 1976-1979*, Kenneth Frampton, ed., with an introduction by Peter Eisenman (Institute for Architecture and Urban Studies, Catalogue 2). For extensive bibliographies of writings by and on Aldo Rossi from 1954 to 1979, consult *Aldo Rossi, Projects and Drawings 1962-1979*, Francesco Moschini, ed. (New York: Rizzoli, 1979).

Rossi's design work is intimately related to his writings. Among his principal built works are the Unità di abitazione for the Società Monte Amiata complex in Gallaratese 2, Milan, 1969-1974, and the elementary school of Fagnano Olona in Varese, 1972-1977. In 1977, working with Carlo Aymonino, Gianni Braghieri, and Vittorio Savi, he won a competition for the design of the Centro Direzionale of Florence. More recently, Rossi has participated in the IBA (Internationale Bauausstellung) competition for a housing project in Berlin, where he won a special first prize; received a special mention in a competition for the redesign of a historic part of Bern, Switzerland; and completed his Theater of the World in Venice. Projects for a cemetery in Modena, a school in Broni, and several houses in various locations in Italy are currently under construction.